CW00381581

Book Design by Out of Box Designs, U.K.

Edited by Lyons Tale Editing

First Edition Paperback ISBN: 9781838497101

First Edition eBook ISBN: 9781838497118

Published by Being Lean Publishing

www.beinglean.net

Fag Pack Calculations Good & Bad Calories

Remote Working

Fasting

Foreword

The ways of thinking described in this book are powerful and infectious. They are like new pair of spectacles revealing unseen opportunities wherever you go - at work, while travelling and at home. You will be hooked!

We discovered them studying how Toyota helps their employees produce the highest quality cars in the world. Not just in the factory but in all kinds of design, engineering and office work. These continuous improvement practices are also being used by hospitals and construction sites around the world.

But you will have fun using them at home - to free up time and reduce stress. As more people are working remotely they provide more effective ways of working together with colleagues in distributed teams.

This book is the first step on your journey to being lean. There is much more to discover once you get going. But beware - there is no antidote to this benign infection!

By Daniel T Jones

Author of The Machine that Changed the World, Lean Thinking and The Lean Strategy.

CONTENTS

INTRODUCTION

Lean is a well-known scientific approach to achieving quality outputs and has, over the decades, been adopted by more than 15 different industries to stay competitive. There is a lot about Lean and leaning oneself for work purposes, but not many apply it privately. When I started work on this book, I wanted to share how lean is applied specifically outside of work.

I thought it would be easy as I have a lot of examples and a lot to say on the subject. I found out, however, that there are still not many lean books about everyday lean living because lean is more consistently applied and more tried and tested in the workplace.

I also realised that applying lean to work is so much easier. There are many relevant examples and much expertise out there for us to learn from and even duplicate. At the same time, we are held accountable for our productivity and quality of work so we do it more consistently as it is necessary for our livelihood. We push ourselves more and we try harder. Whereas, privately, we only have to account for ourselves. There are no immediate consequences, or if there are, we deem them to be of less magnitude as time loss is less apparent than the loss of cold hard cash from a paycheque.

Like a lot of lean practitioners, I found that lean working spilled over into my personal life. Bits and pieces of lean were applied randomly, as and when, whenever I got the chance or an idea came to me. When I started out, I thought that only basic lean was applicable, but now, I find that applying it outside of work absolutely stretches my thinking and application.

There are a lot more tools and techniques to boost that outside-the-box thinking and support your Lean living. With a plethora of very good, thorough self-help, lean and improvement books out there, this is my attempt to carve out a niche. It demonstrates how one's environment can be designed through the structured use of Lean thinking and application, which can help us to get rid of wasteful processes to achieve a better quality of life, whatever that means to each one of us. We can all aspire to be a Lean leader in whatever we do. Most of us "types" who read personal development books like this one will know that leadership is not about our roles at work. Lean leadership is about thinking of the people we are responsible for all of the time, and how we can teach, train, improve and better the lives of ourselves and everyone around us. This may be at work, where we are more accustomed to thinking this way, but it is also very applicable at home with our nearest and dearest.

This book is written from a personal development point of view i.e., working from what is within our control while influencing our surroundings. The idea is to give you the thinking, tools and techniques plus A LOT of everyday examples throughout the entire book. My hope is that lean and improvement pioneers will gain food for thought from this book to improve their already advanced thinking methods. But I also want to reach out to those lean newbies to find a starting point that fits their lifestyle, skills and circumstances to aid them in deploying lean methodology to change their lives for the better. It aims to fuel the urgency of all who read it, and to help you make a start on a deliberate and structured journey in achieving that good quality of life through continuous improvement.

THIS BOOK HAS
3 + 1 PARTS

1. LEAN THEORY & METHODOLOGY

COMPLEMENTARY THINKING TOOLS

2. LEAN TOOLS & TECHNIQUE

3. PRACTICAL APPLICATION & EXAMPLES

+1

The International Motor Vehicle Program (IMVP) was set up in the upshot of the second oil crisis in 1979 to investigate problems facing the world of motor vehicles. The IMVP's initial investigation illuded to new ideas, i.e., Toyota Production System (TPS) pioneered by the Japanese who were gaining market share.

This led to the Phase 2 research programme contributing to the book Machine that Changed the World by Womack, Jones and Roos in 1990, revolutionising the way that the manufacturing industry operated and the accelerated adoption of lean by demonstrating the performance difference between lean production and mass production. The term 'lean production' was coined by John Krafcik, a research member of the IMVP team in his Masters thesis, and since, popularised by the "Machine".

The book is split into two equal halves and within that, four parts. The lean philosophy and methodology have such robust and demonstrable provenance, it is inevitable that the first half should comprise of 3 parts that look at the approach, some complementary thinking plus some hard vbv tools and techniques. The injection of many practical examples aims to show readers how relevant and powerful the thinking and mindset are when they are linked to the doing. It is important to read through this part first to get the most out of the practical examples later on.

The second half of the book consists of the sizeable fourth section and is all about practical thinking and implementation. It is split into the four areas of our daily life, specifically lean thinking and its application at home, in our health, when we're travelling and at work. And with the world growing smaller and more integrated, I touch on the relevance of being a good global citizen from a lean perspective. Theories and thinking usually tend to sound formal, contrived and dry, but they provide the strong foundation required for implementation. They guide and give meaning to what we see, and provide a sound basis for practical action. Some concepts like Mistake Proofing are hard tools and techniques but I have chosen to categorise them in the thinking half as I have used them to illustrate their notions rather than as a hard tool to use in steps while carrying out physical improvement activities.

This is not a recipe book to follow; instead, it adopts an agile modular approach, facilitating you to be your own quality life coach. Certain wasteful processes in life may not be preventable. However, the leaner a thinker you are and the more equipped you are with tools and techniques, the more you will be able to manage and minimise them.

Simple AND Over-The-Top!

Once you've gone through the first half of the book and you're armed with strong lean foundations, we look at the practical examples and you may be surprised about how simplistic some of them are. As a seasoned lean practitioner, it has not been easy to put pen to paper, linking and connecting theory with actions.

This is not dissimilar to when someone asks you to note in detail how you breathe or walk. That's not easy as you just do it without thinking or even being conscious of it. At the same time, some of the practical examples given may seem VERY over-the-top to some of you. This is also the result of being a seasoned lean practitioner. What some may deem to be over-the-top or effortful has become like breathing and walking to me now. Effortless and automated. These over-the-top examples illustrate how the consistency of lean application has induced me to make that initial effort to improve the areas of my choice and transitioned me from Doing Lean to Being Lean. And how my system has been engineered to fit my values, allowing me to achieve the stress-free quality of life that I seek.

However, the examples are just that. To be prompt and stimulate ideas of how YOU CAN apply lean to areas more relevant to you and your interests.

BEING LEAN is fundamentally about waging war on waste to reduce it wherever you see it. Reduce and minimise waste around you to increase value to YOU. If what you read here resonates, adopt and apply it now, no excuses! This book challenges your ability to follow through.

SOME PEOPLE ARE NATURALLY LEAN... NOT

There is no such thing as naturally lean. There is doing lean, which is very different from Being Lean, which is anything but natural. There should always be science and thought behind actions. Thinking is drummed in until it comes more natural, until Doing becomes Being.

Thinking is drummed in until it comes more natural, until Doing becomes Being.

Some people are just naturally organised and efficient but lean is not just about being organised. I was haphazardly organised prior to becoming a lean practitioner, who aims to be organised in everything I do. But as stated, Lean is a philosophy and methodology to help us be more effectively efficient (organised). It is the science and thought behind the doing.

I am good at things, not because I love the activities and enjoy doing them. I know they need to be done and I NEED to find the best and easiest way to do them with as little time and effort as possible, because I dislike doing them. I also NEED to sustain the habits that I do not enjoy or there will be consequences. "But you love training!" my sister says.

I certainly do not. "But you love cleaning!" my in-laws claim. I certainly do not. What makes people think I even remotely like cleaning or training? Apparently, I display quality results and appear to be very good at making it look so easy or so they tell me.

I am very flattered at hearing this and must say it is one of my rewards for Being Lean. Who doesn't like to be perceived as being effortlessly good at things, especially if that is some what true?
I roll my eyes when I hear fitness gurus mention fun training. Build fun into your training routine and you will keep doing it. Frankly, it is impossible for me to make training fun. To me, it is nothing but a chore. I just leverage what lean has to offer to engineer the processes in my surroundings to induce the correct behaviour i.e., do things that I do not like but are necessary.

Automation and occasional rewards help maintain and sustain behaviour and results. Applying and deploying lean is key; it is not a short-cut for efficiency and efficacy are the drivers. Disciplined and efficient. We can be efficient but take the long way around, just because we didn't know there is a better way. A simple example of being organised but not lean is having a larder full of well-organised, labelled foodstuff. We all love those Instagram photos of pretty colour compatible boxes of food in the fridge. That's just simply being neat and organised.

Having the minimal of all that you need (minimal inventory and cash tied u p) at any one time is lean, proven by the fact that you never need to find it, or run out to the corner shops to get something that's missing. This may sound simple, but much background work is required to develop a lean fridge system. If there is no thought or science behind the numbers and types of inventory nor the layout of the inventory etc., then organised waste is still waste, i.e., you're being efficient with wasteful processes. I've got a very functional lean(ish) fridge and a lean home, but it isn't staged or pretty like on Instagram. The same goes for all the photos of real lean living in this book, that's why they are all illustrated.

WHAT IS **EVERYDAY LEAN?**

Every day lean is about everything you do in your life. When you should wake up, how you get yourself and your family up in the morning, how you make breakfast and prepare lunch, how you get dressed, mealtimes, your morning/afternoon/evening rituals, DIY work, fun time, all of work, holidays. It is about every aspect of your life and how you can do things simpler, quicker and safer, using scientific methods to help you obtain your goals without compromising on quality.

Being Lean is about constantly making everything in life a little bit better every day. No drama, we are talking about small improvements, not once, not twice, but when you *"see"* opportunities every single day, consistently for the rest of your life. For me, this is an extremely satisfying and rewarding way to live.

Many things bother me, big and small. If something bothers you, it's usually a sign there is waste in the process, and where there is waste, there are opportunities to improve. For most of us, as long as we are comfortably or mildly uncomfortably content, there is no urgency to be better. Things must usually get bad enough before we decide to do something about it.

Personally, it is my laziness and impatience about doing things twice or taking the long way around that fuels action. I was on auto-pilot and allowed things to keep bothering me. It was only when I understood the lean concept of waste, did I note

that it bothered me. I started asking myself what I could do about it. Whether I like it or not, whether I can do anything about it or not, I was used to waiting for meetings to start. 10 minutes here, 15 minutes there, I was not so much OK with it, but resigned that it happens. Time and again, I allowed the status quo. I got used to being wasteful with my time and wasteful with other people's time. I allowed people to encroach and steal my time, and you bet that I returned the (dis)favour.

Before I was Lean at home, I was blind to waste outside of work. I was OK with forgetting to plan what to eat, and ended up stuffing myself with anything I could find or would compromise the quality of my meal because I didn't have all the necessary ingredients. I was OK with wasting 15 minutes popping into the corner shop to get ginger that I didn't have for a dish.

I used to strive so hard to be productive and efficient at work but seemed unable to do the same at home or in my personal life at first. It's because, back then, I didn't see the bigger picture. Big things that bother us are usually systemic and we, as individuals, potentially have little influence or control over them. But everyday lean is about first being able to see wasteful processes and starting small with things that we can do something about. This inevitably spills out into all areas of our life, making us an all-round effectively efficient person.

Here's a very simple example of everyday lean. I am an avid everyday cook. I noticed that I use onion powder and garlic powder a lot in my cooking. I always have to first shake some onion powder and then some garlic powder into my dry rubs or many other dishes. I noticed that I use onion and garlic every time. So, to reduce a process step, I made a shaker of onion and garlic powder (proportioned the way I like it, slightly more onion than garlic). Once I had done that, I realised that I used salt too. So, for another small step improvement, I added salt to that onion/garlic shaker and eliminated another process step. Every little bit counts, right? Once I saw the power of "consolidation", I went around the house to see what other quick-wins I could get.

Many will be asking what's the point in saving five minutes? You will find a more scientific and in-depth explanation in the time management and standardisation chapter, but for me, it is an indoctrination that every second counts and is precious. For top athletes, to break records, all you need is a fraction of a second. In the manufacturing world, a second or a minute along each step of the production line can produce an extra few units for sale. For me, finding 10 minutes to sit on the couch and catch the weather or joyfully plan which pub to visit over the weekend is happiness and invaluable.

On the other hand, saving 10 minutes in a process may be pointless if it is not enough to accomplish your next task. You will need to find enough time savings to make it worthwhile, or plan in an activity to fit in the minutes you have saved. This is part of what lean thinking, tools and techniques can do. It helps you decide what improvements to take on and if they are worth doing or not.

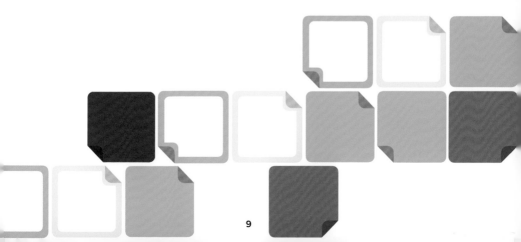

PART
01

LEAN
as a
STRUCTURED
APPROACH

TO IMPROVE
quality of life

As a lean consultant, I have met countless companies and people who pick and choose what they want to improve. We somehow think, by simply putting in the hours or wanting to be better, we will inevitably improve. And since doing something to improve is always better than not doing, we do just that. Unfortunately, the word to use for that is random. You can pick and choose what you want to improve, as long as it is not haphazard or just the most convenient thing to improve. The structured approach means the opposite of random as it is a systematic way of working. At work, only amateurs rely on hoping and wishing, professionals use systems to get results. The same should apply in our private life. Being able to connect the thinking and tools to the deed, action or improvement is important to decide if it is worth doing (business case). Otherwise, it's just random improvements that may not yield the benefits you desire, maintain improvement or sustain the good habit. Many businesses adopt a structured approach and use tools, techniques and formal principles like setting a vision, mission, goals, budgeting and different kinds of analysis to improve productivity and the probability of achieving goals. Some do it better than others, especially those with a consistent purpose.

So, if a structured approach is good for business, why do we only do that at work, I ask? Why not in our personal life? Why aren't we more purposeful and deliberate at home? Don't we need to improve our productivity at home and play or achieve personal goals outside of work? How does that relate to our personal life? I don't understand this. Why does it mean having a shorter life?

Everybody, every company, every project has different processes, even within the same subject area, which is why tailor-made, flexible countermeasures are required. By acquiring the thinking and necessary tools, it enables one to find unique solutions to one's unique process. By introducing lean, the approach allows for thinking before inducing voluntary actions to improve the right things, at work, home or play. It will help you develop a series of strategies and habits to put you in the best possible place to succeed quicker without taking short-cuts and compromising quality.

THE FRAMEWORK
OF LEAN PHILOSOPHY

Lean is the subject of many doctorates. This thinking and methodology is process based and is applicable to all aspects of life. It has since been successfully deployed across various industry sectors including Manufacturing, Construction, IT, Retail, Oil and Gas, Health, Environmental, Accounting etc. Lean, although adopted by many industries, does not have an agreed universal definition. Different industries will have their own interpretation, preferred tools and applications. Whichever way lean is defined, the essence, simply explained is essentially about a philosophy accompanied by a tried and tested methodology that aims to optimise activities to achieve end user satisfaction through the elimination of waste. Waste elimination through minimisation of time, effort and resources without compromising quality.

The key aim for lean is to do it systematically but be flexible in its application; in line with the thinking, principles, attitudes plus tools and techniques. Lean is first and foremost not about finding a solution to a problem. It is about the flexibility of the system to deal with various issues one might encounter in our fast paced and ever-changing society.

In this Part 1, I introduce you to the fundamental framework of lean thinking laying ground for strong foundations.

THE 4 LEAN CUSTOMERS

Lean at work and business is largely successful due to its fervent focus on Customers. Great emphasis is placed in the Customer's perception of value. The word Customer is used when applied by companies and at work. Primarily for people who pay for goods or services. When we talk about customer satisfaction, we all assume that we are talking about the person paying for that something.

That is essentially true but that's where the problem begins. We are all so focused on the fact that payment is power, we forget that there are other important customers throughout the process that lead us to the ultimate end user customer we need to satisfy.

Lean has identified 4 Customers along any one process:

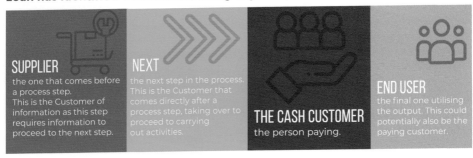

SUPPLIER
the one that comes before a process step.
This is the Customer of information as this step requires information to proceed to the next step.

NEXT
the next step in the process. This is the Customer that comes directly after a process step, taking over to proceed to carrying out activities.

THE CASH CUSTOMER
the person paying.

END USER
the final one utilising the output. This could potentially also be the paying customer.

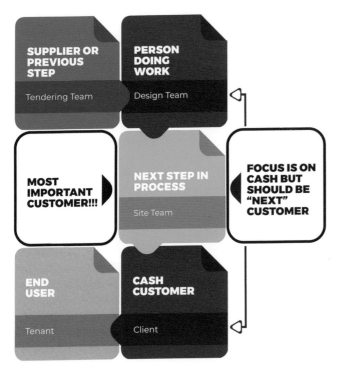

From a lean point of view, it insists that we understand value from the end user's perspective. However, it also insists that to achieve that end user satisfaction, we need to focus on the NEXT customer – next process step. The change over from these process steps (NEXT customers), from one to another is where opportunities for waste present themselves and flourish. It is between each process step (micro or macro) that hiccups appears to break the flow. Another way to see this is whenever there is a start and stop, or whenever payment in any form, is made. In other words, optimising one's own interest without full knowledge of what the end user (System) needs creates waste for everyone including ourselves.

Many in construction that I have preached NEXT customer to, will immediately claim it "altruism" and that it will not work. For example, there is no way the sprinklers are willing to sub-optimise and slow down for the electricians to catch-up and do their bits, for the sake of the whole construction programme. This may be true but that is only if we view processes as linear.

Many micro processes make up a macro process, as stated before. In this particular case, once the electrician is done the sprinklers come back to do their bits, so everyone (trade) will be everyone's NEXT customer more often than not, hence it will work because we're doing it as it benefits ourselves. "Selfish us" will want to give our NEXT customer what they need to do their work and reciprocally, they will give us what we need to do ours as their NEXT customer.

SYSTEM

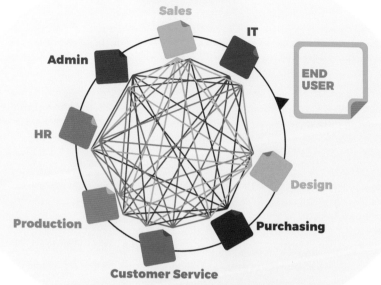

Cyclical process of NEXT customers regardless
of in-house or external services

LINEAR PROCESS OF CUSTOMERS

If you know of the NEXT customer principle, you would not need the Council to print flyers to remind you to pull your bins to the front of your house first thing in the morning. You would know that after putting trash in your bin, on collection day, that the NEXT customer (step) would be the bin person picking up the bins. You would leave the bins at the very front of your house where it is more visible and easier for your NEXT customer to retrieve.

Knowing what the NEXT customer needs allows us to make it easy for them to do the job and provide US with the good service we desire. You may recognise the slight element of mistake proofing here.

The bin being more visible statistically increases the chances of them being emptied and not missed. The bin being out front also means less walking for the bin person which, in turn, means they can do the job quicker and more productively, allowing the Council to pick up more bins in the time they have. Many wins.

Macro Home Example

Good communications at home, letting everyone know what you are up to, so everyone can plan their own activities accordingly, e.g., a missed dinner contributes to wasted effort and food waste. When we do things just-in-case, or we cause people to do things just-in-case, it is because we have not taken the time to consider and understand what our NEXT customers need to do what they have to do and vice-versa.

Micro Home Examples

If the whole family understands the NEXT customer principle, there may not be the need to clean-up after each other anymore, creating more flow.

From a respect for each other point of view, remember that if there are 5 steps in a process to do something and you cut a necessary step or two to make it quicker for you, those steps or two do not disappear.

They will still need doing but by the NEXT person, whoever they are. You have just "fobbed" it off to someone else. The time you "saved" has to be "paid" by someone else. At the same time, you may have introduced extra steps because you did not follow through doing what was required to complete that task at that time.

We may not like our colleagues or cashier at the corner shop enough to give them too much NEXT customer consideration, but to make NEXT customer considerations a habit (standardised behaviour), try applying them consistently with our nearest and dearest at home. A few micro process examples to start you off:

- Replenish toilet rolls after you for the next person who uses the toilet

- Leave the place clean and tidy after use for the next person

- Put things back in their homes so others can find them

YOU, YOURSELF AS THE NEXT CUSTOMER

Bear in mind that you can be your own NEXT customer if the next process step is conducted by you. Ask yourself what it is you need to do the task? A very simple and identifiable example can be food portioning.

You may be tempted to shove a whole chunk of rib steak into the freezer as it is easier and quicker.

But think about the NEXT customer i.e., you, coming home to make dinner having to defreeze that chunk to get what you need. It would take much longer and it would have been quicker to portion up the steak to your needs and freeze them when you first bought it. Whenever I need to do some small painting job at home, I curse and swear each time. I always regret I didn't take that 3 mins to clean the brushes at my last painting occasion.

I end up having to take 15 mins to deal with it instead, when all I want is to just get to the value adding painting bit.

NEXT CUSTOMER CHECKOUT

Do you have a process for how you load and unload your trolley at the supermarket checkout? And now that we have home delivery, do you worry about how the goods will be delivered?

I always feel the person that stands behind me in any checkout queues has chosen the right queue, lucky cheese. My queue will always be the fastest one unless their machine breaks down. I unload the trolley in the way I would pack and categories of groceries in different category bags. All products will be placed on the conveyor belt with codes facing the direction required by the cashier to reduce motion (ergonomic) waste which means least steps to get it scanned.

A micro process but I have three "NEXT" customers. Firstly, the cashier receiving, inputting and registering my products, then myself as I receive and pack away my goods and ultimately the one queuing after me having minimised their waiting time.

QUICK SET-UP

Quick set-up is being ready for the NEXT customer. All set-ups are considered waste, because while you are "setting up", someone is waiting. What sorts of tasks can be done beforehand to allow for more ease when the clock is ticking?

Macro -
Be prepared with your passports, mobile tickets and paperwork at check-in

Micro –
Documents, QR codes in correct direction when handing over to the NEXT customer

Not everyone will do the same for you but at least you will be aware of your own set-up and be quicker with your own processes.

Being Lean and considerate about the NEXT customer, benefits mostly others to start with. Why bother, you may ask? Lean people are not most people. Just because we do not immediately or directly benefit doesn't mean we don't do it. We mirror and lead by good example. It is habit building and natural for us to eliminate waste wherever we see it regardless.

We understand that a war on waste will benefit mankind and all around us. I think of it as selfishness through selflessness. To get what you want, you have to think longer term, the ripple effect. More on this subject and how we leverage and make it beneficial, in the chapter where we plan to change the world!

EVERYDAY LIFE CUSTOMERS

This is also applicable in the case when we use the word 'customer' in everyday lean. Except that our "payment" (value) does not pertain only to money but other valuable commodities like time, emotions, health, wellness, status, affections, rewards etc. It can relate to ourselves, individuals or people that we are carrying out the activity for.

If we are writing a poem for someone to get "payment" in affections (commodity of value), that someone will be the customer we are talking about. Note that from a bigger picture lean point of view, provided that is what that someone wants. If not, the whole exercise is a waste of time i.e., you do not know what your customer wants. If you are trying hard to be efficient in your poem writing and making it good quality (when that is not how you can earn that affection), then that is making waste more efficient.

But if the poem is indeed what will earn their affection, then putting pen to paper composing the poem is creating value for your customer. If we are conducting volunteer activities for the children's football club, then the children are the customers. If we are making meals and keeping house for the family, then members of the family are the customers...and yes, there will be customers with conflicting wants, needs and preferences just like in any business.

The 3 Elements of a Process

It is fundamental in lean to recognise the three elements of any process. Any process you look at, macro or micro, can be classified into the elements of Value, Non-Value Adding (NVA) and Waste.

Value
To identify value, something has to change physically in shape and nature that contributes to the formation of what the customer wants (or is paying for). Taking the poem It isn't above, it's on the previous page if this is in book form. as an example, it will be as soon as your thoughts are formed and you are ready for it to take form. As soon as you concretise it in some form, i.e., the Value Adding bit is when you put pen to paper or type it out. From a macro point of view, the point when your Customer gets the poem and reads it.

Non-Value Adding (NVA)
Non-value adding steps are necessary steps that are a support activity contributing to the formation of what the customer wants (Value). From a macro view, gathering information about that someone to make the poem more meaningful, writing drafts etc. may be necessary as you have to prep and fine-tune it before getting a final version. It remains Non-Value Adding (NVA) until the customer gets the poem. From a micro view, forming the poem in your head, thinking about the language and use of words etc. is necessary as it enables adding value, but it is NVA because you do not physically form the poem. Until you put pen to paper (make a physical change) on the final document/format, it is still only a support activity, i.e., NVA.

We often confuse being productive (VA) with working as fast as we can, every second of the day. We fear that slowing down to do the prep work, i.e., NVA, to ensure we do it right first-time round will kill our productivity. Activities that are necessary to facilitate VA activities, i.e., what customers want or are willing to pay for, are mistakenly deemed a waste of time.

Waste
Waste is any step that is unnecessary and avoidable with no consequences. If there are detrimental consequences then it is most probably NVA. It is anything that takes longer than necessary and we have to do again... and again. From a macro view, for example, travelling (NVA) to that somebody to present your poem but missing (Waste) the train and then, when you get there, they are not home (Waste). And when they finally get the poem, they'd rather have flowers (Waste). Zooming in, on the micro view, it is waste when we start putting pen to paper but there is no ink or we run out of paper. Or when we finish the poem and excitingly send it via email but it gets sent to the wrong person thanks to us clicking on the auto address that appeared on the email To: box.

LEAN NOT MEAN
Raise the ratio of Value Added Operations to Non-Value & Waste.

KEY

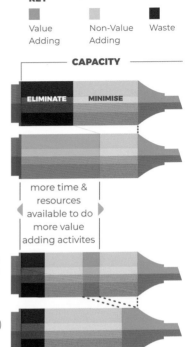

Value Adding · Non-Value Adding · Waste

CAPACITY

ELIMINATE MINIMISE

more time & resources available to do more value adding activites

Increase **VA** by focusing on minimising NVA & **Waste**

All the waste mentioned above is easily avoidable and this is even more the case after the fact; through lessons learnt.

The traditional time and motion principle has never been popular with people in the process being investigated. It focuses on the Value-Adding element to increase productivity, e.g. how to lay more bricks per hour. By focusing on this element, you inevitably introduce further NVA and/or waste into the process. This can also reduce worker morale and the quality of the work.

This principle advocates working harder to get more, plus in reality, you end up with less as quality will suffer when you work faster, as it contributes to rework. Lean works on the premise that we have the right people on board who know what they are doing. It advocates mistake proofing and working on the process first before focusing on the people. Leave well alone, i.e., not teaching grannies to suck eggs in the first instance. By focusing on eliminating and minimising as much non-value adding and waste activities as possible, it frees up more time and resources to do more value-adding work. More on the types of lean waste can be found in the 8 Waste section.

The 5 Lean Principles

If you use only the hard tools and techniques, you will lose the road map that is the power & efficacy of lean. If you use only the thinking and philosophy but not learn the tools, you will not get the optimum results. Hence the importance of thinking and doing.

Starting with the thinking, these are the 5 lean principles:

1 VALUE 2 VALUE STREAM 3 FLOW 4 PULL 5 PERFECTION

1 Value – Not Just Monetary

I mentioned Value briefly in the 3 elements of a process. Something adds Value if it changes in shape, form or function in line with the customer's requirements. Value represents the need at a specific point in time. In its simplest form, for a company, this is any activities that contribute to getting paid (monetary).

In an all-purpose everyday form, it is any activities contributing to the formation of anything that you find of value or need. If someone's affection (commodity of value) is what you are trying to gain, then any process activity contributing to chalking up that affection is of value to you.

If time is the commodity (value), any activity contributing to freeing up time is Value Adding. In this case, it is about freeing up time to be useful to the individual (customer).
I can free up 10 minutes, just to lie on the couch in peace to get some me-time. It contributes to my mental well-being and is a luxury that means a lot to me. But to others, that 10 minutes of couch time could be a waste, when they can be doing something else of more value to them. So, value is subjective to the customer.

2 Value Stream

Value stream is all the steps in the process from raw material to finished job. It is mapping out the process steps of the activity in its entirety. You get a value stream when you start examining each step to see if it is of value or waste. Here is an example of a Value Stream Map of doing the laundry where each process step is allocated its element.

Whether the steps are NVA or Waste is dependent on the circumstances. The only value-adding step here is Step 17, when the machine starts contributing physically to the cleansing of the clothes, contributing to what the customer wants i.e., clean clothes. All the other steps are just facilitating this one step. The idea is to reduce as many NVA and Waste steps as possible in this process within the premises that the current circumstances allow at that time and situation, i.e., the budget, space, technology available etc.

It would be impossible to get rid of all the steps but being able to see and know what the wasteful steps are enables us to do what we can to improve the process, free up time and improve quality wherever possible.

Steps	Activity	Elements
1	Remove clothes from laundry basket	W
2	Sort clothes into piles, e.g. black if doing black laundry	W
3	Put non-blacks back into laundry basket	W
4	Put blacks into laundry bag	W
5	Take laundry bag and walk to washing machine	NVA
6	Empty laundry bag contents into machine	NVA
7	Close machine lid/door	NVA
8	Walk to cupboard to get washing liquid	W
9	Open detergent cap	NVA
10	Pour liquid into measuring cap	NVA
11	Open detergent compartment	NVA
12	Pour detergent in cap into compartment	NVA
13	Wipe cap	W
14	Put cap back on bottle	W
15	Turn dial	NVA
16	Press start	NVA
17	Machine starts washing your clothes turning them from dirty to clean clothes	V
18	Walk bottle back to cupboard	W

Improvements can include:

Segregating laundry upfront from the source into whites, blacks and coloured e.g., putting a white T-shirt directly into a white pile when you take it off.

Having the laundry basket situated next to the washing machine, reducing walking time.

Having the detergent situated next to the washing machine will also reduce walking time.

A smart washing machine that's been programmed with the correct doses and dispenses whatever is required for whatever wash cycle you choose in one touch.
Every little bit counts.

3 Flow

Flow is about linking together the value-adding steps by removing waste. Every wasteful step is a hiccup in the process. In lean, we want to remove all hiccups to establish flow. There should be little or no wasteful steps. In the laundry example, turning around and taking a few steps, reaching out for the detergent is a "hiccup". It breaks the movement for a steady flow of steps.

Inconsistencies, ups and downs, starts and stops mean choppy processes with no flow. Most people will have an immediate understanding when it comes to work. But once you have the lean waste glasses, you will be able to see when things don't flow all around you. They'll stick out like a sore thumb and jump out at you.

When you are in a café waiting to be seated and the server is more interested in wiping a table than attending to a paying customer, can you recognise what the waste is? This might be obvious now, but before you started thinking using Lean methodology, you wouldn't have given this process a second thought. For example, mood swings can contribute to huge inconsistencies in everyday performances and disrupt the flow of activities. Just understanding the concept of flow changes the way you see processes.

4 Pull

The idea of the lean pull principle is to produce what the customer wants and not force what you have to offer on them. It is the system of controlling supply to match demand. This is similar to unrequited love, where things are very one-sided. It is about not being too needy or stalky.

PUSH   PULL

Regardless of the benefits of a pull system, unless a customer wants what you have to offer, everything you do is of no value to them, like the earlier example of working hard on writing a great poem when they prefer a flower. Whether it is a product, a service, a task, an improved process, help, love, money or time, if the recipient does not want it, no matter how fantastic the offer is, it will be a very difficult sell.

The pull , as opposed to the push system, lets the customer decide what and when, based on a need system. You don't *need* another can of tomatoes when you already have one waiting, but a pull system would trigger you to buy one on the next shopping round if you knew the current can would be used by then. If you keep buying canned tomatoes each time you go food shopping and have a dozen sitting in the larder, that would be a push system.

5 Perfection

Perfection is the goal and aspiration. It is a realisation that improvement is infinite and just better is not good enough.

I've been asked by quite a few people, "why don't I have a sexier title, like '101 Life Hacks to Help Save Time and Effort?'" Frankly, I do not like the word 'hack' as that seems to have the connotation of short-cuts and cutting corners. That is the total opposite of what lean is about.

Short-cuts, more often than not, create more problems as they either use more time and effort to fix or you have to do it the a second time round. Lean is the genius of finding the optimum cusp, just before you hit the short-cut limit, without doing too much and *Never* doing too little to compromise quality. You will never attain that perfection but can try and each time, get nearer to it.

CUSPS BETWEEN LEAN & SHORT CUTS

Car

Waste
Lean
Waste

THE PROCESS AND CONTINUOUS IMPROVEMENT CYCLE

THE PROCESS CYCLE

One of the main reasons why lean is so adaptable and transferable is because it is process-based. Everything we do is a process, whether it be a simple micro or complex macro activity. The diagram below shows that processes can be broken down into the components of Inputs that we can manage, Methods that we can control and Outputs that we can measure.

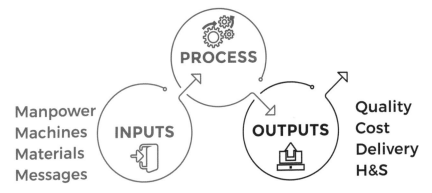

Manpower
Machines
Materials
Messages

Quality
Cost
Delivery
H&S

With everything that you do, you will need inputs. These inputs are Man, Material and Machine, Messages (information), which we have to manage.

Then you have the process of the doing itself, which we have to control e.g, who, when, why, what, where and for how long. And every process produces an output, which we can measure or test the level of satisfaction in terms of the quality, cost, delivery (time taken) and health and safety (H&S).

To use a simple, small process example that everyone can identify with, let's say we are making spaghetti bolognese for a dinner party of 20 people.

MANAGE INPUTS

Man	Chef
Material	Ingredients
Machine	Cookware
Messages	Instructions (recipe)

To manage the inputs, we will need to ask how many cooks do we need? In this case, just myself as it's nothing fancy, just spaghetti bolognese.

With regards to material, what are the ingredients I will be needing and how much of them? This is basically the top part of the recipe, if you are using one. I will have to scale up, as Delia's recipe is for four.

What information do I need? In this case, the bottom half of the recipe, giving me the instructions.

Once I've managed my inputs, I need to control the activity of making the dish. That will involve me looking at the sequencing, e.g., when do I need to start for it to be done by the time people begin arriving. This includes controlling the process during cooking. It would be a waste of time if I stood and watched the kettle (or even worse, the water in a pot) boil when I could be doing mise en place (food prep e.g., chopping up the onions, garlic, opening cans of tomatoes, weighing my pasta etc) and having a sip of wine.

CONTROL PROCESS

How much preparation time?
How much cooking time?
When to start?
What to start with first?
Where to do it?
How long will it take?
How much time do I have?

MEASURE OUTPUTS

Was it on time?
Did it taste good?
Is it to budget?
Was it done safely?
Were all guests happy?

Once all of that is done, ultimately, my guest will decide how it tastes (quality). I will decide if I stuck to my budget (cost) for the party. Was I done in time to meet my guests? Did they all get their food at the same time or did some have to wait longer (delivery)? Finally, did I burn or cut myself during the process (H&S)?

Once we've been through a process, we would like to think we could do better the next time, which brings us to the next section of the Continuous Improvement Cycle.

CONTINOUS IMPROVEMENT CYCLE

Kaizen is the popular Japanese word used in the lean circle that means "take-apart and put back together in a better way". This is synonymous with continuous improvement.

Continuous improvement is a philosophy but also a methodology and a standardised procedure. As opposed to "Kaikaku", which means radical change (innovation), Kaizen should be undertaken as part of our lives and not as some big initiative, where you need to take out chunks of your time on top of your daily process to work on it. It is step-by-step daily activities that go beyond simple productivity and become a mentality and automation of habits.

There will be the time and occasion for spurts of time and effort innovation and initiative type improvements but that can and will be decided by the lean business case we will talk about down the line. Meanwhile, Lean is mainly about continuous improvement. It is NOT about the immediate satisfaction of everyone's needs but small improvements in processes to achieve a better quality of life. It is long-term thinking and doing; a lifestyle. For better or worse, it is a forever task that never ends as the world and circumstances change around us. It is not a project that you look forward to finishing, hence there is no need to overload yourself and do it all now. The important thing is to actually start and take it one step at a time.

Because the world is changing, new waste occurs even as we minimise it. In reality, not striving for improvement is not a choice. By not striving for improvement, the natural law of entropy prevails. Through some effort and continuous improvement, we maintain the status quo and with increased effort, we achieve a better quality of life every day. Luckily for us, our understanding and embracing of continuous improvement will make us leaner and ready to meet entropy.

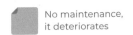 No maintenance, it deteriorates

 Service and maintenance prolong life

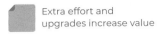 Extra effort and upgrades increase value

Entropy = Spontaneous Degeneration

With no energy applied (human effort), things deteriorate
With some service and maintenance, we prolong life
With extra effort and upgrades, we increase value

Entropy is endemic in all aspects of life, like rust in a car depicts ageing and deterioration, illnesses for our bodies, divorces for relationships etc. So, the effort is required to combat entropy and just maintain the status quo. Extra effort is required to continuously improve and make things even better.

CONTINUOUS IMPROVEMENT

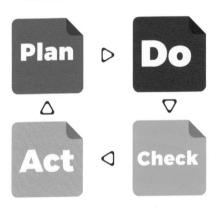

The continuous improvement cycle is also what we call the Plan-Do-Check-Act (PDCA) cycle. This is a continuous feedback loop to ensure that value requirements have been met. This allows us to set sensible objectives, provide standards for comparison, and provide visibility to monitor our performance, highlight issues, if there are any, and ultimately keep getting better and better at what we do.

The PDCA cycle can be applied to any process, as depicted in the process cycle where a process is a series of interrelated tasks that change inputs into outputs. You need to Plan the inputs (man, material, machine), Do the changes (activities) and Check that the outputs are in line with customer (our) Quality, Cost and Delivery requirements. Where the outputs do not meet targets or expectations, you then need to carry out analysis to understand what has caused the gap.

These gaps represent opportunities for improvement and the analysis provides information on where to improve. In order to survive long term, you need to Act on these opportunities for improvement by applying improvement tools and techniques as required.

PLAN: PLAN OUR INPUTS

DO: DO AS WE PLANNED

CHECK: CHECK HOW WE DID

ACT: ACT ACCORDINGLY WITH THE FINDING

Going back to our dinner party of spaghetti bolognese. How do we apply the Plan-Do-Check-Act cycle to it? Now that I have **Planned** and **Done** the party, let's **Check** how the party went through feedback, from ourselves and our guests.

QUALITY
I am usually very good at making spaghetti bolognese and can always get it the exact way I like it. However, I've never cooked it for 20 people before. It's usually double meal portions so I can freeze some for future quick meals. I normally never need a recipe but I printed out Delia's as who else can do good old school food like her?

The recipe is for 4, so I upped all the ingredients by five. By doing that, the five cans of tomatoes seem to have been too much and caused it to be too saucy and runny, which, in turn, needed thickening with flour. According to my guests, the taste was good but it could look a bit less lumpy and starchy. Also, because I took on all the responsibility of cooking and hosting, some of them got their food first and were polite enough to wait until everyone had theirs before eating, making the food colder than they preferred.

COST
I usually just go for the supermarket house value brand for larder stuff, like pasta, canned tomatoes etc. but since it was a party, I decided to splurge and go for the luxury ones. From a cost point of view, it was more expensive than normal but it is fine as I budgeted for it and it came within that budget as planned.

DELIVERY
Execution of the dish was fine; I did lose a bit of time boiling the water for such a big batch of pasta as I only had one electric kettle. I was, sort of, on time to meet the guests. I had to leave my best friend, who arrived earlier for a pre-drink, to welcome the first couple while I finished off curling my hair. Another point on delivery that I mentioned earlier, I was not able to dish it out quickly enough so some guests had to wait while their food got cold.

H&S
I did not hurt myself in any way while making the food and no guests fell over from too much drink or clutter in the house.

HAVING DONE A CHECK, HOW WOULD I DO THINGS DIFFERENTLY THE NEXT TIME? THERE ARE IMPROVEMENTS ALONG THE ENTIRE PROCESS OF INPUTS, PROCESS AND OUTPUTS THAT I CAN ACT ON FOR THE NEXT TIME.

 I plan to stop being a control freak and not take on the whole party myself. I'll enlist more manpower and delegate.

 I plan to either borrow another kettle or boil water in a pot simultaneously with the kettle.

 I plan to take my "me prep" time into consideration so I do not leave my friend to meet and greet strangers at my party or leave my guests high and dry while I get ready.

 To be honest, I've used this recipe before and vaguely remember a few issues with it but have never bothered to make notes as I was sure I'd remember. This is the case with many of my recipes, I am always so very sure I'll remember. So, I've pledged to make a note on the instructions part of the recipe to use less canned tomatoes.

The below diagram is an amalgamation of the Process and Continuous Improvement cycle. It looks complex but it's actually a very powerful visual aid that depicts a template for use with any process.

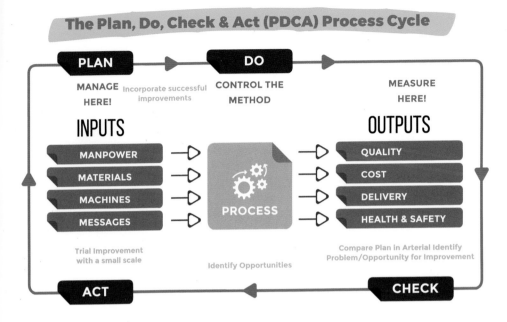

The quicker we go around the cycle the better. We need the system to be flexible and agile. Instead of trying to achieve big wins, many small improvements add up to a lot. Big wins need a big effort and take longer. Small efforts with immediate, accumulated small wins provide the will to do more. A quick PDCA around the process cycle to get immediate feedback gives us a better, more flexible and agile life management strategy.

MACRO AND MICRO VIEWS

The ant and eagle view are common ways to describe macro and micro views; the macro view is the bigger picture while the micro is zooming into the details. It is important to always have these two views in scope, because the more you see, the more opportunities there are to improve.

Let us take the process cycle as a framework to look at the macro and micro view, using our spaghetti bolognese example. The pasta dish is an example of a micro view of one simple process. Already, with just one dish, we can see there are things we can easily do to improve. So, imagine the multitude of quick win improvements you could achieve from a macro, bigger picture view.

I would not be very popular and no one would turn up for my parties if I only served spaghetti bolognese. For a party, it is more likely that I'll have pre-drinks and snacks, maybe a Caprese salad as a starter, pasta bolognese mains, and ice-cream for dessert with drinks to pair with each course. These would be a few micro processes in tandem to form the macro process of the meal. This makes the process cycle a bit more complicated with the increased overlapping of micro processes. Not to mention if we zoomed out even further from the meal alone to the whole party and included other activities. The way we would manage our inputs and process activities, meaning outputs would be very different.

When you try to relate it to your everyday life, it may look overwhelming. But how do you eat an elephant (make improvements)? One bite-sized chunk at a time. Break your processes into manageable activities and tackle them a little at a time with quick rounds around the PDCA process cycle, making it an easy, automated habit.

The sidebar gives us examples of micro and macro ways of viewing things and activities. Whatever it is we choose to look at can always be zoomed in or out, as much or as little as we want.

MACRO

MACRO	MICRO
House	Rooms
Family	Individual members
Room - Kitchen, bedroom, bathroom, shed	Desk, wardrobe, cupboard, table, bag
Desk	Drawer
Car	Boot
Bag	Wallet, keys, make-up, medication
Cupboard	Shelves, drawers
Shelves	Spice, dish, wine racks
Meals	Dishes
Dishes	Ingredients
Travel	Holidays, commutes, trips to supermarkets
Holidays	Pre-planning hotel stay, tickets
Health	Nutrition, fitness
Fitness	Meal, food, training regime, exercies

5 LEAN ATTITUDES OF SUCCESS

Working as a lean consultant, my colleagues and I are very much in consensus on one of the keys to successful projects. We can more or less gauge how well a project will do after the first workshop with the project team. Nothing tanks an improvement project like a team that doesn't tick a few of the 5 lean attitudes required for success.

Personally, having witnessed the power of these attitudes, I am keen to make sure I indoctrinate myself with them. I used to have a list of daily tasks and habits under each of the attitudes and made sure I ticked them off daily just to get them anchored into my being.

The tasks and habits changed over time. I started off not necessarily ticking all 5 attitudes daily but ensured they all got ticked within the week. I stopped using the list when it became more habitual. It gave me the confidence that these attitudes have become ingrained into my thinking and demeanour. However, writing this section of the book makes me think it's time to do a round of the PDCA cycle and bring back the list for a quick check.

DO IT NOW, NO EXCUSES!

The main reason most of us make excuses for not doing something or making necessary changes is mostly because it is easier to succumb to the instant reward of "freeing up time" or "ostriching" i.e., not having to face challenging tasks immediately. I am very pleased to say that I currently have fewer personal examples of this as I no longer make excuses for doing things I have to do.

Audre Lorde was an American writer, who was a woman, black and a feminist, and those are not even excuses, making our usual pretexts a bit trivial. Break that cycle now! Want changes? Make changes now! No more excuses. There will never be a perfect time.

"Sometimes we are blessed with being able to choose the time, and the arena, and the manner of our revolution, but more usually we must do battle where we are standing."

Audre Lorde

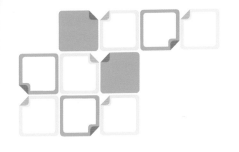

EXCUSE:	DO IT NOW:
My wife is such a good cook, she makes all that good food it's impossible to lose weight!	Get all relevant parties, including yourself, and start deciding the menus and cook together with her now!
Work is so busy right now. I've got 100 emails in my inbox!	Don't find time but make time! Pen it in the diary like an official appointment.
I travel so much so cannot train or eat well	1) Find a 10 minutes body weight programme. No hassle, no equipment. Do it now, no excuses, 2) Bring/buy your own snack and choose food you will eat beforehand from the restaurant menu online

USE YOUR WISDOM BEFORE YOUR MONEY

The construction industry, where I started as a lean practitioner, is like many other industries. They have slim profit margins, strong (global) competition, but at the same time, are very wasteful and, contradictorily, very willing to throw money at problems. They throw more labour at projects instead of going to the root cause, buy cheap knowing it'll pay double later, but can then dip into the "just-in-case" pot earmarked for throwing away.

We will talk about human potential waste in another chapter but in essence, the industry is filled with world-class expertise and experience at its best. Around any supply chain table, at any one time, you will find over a hundred years of experience. It is as simple as leveraging the "been there done that" know-how to eliminate waste. Even better if one of them has a pair of lean waste glasses.

A great deal of head-shaking and smirk inducing anecdotes regarding this attitude can be found in the myth about NASA spending millions of taxpayer's money on R&D to come up with an anti-gravity pen that could be used by their astronauts during the 60s space race, while the crafty but thrifty Russians handed out pencils and chalk.

Capitalising on the expertise around you is wise, but always recognise when that is not possible. There is advice out there to buy skills and not waste time doing everything yourself. That is sound if we are talking about things someone else can do better and not necessarily just anything. In other words, splurge if you have to. Free up time to do more important stuff. This can be a problem for stinging organisations that make their staff take on multiple roles without the appropriate training or skills. This, in turn, creates more waste.

Closer to home, our first port of call is eBay or the like, throwing money at our problems. By using our wisdom first, not only do we save money, but we also get to do our bit as global citizens with regards to the environment.

CHALLENGE THE STATUS QUO

I used to be an employee, driving 30,000 miles a year and was a frequent flyer with most budget airlines. I worked 80 hours a week and was never home. I had a self-imposed no alcohol Sunday policy and tried to avoid social activities with family and friends on that day as I wanted to remain 100% for a long hard week ahead. Even when I made some life choices and put an end to my stress-filled hectic work life, I was still so stuck in my usual routine I don't see friends and family or drink on Sundays.

It might sound trivial and a silly example, but I lost out on so many sociable and happy Sundays because I kept on doing something that I've always done, not rethinking processes (going round the PDCA cycle) in line with changes around me. If you don't even question your status quo, you wouldn't know when to challenge it.

On the other hand, "Why fix what's not broken?" is what I get a lot at work. This is especially true for people who think they are good as they are. It may not be broken but it may no longer be as good as you once thought.

It does get more and more difficult to challenge fixed ideas, especially when the process or activity you're looking at has minimal waste or rather, we perceive is a good process that's been improved many times.

When I work with customers who are so fixed on doing something one way, I ask them to give me their logic. They may/may not falter and start running through the whys through their own heads trying to give me logic that sounds as reasonable as it does in their own minds. I can then push through a bit further, getting them to explain the thinking behind the logic. This is fine if the logic is sound, but when it isn't, by then, they will be more open for discussions.

Personally, I find constantly questioning the logic behind my thinking and demanding explanations for my own actions helps. I find this works very well and it's a great way to catch myself out.

FOCUS ON ROOT CAUSES

Getting to the root causes explains itself. Weeding by chopping off the growth alone is not enough, as it grows back. It's not until you put in the effort to, once and for all, rid the weed of the root, will it truly go away. The whack-a-mole game portrays how we unknowingly, but worse when knowingly, subscribe to this in life. This may be fun when it is a game, but are you willing to play with real-time in your life? Would you want to take the unplanned long way round all the time?

There was an occasion when I was working with a project team on a care home. We worked with the different trades from the timber frame to plaster borders and painters etc. But section after section of sub-standard work was produced by this great and earnest team. In the end, our root cause investigation found something totally unexpected. There was a wave of thefts at the building site and no traders were willing to bring their own lighting. Working in dim light was the root cause for bad quality work. It was nothing that a new lock-up and better security couldn't fix.

I cannot imagine a hungrier attitude for perfection and success than elite, world-class athletes. They have to be quite narcissistically greedy to need and want that fraction of a second or point to put them at the top... for that particular moment, because someone else can and will top them at any time. But because they are hungry and greedy for it, they are world-class. Their insatiable hunger and quest for perfection gives them better chances of success.

That is the opposite of most of us in the ordinary world. Elite athletes are hungry and greedy for titles (and monetary rewards) that are relatively superficial. Yet, we are less than half as hungry and greedy as them when it comes to losing the most precious commodity we have i.e., time (ergo quality) in our life.
The lean attitude of the quest for perfection is probably one of the most unnatural and hardest to achieve. Elite athletes get hungrier and needier the nearer the top they get but many of us become complacent rather than hungrier when we are in the top-ish percentile. Ironically, at the same time, the biggest hindrance to being better is not even perfection, it's complacency i.e., "been there, done that" and "I've been doing it for donkey's years" attitude.

My layman take on this is that there is such a thing as a hungry gene. The athletes (whether based on hard work or talent) who become world-class have that. Steve Jobs, Elon Musk etc. have it. Most, including me, don't. Like every aspect of lean, there is the need to make the effort to hone that skill through the correct attitude.

ELITE, WORLD CLASS ATHLETES

Like everything we try to do, I had to start small. I needed a "vision", something I really wanted. I needed to sow the seed and then grow it. Without that seed (want), there was no growth or desire to do. And as I got better at it, I started to become "hungry" and wanted to be even better, just like elite athletes. Without needing to reveal what this elusive "it" is, I can say that I am now the best in my relevant circle. It took me a long time but I would not have gotten there without my fervent quest for perfection attitude driving me on. I am still on the quest for perfection because, as tiresome as it is, I am now my own worst competition. My perfection voice is forever nagging me.

The good thing is that the nagging voice of perfection has started on many other aspects of my life. I dare say it has become a good habit of mine, which I value.

THE 4-STEP LEAN APPROACH TO IMPROVEMENT

Finally, in this last section of the first part of this book on the Lean framework, we look at how to deploy Lean practically. There are 3 levels of fixing problems. We can focus on outputs, processes or the System itself. According to the business management author Peter Scholtes, companies normally spend 30-40% of their efforts fixing outputs and checking processes and only up to 4% of the time changing the System. You can easily tell which is easier.

Focusing on outputs means putting resources into correcting a problem situation. For example, if my guests are unhappy with the cold spaghetti bolognese I served, I can fix it by heating it up immediately in the micro-wave. This is what we call "firefighting". And like firefighting, there are a lot of fires to fight. The more we do this the better we are at firefighting and we get rewarded for being so good at it, unfortunately.

Focusing on process is about finding and fixing a problem before it manifests itself. The logic is that it's less expensive than trying to fix the output. As good as a preventative measure this is, substantial time and effort are still required.

THE 4-STEP LEAN APPROACH

Focusing on the System works by changing or improving the System. Lean systems are about building a culture of continuous improvement, not just conducting lean improvements with the focus on outputs and processes. This is not an easy upfront task but it is, in the long run, the most efficiently effective way to achieve flow to get value.

This is Waste elimination at the highest possible level. It may be as costly as focusing on outputs and processes upfront but, in time, the cost tails off and the rewards include automated upward returns, while the other two levels continue generating more and more costs.

THE LEAN APPROACH TO IMPROVEMENT

Understand the bigger picture

Investigate the process in detail

Team based approach to identify and eliminate wastes

Generate actions for sustainability

We will always need to work on all three levels. Lean thinking encourages us to focus on changing the proportions of where we put our efforts. The more effort we put into the Systems level, the less effort needs to be made on the other levels.

To achieve a lean culture, we first need to get into and adopt this new way of Systems Thinking. With thinking comes the doing, and with doing, comes a more permanent and progressive change of habits in us as individuals contributing to the System. Without taking the lean approach of systems thinking, deploying (doing) lean can just be another random flavour or initiative of the month.

We work within many Systems; hence it is important to educate everyone around you on the lean principles, whether it is family, friends or colleagues. You reap the most rewards when everyone around you works towards the same goal of eliminating wasteful processes.

UNDERSTAND THE BIGGER PICTURE

The first step in the lean approach is to understand and see the system for what it is in the current situation. Feel free to envisage your system throughout this walk through of the illustrations, with work, household or any communities. It may then make more sense.

Process Start
(First Orders)

Process End
(Money in the bank)

All Systems have processes and every process has a start (A) and an end (B).

Flow / Perfection

In between the start and the end is the ultimate perfection of flow of all the activities within the System

Hiccup (waste) along the way

But in reality, the System looks more like this. With many hiccups (wastes) in the processes. Some will be bigger hiccups than others. The illustration shows so many more hiccups than flow because the lean community is in consensus that when we start investigating wasteful processes, only as little as 10% is actually of value to the customers while everything else we do is either facilitating value adding or standing in the way of it.

Waste Identification & Elimination

Once we see the system for what it is, we can do the business case and make plans on how to deal with all these hiccups. We can allocate budgets, timelines, people, and resources to systematically eliminate waste from the system. We can use some hard lean tools and techniques to help choose and prioritise which wastes to tackle first.

With a bit of science behind the prioritisation of waste elimination and root cause, you will not only see targeted wastes eliminated but many hiccups will fall away without even having to address them due to the knock-on effects. The idea is to achieve more flow to the system.

Waste Minimised Flow Increased

Without seeing what the system really looks like, we would really have no idea that we are living the whack-a-mole game for real. We know and may have a rough idea that there are different kinds of waste, but not how hopeless it is and what a waste of time it is putting in all the effort we have so far to improve things when the effort itself is a waste. Yes, lean says we should NOT waste time improving for the sake of it. We need this initial macro view of the System.

INVESTIGATE THE PROCESS

Having stated this, there will be many firefighters who are happy fixing recurring outputs, as that's where their rewards lie. But this book is not for them. So how do we start the overwhelming task (extra-large hiccups) of minimising waste in the system? How do we eat an elephant? One small chunk at a time.

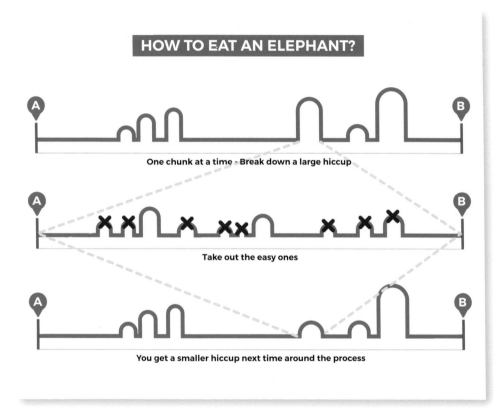

HOW TO EAT AN ELEPHANT?

One chunk at a time - Break down a large hiccup

Take out the easy ones

You get a smaller hiccup next time around the process

To make system changes, we need to zoom-in to investigate the micro processes by breaking processes down, prioritising areas and SEE what the process says and where the different kinds of waste are. Rinse and repeat. Plan, Do, Check, Act (PDCA). You may not have removed the large hiccup entirely, but it would be smaller the next time it comes around.

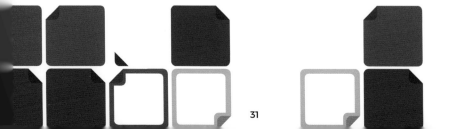

USE A TEAM-BASED APPROACH TO IDENTIFY & ELIMINATE WASTE

You would have involved the relevant people while trying to understand the bigger picture and investigate the process. Just as management will be involved in a company, involve your whole family when trying to understand the system of how your household works. It's the same if you are looking into the system of your volunteer charity organisation, or the children's sports club etc. You alone or a randomly chosen few cannot represent the system alone.

While using the team-based approach, there may be revelations on how things actually work as opposed to how we think they work in our minds, but essentially, the problems and areas identified will come as no surprise. The exercise will have given you a more coherent and realistic view, enabling you to see better to make better decisions.

It's no surprise part that the relevant people involved in the exercise are those who are actually living the system. Who could be better than these people to identify the problem areas, come up with what should be done to eliminate the identified wastes and execute the plan?

You will recognise the hardship of pushing rope when imposing tasks or improvements as opposed to soliciting volunteered ideas and actions. Similarly, always remember to bring everyone else around you along the lean journey, before you get too far ahead of yourself and end up creating the waste of having to come back for them – the long way round.

GENERATE ACTIONS FOR SUSTAINABILITY

Imagine a pot of white paint. The point of the whole exercise is to identify at which point we allow black flecks to contaminate the paint, and so end up using grey paint instead. If we find that the current process allows many black flecks to enter the system, we need to take action and put things in place to make sure it does not happen again. These measures need to last and be sustainable.

This way, we won't have to worry about those areas again and can move forward trying to remove more black flecks caused by things that are not within the system's control along the way. We want to see the shades of grey getting lighter in the quest so that it will be white (Perfection) to start with.

Sustainability of actions means the household or organisation can attain a system's shift in behaviour to self-maintain the process.

PART 1
SUMMARY

To summarise Part 1; the framework of Lean principles highlighted will help readers to:

Distinguish the 4 lean customers as the Supplier (customer of information), Next customer (the next process), Cash customer (paying person) and End User (this could potentially be the same person as the Cash customer) and understand their needs in everyday life.

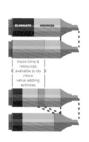

Recognise the 3 elements of a process to differentiate value adding (VA), non-value adding (NVA) and Waste activities.

Understand that the 5 lean principles are about defining value from a customer standpoint, identifying value stream for waste elimination, creating flow using a pull system, and understanding the importance of pursuing perfection.

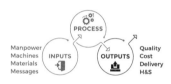

See that processes can be broken down into the components of Inputs (Man, Material, Machine, Message), Methods (Who, When, Why, What, Where & How) and Outputs (Quality, Cost, Delivery & Health & Safety) for scrutiny and waste hunts.

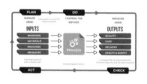

Realise that continuous improvements can only be achieved through continuous Plan, Do, Check, Act (PDCA) jaunts around the process cycle.

Appreciate that both the macro and micro view is necessary to maximise opportunities and optimise the results for improvements.

Be aware of the 5 Lean Attitudes required for success in Being Lean.

Know how to deploy lean practically through the 4-step lean approach to improvements.

COMPLEMENTARY

THINKING TOOLS

&

MINDSET

In this second part of the book, I will introduce some key complementary thinking tools through a lean thinking perspective to optimise lean application in everyday life. This includes introducing a few hard lean tools and techniques e.g., modular, batch size reduction, mistake proofing etc., in the form of concepts and mindset, instead of the original method-based deployment tool specifically used for work.

If you are reading this book, I believe you will have read quite a few other types of personal development books, including those on leadership and management, that have inspired you to continuously improve yourself. I am no different. My thinking and being are guided by lean and it's constantly being enhanced with the works of Edward Deming, Jim Collins, Stephen Covey, Brian Joiner, Peter Drucker and many others.

More complex and critical thinking is vital, as the more thinking tools you have in the bag to use the better. The overlaps actually help you with the critical thinking required for better decision making and prioritisation. This has helped me out with the dilemmas of prioritising which waste is less wasteful on many occasions. Furthermore, this thinking process makes you search for hard tools and techniques to facilitate the doing. This is a quick introduction to some of the underlying thinking that's complementary to lean, which I find helps me to achieve better results.

It's worth noting again that certain kinds of thinking, like Mistake Proofing, Modular and Batch Size Reductions, are hard tools and techniques but I have chosen to categorise them in the thinking part as I have used them to illustrate their concepts rather than as a hard tool to use in steps when carrying out physical improvement activities.

THE LEAN THINKING WAY OF
TIME MANAGEMENT

We all know that time management is an important aspect of being efficient. Time is, after all, the most valuable commodity we own and it's what Being Lean is all about.

There are different schools in the lean community as to whether the focus should be on quality or time. Regardless of which camp you're in, to me, the desired outcome is the same. It's important to achieve quality by doing things correctly the very first time round, so that we do not have to waste time revisiting (rework). To save time, we have no choice but to achieve the correct quality first time round so as not to waste time doing it again. Whichever way we see Being Lean, we need to eliminate waste to free up precious time and achieve the quality of life we are all after. We all have only one life to live and we want to do it as correctly as possible the first (and only) time round.

Time is a non-renewable resource and, to me, is so much more prized than money. Money can always be earned and will eventually and naturally follow when we value our time. Hence, my fervent journey to Being Lean. This fuels my quest for perfection in achieving quality in my life. Like most people, I have always thought and known the importance of time management but I never truly understood the value of time until I encountered Randy Pausch's time management lecture, and never felt so hungry about it. This was a dying man sharing his insights into time management. To him, there was less time than he thought and time was all that mattered. I now value time-wins by the second.

Prof. Randy Pausch
(1960-2008) author of

" **The Last Lecture** "
Time management lecture

www.youtube.com/
watch?v=blaK_tB_KQA

How does one manage time?
We all want answers to that and there will be a whole host of specifics we can do to achieve that. But ultimately, I've discovered that all the things I do in the name of time management are because I manage my time OBSESSIVELY.

LEAN TIME MANAGEMENT

The same applies to naturally organised people (as opposed to lean people), naturally good time managers and lean time managers, which is an applied waste elimination methodology to time management as opposed to random improvements. Being efficient with wasting time on wasteful activities, unfortunately, still renders one ineffective with time.

I am always amused when people exclaim how busy and stressed they are and how little time they have, even when they are supposedly such good time managers. These "firefighters" lament about how much they have to do and how little sleep they get, but are secretly pleased with how capable they are at fighting fires, managing chaotic situations and saving the day (project).

What about those people who send late-night emails and are proud of how late they have been working? As aspiring lean leaders, do we think this proves how hard-working we are? Or does it demonstrate how ineffective and wasteful our processes are?

It is not uncommon to hear that good time management is to do things in the least amount of time possible i.e., cram in more. If we go by that, you can be assured that more often than not, you will inadvertently introduce waste into the process. This is very short-cut inducing thinking. What lean advocates is to do the right things and do them correctly the first time round, whatever time it takes, because having to do it a second time will always take more time!

Another important point to mention, which makes lean different from just good time management, is the popular idea of getting more done will make us happier. No, we will just get more of the same done.

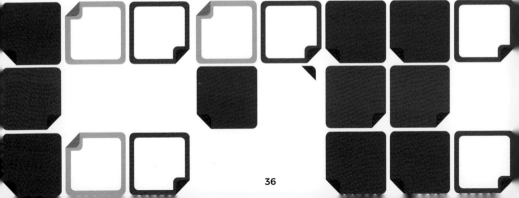

PROCRASTINATION

Time is a non-renewable resource and, to me, is so much more prized than money. Money can always be earned and will eventually and naturally follow when we value our time. Hence, my fervent journey to Being Lean. This fuels my quest for perfection in achieving quality in my life. Like most people, I have always thought and known the importance of time management but I never truly understood the value of time until I encountered Randy Pausch's (insert photo of Paul) time management lecture, and never felt so hungry about it. This was a dying man sharing his insights into time management. To him, there was less time than he thought and time was all that mattered. I now value time-wins by the second.

There are many ways to deal with this, but the few I find that work for me are:

Following the lean approach to improvement by diligently breaking macro tasks into micro tasks and keep ticking to get your rush. Ultimately, that contributes to closing your macro task.

Having your to-do list but having only one macro task that MUST be done each day to make the day less daunting.

Do a Brian Tracy and eat the biggest frog. Choose to tackle the biggest and ugliest micro task on your macro task first.

Design your surroundings to induce the correct behaviour. I hate vacuuming, so I got a cordless Dyson (to "play" with). For the home office, I surround myself with comfort and lovely things. I got a really comfy ergonomic chair, eye-pleasing colourful charging cables and Post-its, and a German design Leitz Juwel Stapler that makes me want to keep stapling things.

Reframe any onerous assignment or chore into a more positive opportunity instead of the chore you perceive it to be, e.g. instead of having to go to the gym, I think I get to go to the gym.

TYPES OF PROCRASTINATORS

What procrastinator type are you, and what about those around you? From a lean point of view, always know what you are up against and "see" potential wastes. Knowing what procrastinator type you are will help you to choose how to deal with it or overcome it. Here are a few that I've come across. You may be a few of the types, depending on the procrastinated subject area.

Perfectionists	- ...BUT it's not perfect!
Dreamer	- ...BUT it's so difficult!
Worrier	- ...BUT I'm afraid to make changes!
Rebel	- ... BUT I like to do things my way!
Defier	- ... BUT why should I do it?!
Overdoer	- ...BUT I have so much to do!

I am very susceptible to a couple of them. But knowing which they are helps me flex my discipline muscle each time I recognise that they are rearing their ugly heads.

TIME ROBBERS

Time robbers work in stealth and are worth recognising. I am deliberately harsh using the word robber because that is the only way to describe it. We are all time robbers. We rob time off others and rob our own time from more important things that need our attention.

We are very precious and cautious about our money, saving it for essentials or to do fun stuff. We would NEVER allow someone access to our debit card to get their hands on the money we have worked so hard to earn. But when it comes to time, we are happy to spend it frivolously. We allow all strangers into our time vault to take however much they feel they can get away with. And while they do that, we feel justified to return the favour and do the same, contributing to a time-robbing culture around us.

With that happening, we need to save time to have more to spend and compensate for the time stolen by time robbers, which you have less control over. However, having no control does not mean there's nothing we can do about it. Recognising this crime and the severity of it makes us stricter with how and how much we allow our time to be spent. And there are tools to help us make those decisions.

COVEY'S CIRCLES AND
PRIORITISATION QUADRANTS

Many will be familiar with and hugely influenced by Stephen Covey's work. His body of work is prolific but I find time and again, when practising lean, that his famous circles and quadrants are of great stimulus to my thinking and induce me to do things. Here's a quick introduction to them and how we can use them to combat time robbery.

STEPHEN COVEY'S CIRCLE OF INFLUENCE AND CONCERN

Like types of procrastinators, it helps to recognise time robbers by separating them into self-inflicted or environmental – whether we can do something about them or not. Stephen Covey's two spheres of concern and influence, from his 7 Habits of Highly Effective People, can help us separate things that we can do something about, things we can influence to bring more control to us and things we should not waste time on or even think about for now. Make a list of time robbers, for example, self-inflicted or environmental causes or note down things that waste your time daily and then attribute them to the two spheres before moving to prioritise them for action.

Bear in mind you can utilise the Lean Attitudes to help in this task or many may find that everything will come under things "not within your control". Personally, having become a control freak from Being Lean, my preference is always to try and find ways to put time robbers in the proactive sphere of influence so I have control and can do something about it while widening my influence and encroaching into the sphere of concern. More on Covey's Circles in the Changing the World section.

Concerns and Influence

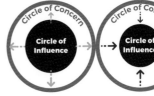

The Circle of Concern
Things we are concerned about but which are beyond our control

The Circle of Influence
Things we can actually control

Proactive energy
positive energy enlarges the circle of influence spelling

Reactive energy
negative energy reduces the circle of influence

TIME ROBBERS

Environment	Self-Inflicted
Interruptions	Failure to delegate
Waiting for answers	Poor attitude
Unclear job definition	Personal disorganisation
Unnecessary meetings	Absent mindedness
Too much work	Failure to listen
Shifting priorities	Procrastination
Lack of authority	Poor planning

Visual management is one of the foundation hard tools and techniques that lean has to offer in its toolbox and Covey's quadrants are brilliant at helping us visualise where our time should be spent.

NOW MONEY OR FUTURE MONEY

Whether we've thoroughly investigated or have a fag pack look at who and what our time robbers are, how do we prioritise the counter-measures? It is never easy to pit "now money" with "future money" as they are just as important. If we spend too much time doing work to earn money now and not enough time on business development to find work for when our current work ends, we will not have Future money.

On the other hand, if we spend too much time lining up work and not doing enough work currently, we will not be able to get through the Now. This situation is less likely because the effect of not having Now money is more immediate. There are similar considerations when it comes to pension saving; pay the bills now or save for old age? With current bills knocking on the door loudly, it's easier to deal with them now rather than the seemingly less urgent matter of saving for later.

This is why many of us do not plan as much as we should. This is why we "do what can be done tomorrow and not today" as we can take our reward of "freed up time" immediately. At the same time, if we spend too much time finding future money or scrimp and save for the future, we may lose out on enjoying living our life now.

We have to agree that it is not a choice between do-it-now or long-term planning. Both are as important and must be done in parallel. So, how best to prioritise? This is where Covey's quadrants come into play. Not only do they help prioritise immediate now money, they also help us to put now and future money into a balanced perspective.

During my time writing this book, I had a writing schedule that I had to toggle with everything else that needed doing. It would have been easier to give in to everyone advising me to keep writing while I was on a roll. But I had to be disciplined about sticking to only allocated times. That is where lean time management features strongly. Stick to the approach and do not "play by ear".

If you follow the plan that you've already spent the time and effort to come up with beforehand, backed by science (prioritisation and business cases), it will remove the decision of what to do. Going off-piste is random and undesirable in lean. On this occasion, I consider the book writing future money and the "day job" now money. Both are just as important, even though I instinctively wanted to get the book done while I had the spur.

Covey's 4 quadrants represent the time you have, so the size of this cannot be changed, but each quadrant can be changed, depending on how much time you spend in it. The general idea is to try and shift, according to importance and urgency.

You want to increase the amount of time you spend in the Quality and Personal Leadership quadrant number two, whilst reducing the time spent on others.

Covey's Quadrants

The 4 quadrants simplified are:

Q1: Do it now – Manage
Q2: Do more of – Focus
Q3: Delegate – Limit
Q4: Do NOT do – Avoid

Urgent – Due soon	Not Urgent – Not Due soon
• Crisis • Medical emergencies • Pressing problems • Deadline-driven projects • Last-minute preparations for scheduled activities	• Preparation/planning Prevention • Long term goals • Exercise • Recognising new opportunities • Relationship-building • Pure recreation/relaxation
Q1 – Non-Value Adding Manage	**Q2 – Value Adding Focus**
• Interruptions, phone calls • Ding "You've got mail" • Many "pressing" matters • Many popular activities • Unnecessary reports • Unimportant meetings phone calls, mall • Other people's minor issues	• Trivia, busywork • Junk mail • Irrelevant emails • Time washers • Poor planning • Personal disorganisation • Lack of self discipline • Procrastination
Q3 – Limit Waste	**Q4 – Waste To Avoid**

Urgent – Due soon	Not Urgent – Not Due soon
• Crisis • Medical emergencies • Pressing problems • Deadline-driven projects • Last-minute preparations for scheduled activities	• Preparation/planning Prevention • Long term goals • Exercise • Recognising new opportunities • Relationship-building • Pure recreation/relaxation
Q1 – Non-Value Adding Manage	**Q2 – Value Adding Focus**
• Interruptions, phone calls • Ding "You've got mail" • Many "pressing" matters • Many popular activities • Unnecessary reports • Unimportant meetings phone calls, mall • Other people's minor issues	• Trivia, busywork • Junk mail • Irrelevant emails • Time washers • Poor planning • Personal disorganisation • Lack of self discipline • Procrastination
Q3 – Limit Waste	**Q4 – Waste To Avoid**

PERSONAL EXPERIENCE OF LEAN TIME MANAGEMENT

Time management issues are systemic. We know by now that finding the time to do important things will not solve the time problem. We need to make time for what is important and do that, we have to have intent and deliberately do what can be difficult.

There is no way anyone can give you a set of what to do to lean your time management. You need to build it around your own situation. It may or may not help, suit or be relevant to you, but here are some things I deliberately install into my daily life in order to be Lean.

NOT-TO-DO LIST

We all have to-do lists, some longer than others. Personally, I prefer a very short not-to-do list. I feel this works better for me and helps me with immediate prioritising and decision making. I use this as a demarcation to help me rid two of the enemies of lean; Muri (overburden) and Mura (unevenness). The third being Muda (wastes). Overburden is when I take on too much, more than I can do, and unevenness is when I consistently start and stop what I am doing because I am interrupted.

A couple of my sacrosanct not-to-do list include:

▶ Never say yes to something you know you cannot do or do in time. That includes throwing the time you spend on well-planned important activities off-kilter just because you cannot say no.·

▶ Never give a deadline you are not sure if you can achieve. If you do give one, you must achieve it (see mirror effect).

They are not at all easy to achieve, especially if you are the kind that needs people to like you or love your reputation of being "efficient", like me. I am still working on it but it has gotten much easier over time and I find this to be very beneficial in the longer term and a game-changer to my System.

To-Do List – Vital 1, 2, 3s

I know my Covey's Quadrants and stay focused in Q2 by sticking to a Vital 1 each day. This can stretch to 2 or 3s dependent on the size of that macro task. I am constantly structuring around what is "most important" to me from both a macro and micro view.

I decide what I absolutely, no matter what, WANT to get done that day. I block off the required amount of time to get that done first. Throughout the entire day, I will fight for the time to make it happen if I have to. I never manoeuvre the daily Vital 1, 2, 3s, as they are sacred.

Everything else on the list from Q2 – Q4 can be moved and used to plug or free-up time. I build in and set limits for each item on the list, e.g.

I'm able to move some only once and some twice etc., so, it is easy to make decisions and move things around without affecting my plans. I know exactly how and when to move items when I really need to, without any detriment to my schedule.
This is how I build flexibility
into my time management.

Instead of hoping and dreaming, this strategy has helped me to realise every one of my quests and pursuits, including this book. With such deliberate conviction in managing my time, I believe that success is *when* and not *if*.

FLEXIBILITY & AGILITY TO MEET THE CHANGING **WORLD**

Many believe that organised people with lean minds are sometimes rigid and inflexible. I do not believe that to be true but even if it were, there is no need for them to change personality if they learn to use flexible life management techniques.

The only guarantee we have in life is that everything around us will change. We cannot control what happens but I fully believe we can influence and control how we respond to it. Continuous improvement is the way to meet these changes and, when paired with flexibility and adaptability, it can put us in front of the change.

Flexibility is key; solutions should not be found for particular problems at a particular moment. Lean thinking advocates flexible solutions. Instead of a one-size-fits-all solution, have a series of countermeasures. A structured approach with built-in flexibility is like a magician who knows which card you are thinking of no matter which one you have in mind, because he already has the correct card ready for display.

Process experts (people within the process) are best placed to come up with flexible solutions and countermeasures. Fixed solutions can potentially miss out on satisfying needs for all involved, hence consulting the people involved is vital when identifying all wastes before the countermeasures are applied.

Wastes never stop occurring, I recently came up with another simple flexible solution to a long time niggly issue I have at home. My husband and I are used to having a night lamp each, on each side of the night table. We've always had it that way. But we can never find the perfect solution to meet our different needs i.e., differing light dispersal at differing times.

We tolerated this for a while until I finally gave it some thought, and we came up with the simplest of flexible solutions that fulfilled both our needs at any given time.

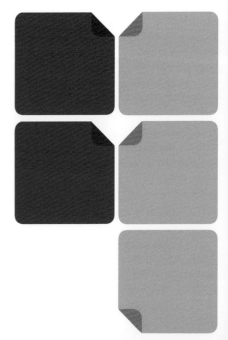

We relocated the static bedside lamps in exchange for two gooseneck lamps that we fixed above the headboard in the middle between us. With one 6 watts bulb in one lamp and one 4 watts in the other, we can use the different "strength" lamps interchangeably between us. The gooseneck allows us to aim our light source where it is needed. In addition, we no longer need reading headlamps.

Just making this little change has been double happiness for me, as it's actually helped me clean better too, especially vacuuming under the bed along the wall. I just shoved the vacuum hose in and made random moves hoping I got everything.
Now, I can position the gooseneck and aim the light onto the floor and see clearly to vacuum behind it. I never realised how much of my very long hair was entwined with the extension cord, which I have missed all this time!

We just need to take the time to understand the different needs of the different Customers involved to build in flexibility into the solution.

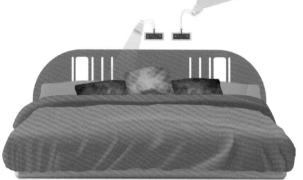

There are many tools, techniques and thinking processes we can use to come up with flexible solutions. I cannot cover them all extensively in this book, but I have chosen to touch on the few key ones that have helped me tremendously.

FLEXIBILITY OF THE MIND

Before going into ways of coming up with flexible, agile solutions, there is a need to address the flexibility of mind. Without that, it limits our creativity in coming up with such ideas.

Like all other muscles in your body, your mind needs training to get it to do what you need it to do. To achieve flexible solutions and systems, one of the 5 lean attitudes needs to be adopted, specifically "Challenging the status quo". Flexibility of the mind means not having any fixed ideas and being open to anything, even the impossible.

"Impossible" and "Cannot" are words that are enemies of being flexible. Never start with how we cannot, or what is impossible, but start with how we "Can" and what is "Possible".
The former, we are all naturally good at, but the latter is the challenge.

Once I let go of the fact that salt and pepper mills are not only for salt and pepper, I no longer need to pound my very frequently used onions and garlic

granules into powder in a mortar and pestle. Once I convinced myself that I actually did not need to eat just because it was mealtime, I ended up eating less but had higher quality meals that I thoroughly enjoy.

Once I convinced myself that I am allowed to say no sometimes, I felt a release. My mind is much more pliable now after years of practice.

GO MODULAR!

In construction, modular buildings have been a great contribution to improved quality, delivery of the construction programme and costs. This, I

found, is surprisingly transferable to all aspects of our life. The opportunity comes from applying it in different parts of my life and when they are investigated from the macro and micro view, these time-saving benefits are incredible.

Modular means constructed with standardised units or dimensions for flexibility and variety of use.

A modular system consists of different parts functioning together and individual modules should be easily reconfigured without the need to make new changes to the whole system.

This is a cost-effective way to provide flexibility, as opposed to the old school concept of customisation being inflexible and bad.

Modular changes actually make customisation more structured and less random, turning it into a good thing, in line with what the customer (we) wants.

Modular inserts of all shapes and sizes are great examples of applying the modular concept. Compartmentation allows the flexibility of changes according to circumstances.

SOME PRACTICAL EXAMPLES

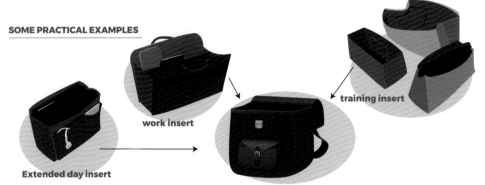

work insert

training insert

Extended day insert

Handbags, workbags, travel luggage, toiletries bags and make-up bags let you transfer the contents of one bag to another in a pinch. Changing bags at the last second and remembering all your necessities has never been easier.

Imagine an empty bag going modular, where you have inserts (bags, pouches, smaller bags, plastic bags etc) for different things and occasions. You can then easily switch from a weekend bag to a work bag in one swift exchange of modules.

Bag with Inserts

We have all been there. I have a basic handbag with the essentials, e.g. wallet, keys, compact mirror, lipstick, tissue, sachet wet tissues etc. By the end of the week, I will have used the bag as weights, having added chargers, cables, mints, more make-up, water bottle etc. along the way. It's worse when I change to a smaller handbag plus a sports bag and start moving things about. I'd like to think that I have an improved modular system lean bag now. I start with an essentials pocket within the bag and expand using inserts, according to the day's and week's activities:

▶ Extended day insert: earphones, deodorant, vitamins and medication etc.

▶ Work insert: laptop, cable/charger, access card, post-its, marker pens, water bottle, notebook with pen etc.

▶ Training insert: water bottle, clothes, towel, shoes, Fitbit etc.

An empty car boot allows you to bring the appropriate modules e.g., PPE for work, a baby bag, sports bag and shopping bag that are all interchangeable without messing or filling up the boot. This helps to maintain and sustain tidiness. You can change from a work boot to a weekend food or DIY shopping boot to make space for the daddy-taxi boot. Going modular and removing excess weight from your vehicle will also help improve fuel efficiency and your carbon footprint.

The same can be done for a fridge. Using pull-outs (inserts) allows flexible change and the location of content according to the season, depletions, family circumstances etc. What about wardrobes? Instead of drawers, lidded boxes can be used and the content's location can easily be swapped according to the frequency of use. The summer top box can be lidded and exchange places with the winter clothes box when autumn comes.

What about short-cut email folders? Flexibility means being able to chop and change your short-cut folders, making changes and updates according to new or ending projects. The same goes for presentations. Instead of the traditional way of saving slides by the speaking occasions (this or that conference/workshop), I save slides by the topic or message. The modular concept helped me free up a lot of time prepping for workshops and speaking opportunities as I can pick and choose standardised slides from relevant topic areas for different occasions, customising my presentations to the current need. Nonetheless, all slides come from a pool of standardised material.

THE CONCEPT OF CONSOLIDATION

Another excellent way to get flexibility is through consolidation, where you combine many functions or solutions into one source to enable the meeting of a variety and host of requests and needs. Some may need to stretch their imagination on this one.

Finding consolidation solutions should come from a pull-system (need). For example, versatile visual management boards are good for communicating information and updating fast-changing information. This is a great platform for displaying the different types of information required, depending on the needs.

Other more straightforward consolidation examples that I absolutely love are the many-in-1 gadgets and solutions, the smartphone being the epitome of such an example. I will need to explore and write about all the lean features they provide.

I have my eye on a 7-in-1 instant pot that acts as a pressure cooker, slow cooker, rice cooker, sauté (browning), yoghurt maker, steamer and warmer. Imagine all the space I can free up in my gadget-filled kitchen.

Looking for purpose-built versatile gadgets and solutions may not be easy as not all purpose-built products are suitable for our needs. For example, I will use most of the features of the 7-in-1 instant pot but I may not use the sauté function, steamer or yoghurt maker. Also, as I slow-cook and make rice a lot, having to toggle using one appliance may not be the most time-efficient or convenient for me.

Funnel   Mesuring cup

Squeezer   Egg masher

Spice grater   Egg separator

Cheese grater   Can opener

Multi-usage is a tricky one. There is a difference between multi-use and reuse. Multi-use is doubling up the use, e.g. using a salad spinner to hand-wash delicates, a lip tint and doubling that up as a blusher, tea strainer to shake icing on a cake or flour into a sauce without clumping. Reuse is finding another use for something when it's at the end of its life. More on reuse in the Lean Green section.

Using the lean attitudes of Wisdom and not money first and challenging the status quo, means homemade solutions can be more customised to our needs. They are cheaper, more fun, satisfying, and we're doing our bit for the environment.

I use lip tint for my cheeks so I don't need to buy blusher too. I double up eyeliner with eyeshadow, use shampoo to shower and use my hair straighter as an iron for small creases when I'm travelling.

Outside the box thinking while looking at consolidation can also mean consolidating needs with usage.

My husband and I now use the same face creams, shampoos, body creams etc., reducing the need to buy different types and pack different things when going away together. It can also mean consolidating tasks through the more efficient use of time.

This is the flexibility through batch size reduction technique, looking for areas where we can reduce waiting time, e.g. folding laundry or chopping something while waiting for the water to boil or microwave to ping.

Do some sit-ups instead of going on your phone to "kill time" when un-skippable commercials come on while streaming movies. It can also be more extreme, like Paul Rausch, whose every dying minute counts. He makes appointments while on his treadmill.

BATCH SIZE REDUCTION

The checkout process at supermarkets offers a simple lesson in lean. In the cashier checkout lane at one supermarket, I scan an item and then place it on a conveyor belt, which carries it towards the cashier and then a bagging location.

After paying, you walk to the end of the checking area and must handle each item a second time while placing it in the bag.

The customer behind you in the line has to wait until you are finished. This is an example of over-processing — each item is handled more than once and by different people.

Additionally, there is an extra inventory of scanned items that aren't yet bagged.

At a self-checkout, you scan the item and put it immediately into a bag located next to the scanner. You scan and bag, scan and bag, pay, take the bags and leave. Look what happens to throughput time. This is a great example of a single-piece flow. You don't have batch processing here, and no inventory or people waiting around.

You handle each item only once, making the process faster for you, and the person behind. Self-scan as you shop is even better as it reduces the handling even more.

Small batches go through the system quicker and with less inconsistency, and promote faster learning. This reduces the work in progress (inventory) and improves flow. Imagine making a 3-course meal while your guests are waiting. You wouldn't wait for all 3 courses to be done before serving the starter as the guests would wait a long time and the other 2 courses would be cold. Reducing batch size reduces the waiting time and achieves better quality. Meanwhile, for every course your guests partake in, you learn about their tastes and preferences, which you can incorporate into making the next course, enhancing their experience.

Faster feedback and learning with small batches enables quick adjustments to meet changing circumstances and environments.

MISTAKE PROOFING

ADOPTING PREVENTION BEFORE MANAGEMENT IS ALWAYS BEST

Mistake proofing is all about prevention before the management of issues, enabling you to get it right first time and reduce the chances of doing it again.

Think of it as preventing dust before the creation of it, plus the need to wait for it to settle.

By mistake proofing a process, you increase the chance of consistently achieving quality and reduce the wasteful need for inspecting and checking to make sure all is well time and again. Creating a lean culture in an organisation or around you personally is the ultimate mistake proofing you can do to achieve an overall better quality of life with minimal waste.

The most simplistic and classic types of mistake proofing include templates and checklists. When travelling, hotel key cards are great examples of preventing the waste of energy and reducing costs. By cutting the electricity when you remove the key card on your way out removes the potential of you forgetting (or deliberately not wanting) to switch off everything before you leave.

Engineering and designing your surroundings to prevent bad quality, rework (loss of time) or bad habits removes the burden from individuals.

We are inevitably and humanly inconsistent. By consciously engineering and designing our surroundings for mistake proofing, we can help automate good decisions and reduce bad decisions and behaviour. To do this, there are some things we should consider when investigating the use of mistake proofing through engineering our surroundings.

PROCESS EXPERTS' ROLES IN MISTAKE PROOFING

Whether at work or home, a simple and must-do way of mistake proofing is consulting people within the process.

This is not just to leverage their expertise but also to increase the chance of "it" being done.

Instead of dishing out chores to your children at home, separate and delegate chores based on their capabilities, skills and interests as there is a better chance of them doing it if they get to choose the chore, and this also gives you a better chance of sustaining it. Breaking down chores (reduce batch size) to, for example, cleaning smaller areas each time will also increase the chances of it being completed.

Instead of coming up with the perfect nutritional programme for someone who wants to lose weight, there's more chance of them following the meal plan and training regime if we plan around what they will and will not eat or do. This is simple mistake proofing.

Without this first consideration, we start introducing waste into the mistake proofing process before we've even begun, reducing the chance of success & its sustainability.

Engineer & Design Your Surroundings

On a personal level, engineering and designing your surroundings is an absolutely invaluable thinking tool I treasure in my quest for Being Lean and achieving a better quality of everyday life. By not having food, I shouldn't be eating in the house at all, I never get the chance to fall off the wagon. Knowing how I am very indecisive on certain things; I make sure I am never put in that position in the first place. It takes a bit of legwork upfront to investigate these "risks" but the amount of effort I expend to live the way I do now, compared to how my life was before, is like chalk and cheese.

I design my environment by leveraging my laziness. Some examples:

- I know I get less sleep when I am distracted by TV and mobile. I reduced the time spent watching TV in bed and got rid of the remote control so I have to be more intentional about turning it on and have to get out of bed to switch it off. Positioning it awkwardly helps reduce the pleasure (reward). At the same time, if I do watch TV and have to walk over, I console myself that I've burnt a calorie (positive thinking). I leave my mobile at the configured home of the upstairs charging station outside the bedroom on the landing, far enough away so that Siri doesn't work. This doubles up in usefulness so that: 1) I do not check and use my phone before bed or when I just wake, and 2) I cannot snooze 10 minutes when the alarm goes off, but have to get out of bed to shut it up.

- When working from home, I tend to have a drop in productivity around 15.00hrs, so I time and schedule a change in focus. I set up virtual meetings, or schedule in a walk to the Post Office or corner shop for a planned task or purchase.

- Knowing how often I justify skipping training when travelling for work, I only book hotels with gyms. At home, to encourage more willingness to do cardio workouts, I put up a folding shelf on the wall for my laptop to allow me to watch a movie while on the elliptical. This, most definitely makes the activity less painful and I had no idea that a good documentary can make the time fly by so quickly. Researching griping 30 - 40 minutes programmes has now become an invaluable task.

- Everyone will love you for this; offer to be the designated driver to avoid drinking because will-power alone never works for me. Legal requirements should do the trick.

Notice how many times I used the word "knowing"? Well spotted, because you can only engineer and design your surroundings for preventative purposes if you are aware of waste in your processes. Have a look at the Lean at Home section to get some pointers for consideration when designing your workspace for remote working.

AUTOMATION TO GET IT DONE

Using finite unnecessary brainpower is a waste of energy. Trying to remember trivial things is overprocessing waste i.e., using a hammer to crack a nut. Many argue and give the excuse that it is brain training. There are more productive ways to train your brain like learning a new language. At least you get something for the effort. Trying to remember things gives you inconsistent results and will definitely waste a lot of time if you forget.

The older I get plus the more I have to do, the more reminders I use. My calendar, which doubles up as my to-do, is filled with reminders and alerts for daily, weekly, monthly and recurring activities throughout the year. The less frequent the task, the more likely it can be missed.

At my busiest, the standard for important tasks is three spaced-out reminders as it draws nearer the task. This helps with my Vital 1, 2, 3s in time management. It keeps me on top of movements in the calendar with a good overview, in line with building flexibility in my dairy. At home, I set alarms, counters and timers all the time.

Why make the effort to remember to feed my cat and risk them going hungry if I forget or I'm late?
I don't really need a cat feeder but I use it to eliminate the risk (one involuntary skipped meal is one too many and unacceptable) and free up a few more minutes of my time.

This way of thinking can be extended by using visual cues to automate behaviours and actions. For example, a half-empty bottle or decided trigger line drawn in a box/drawer/bag etc., triggers action e.g., buy more on the next trip or put it on the shopping list.

They can also be used to deter an action e.g., a full, almost over spilling container means DO NOT buy any more even if it is on sale or BOGOF.

Always Try To Reduce Decision Making

Other do-not-do triggers include setting boundaries and key rules to help prevent bad decisions or any decision-making at all. By specifically deciding limits, you can make it a simple go/no-go situation. On what occasions do you have difficulties saying no, or end up taking on more than you have time or strength for?

Occasions like this end up not being optimal for those you've made the promise to. By not delivering you're putting a spanner in their works plus you lose your integrity, which is an extremely hard commodity to earn back. This kind of behaviour gets mirrored back as it will now be OK for them to break their word to you, without much consideration. It becomes the norm and acceptable.

With a go/no-go criterion in place, you've already done the decision making upfront, you just have to say go or no-go (Yes/No).

The reason why a lot of us have Plan Bs is because we want to have something in place that is quickly accessible when Plan A goes wrong. The idea is to make Plan A as easily deployable as possible, so that it does not go wrong or not happen at all.

For example, the reason why some exercise apps work a treat is because they take the decision of what exercises you do. It's the same with any of the exercise classes led by a trainer.

When you're told, "One minute of sit-ups" or "Downward dog and hold for 20 seconds", you do it. There's no need to think, just do. If you had to think of what exercises to do, especially if you did not have the skill or knowledge, half of the allocated time would be spent on coming up with a routine rather than spending the whole time actually exercising. Or worse, you just wouldn't do it at all.

As a simple example, I've got a lot of mini (DIY) chores to do but I never get around to doing them. I've since written them up on bits of paper, put them in a glass jar and added new ones. I agreed with myself to pick one from the jar each Saturday and Sunday, plus whenever I get time on the weekdays instead of watching too much TV, or spending too much time on WhatsApp with family and friends. This has happened 98% of the time each week so far. It's still not perfection but at least a lot of the mini chores have got done compared to when I did not have that jar.

A STRATEGY TO GETTING IT DONE – LITTLE IS BETTER THAN NONE

According to Charles Duhigg, bad habits are easy to latch onto because of the rewards. If you have a drink after work, the reward is the wonderful taste of a good glass of wine and the enjoyable, peaceful, calming and relaxing moment in the kitchen. I'll have some more of that, thank you.

This can easily become a habit every day after work, potentially leading to alcohol consumption creep. However, good habits are hard to build due to the lack of rewards.
That is indeed true but I felt that I needed to push myself a bit further because, unfortunately, we need to build good habits even if we don't always get the rewards, especially when they are not immediate. And this happens much more often than when we do get rewards.

A Big Mac after training will wipe out the training gains, a binge or a celebratory meal may wipe out being good for the past month, creating further bad habits on top of good intentions.

To mistake proof it, we need to identify these occasions (i.e., no reward moments) and put in place a plan on how to get through them i.e., get it done. To identify such occasions, we need to do a risk assessment (FMEA). What are the very important things (80/20 rule) that we make excuses not to do or do not stick to the plan more often than not? There will be more practical examples under the relevant aspects of life, but I will use training here as this is my Achilles heel. I dislike training and this thinking has helped me get it done many times and is a revelation with some afterthought. It has helped me stick to my exercise regime and practise flexing my flexibility muscle.

Learning and improving to challenge my status quo way of thinking, including the fact that consistency doesn't mean I have to train exactly as I planned every time, just means showing up consistently and doing what I can. Consistency beats quantity any day. We'll have a much better shot at achieving our goals if we do something consistently, as opposed to doing something perfect infrequently.

I am almost embarrassed to say that I've been lean thinking for so long and yet I missed the ultimate concept of the minimum effective dose until recently. Instead of the predisposed training programme of reps and sets, I do the absolute minimum (naturally, you have to have some science behind setting that minimum dose) to maintain my strength and fitness without deterioration.

This helps with trigger habits i.e., a small initial action that leads you to finish the rest of the activity.

Further disclosure, I am also ashamed to reveal the number of times I do not feel like training. That I have a strategy to get me through it helps me to get started, which is usually the worst and most difficult hurdle. I usually start with whatever I can do or muster up enough energy to do. In my mind, I will do as much as I possibly can with no pressure. But more often than not, once I get started, I usually go through the full monty.

My usual week of flexible training regime includes 3-4 strength training sessions, 3-4 short cardio passes and being active every day. There are many occasions that I cannot muster enough energy, enthusiasm at all or I'm having visitors or travelling. But no matter what, from a macro point of view, I stick to my minimum effective dose of 2 shorter than normal strength training sessions, 2 short cardio passes and everyday activeness.

From a micro view, my usual strength training consists of 6 sets of strength circuit exercises of 8-12 reps with relevant weights for about 45 minutes. My minimum effective dose is flexible and officially any effort is equivalent to half the usual training. 3 sets are good (for those interested, see more details in the Health and Fitness section).

Fewer sets, more reps, fewer weights or any combination. I listen to my body and whatever works to get me through a training pass is good, even 2 sets of 10 reps of weighted squats and lunges in 10 minutes. I will call it a day and pat myself on the back for having done something rather than nothing at all.

However, a HUGE, IMPORTANT lean caveat. When we say get it done, we NEVER mean sacrificing quality. With the training example, get it done can mean I choose the easiest exercises to do, with reduced repetitions and sets, but we never advocate you sacrifice form (quality). Using proper form when lifting weights is important to maximise the gains and reduce the risk of injury.

So, if cleaning the house is as huge a pain for you as it is for me, there is no need to schedule in a full or half-day, or make it the perfect occasion to clean-up the shed.

Instead, work out what is the minimum effective dose to get it done? Do the obvious areas in the living room today, part of the kitchen tomorrow and bits of the bathroom when you're on the way to shower etc. Just get something done, however little.

YOU CAN CHANGE THE WORLD AROUND YOU
A LITTLE AT A TIME

NOT ALL ALTRUISM – THE BIGGER PICTURE SELF-SERVING MOTIVE

Many good leaders try to be altruistic. I do try to be a good person, but like most human beings, I am generally a tad selfish and self-preserving. We are not all inclined to do things for free. It takes hard work to be altruistic. Even though I try to give without expecting any returns I catch myself wanting acknowledgement from the restaurant wait-staff for my big tip. Instead of fighting hard against this natural behaviour, I try to leverage it instead.

As stated in the NEXT Customer section, there are 4 customers in the process. We spoke about all the customers, including the "Supplier" (the step before in the process). The supplier (step before) comes before the NEXT customer (the next step) and is seen as a customer of our inputs (man, material, machine and messages).

The question to ask is, as the NEXT customer, how do we make a good supplier? The answer is by giving the step before (Supplier) all that they need to give us what we want.

I order a steak and glass of red wine in a restaurant. The chances of me getting my preferred medium rare steak and glass of specifically Chilean Cabernet Sauvignon is minimum. Unless the wait-staff ask me specifically, I will probably end up with a 25% chance of my steak medium rare and my wine will probably be whatever house red they have on the menu. My chances increase if the wait-staff asks me both how I like my steak and what specific wine I'm after i.e., the

grape and from where. But that will depend on the wait-staff being good and knowledgeable, which can be hit or miss.

You can increase your influence on something not within your control (good wait-staff) by mistake proofing the process, which increases your chances of getting what you want each and every time. I have to treat the wait-staff as a Supplier customer of my messages (information) in this particular case and manage that.

Just like the binmen, we spoke about in the NEXT Customer section, making sure the bin is left out so they can easily access the bins helps them to supply us with a better service.
What do the wait-staff need to give me good service? The best quality information I can give them, such as am I allergic to anything, or are there potatoes on the menu when it's unclear? Ask or state how you want it to avoid increasing the chances of disappointment. So, with a bit of self-serving altruism, it's a win-win for all.

Customer Satisfaction

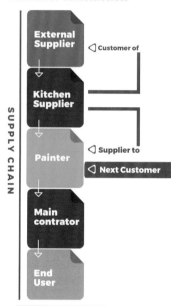

The Supplier as a customer of information does not necessarily aim to be altruistic; it's more of a delayed reward case of bigger picture self-serving reasoning. My reason for showing perseverance and being consistently lean without an immediate reward is to see the bigger picture. The future is made from compound interests and delayed gratification. Slowly and steadily, it will make your life easier as you influence your surroundings. That must be a huge win for anyone.

INFLUENCING COVEY'S CONCERN AREAS THROUGH LEAN CULTURE

How many times have I heard people around me complain about how unsupportive their organisation is, or how some bosses are chasing numbers? With no intention of trivialising the situation, we have all been there. The only way to get out of that situation is to focus on what is within our control, improve ourselves and strive to make effective systemic changes i.e., the long game.

When you do that, you become a prized commodity and your sphere of control changes. You may even realise that it is no longer tolerable for you to be in an organisation this wasteful with human potential (i.e., you). It may give you the courage to change organisations and choose one that will facilitate your growth and leverage the leaner you. You can choose to influence or control your surroundings by having confidence to make better decision. Like Covey said, we all have choices. Yes, we really do. We just need to engineer our surroundings and make those choices doable. Either that, or nothing changes; if that is acceptable to you.

> **We may find it convenient to live with the illusion that circumstances or other people are responsible for the quality of our lives, but the reality is that we are responsible (- respond-able -) for our choices.**
>
> – Covey

"My other half doesn't do this and that, so I can't do this and that." "My situation doesn't allow me to do this and that, so I can't do this and that". They sound like excuses, because they are. Change yourself first and they may follow and things may fall into place.

First, we manage what we can control. For example, living a healthier lifestyle is about making little adjustments that add up to big results. Start with something manageable and think about the aspects of your life that you are in control of. This can be cooking an extra meal every week instead of going out to eat or simply drinking water instead of sugary soda.

If your other half is serving up less than healthy meals, take over the shopping and cooking once or twice a week in the guise of contributing to gain some control and make some changes.

Volunteer for key tasks that contribute to systemic changes, e.g., volunteer to lead a process or activity so that you can "dictate" a better way with less waste e.g., change to a better template (literally or process wise) with less waste and steps, produce a more effective agenda, design a better surrounding to get better flow etc.

Certain aspects of life are out of our hands, which makes it imperative to try and stabilise the parts we are able to and encroach more and more into the areas not within our control. This helps increase your influence a little at a time.

INFLUENCING A LEAN CULTURE AROUND YOU

I spend a lot of time and effort very focused on eliminating waste and continuously improving as many of my processes as possible. As I got better at it, I got more and more frustrated and impatient wishing everyone would stop causing me so much grief and be lean like me.

In reality what I needed to do is to stop moving forward alone but slow down and bring everyone around me with me on the journey. I needed to slowly build a culture of lean around me through choosing the right lean thinking people to surround me, plus demonstrating, preaching and training people around me.

Being Lean alone can be very lonely and hard (pushing rope) work. It can be frustrating being the sole driving force behind the war on waste. Whether it's at home or at work, as long as I was around, things will improve and happen. It was inevitable that I learned from "giving out fish", I had to "teach fishing". This is not only to empower others around me to have a better quality of life but to influence surrounding processes around me which are not necessarily within my control, as discussed before. This is a longer-term view of influencing surroundings in order to further improve your own quality of life. You need to surround yourself with people that facilitate your process improvement, whether you find them or whether you have to "train" and influence them.

To achieve a lean culture, must we do lean to be lean or be lean to do lean? Chicken or the egg? With the goal of creating a lean culture, because we know, we have to start doing, leading and teaching by example. We learn, apply and pass it on to get the ripple effect. This is us being "selfish" with a bigger picture view playing the long game.

THE MIRROR EFFECT

There will always be givers and takers in life and I choose to be in the better position of giving rather than taking. This is a way of maintaining the thinking, building and sustaining good habits regardless of reciprocation. I try to adhere to the **NEXT customer principle** even though the favour may not be returned.

Cleaning something after use so the next person (may be myself) gets it nice and clean and able to use it immediately. Putting things back in their homes so that the next person (may be me) who needs it does not need to waste time finding it. I truly see how precious time is and will not waste mine or anybody else's, where possible. By being consistently lean, it becomes automated, reciprocated or not, and not selective good behaviour which can lead to inconsistencies.

There are a lot of takers in the construction industry. However, I find that consistent, good behaviour ends up being mirrored (reciprocated) even with takers. I have personal experience of when I consistently and obviously am precious with someone else's time. They will take note and mirror that integrity. I am particularly proud that my work performance stats show the least change in scheduled meetings and workshops and consistently, with upper 80% in closing of actions by project teams even in volatile circumstances.

This does take time and patience and works in the longer term. That's why it is changing culture by consistently Being Lean and not just Doing lean. Having as many thinking tools, lean tools and techniques definitely helps in this effortful endeavour.

EMAIL PROTOCOLS

I get absolutely annoyed that people who thoughtlessly bombard and cc every one of the 20-people project team with emails, "just in case".

This is so that they "save" 5 minutes of their own time while wasting 19 x 5 minutes i.e., 95 minutes (each email) of the whole project team's time, while making insurances to cover up potentially shoddy work or bad communications. This is you and me.

Whether you are at work or home, email protocols are a must. It is a courtesy for everyone, as it eliminates time-wasting, especially if the group is big. For example, To: is directly relevant and must-read. Carbon Copy (CC) is relevant, indirect attention that's required and should be read whenever possible. Blind Carbon Copy (BCC) is good to know, so you can read it in your own time. And those who don't need to know should not be included. This helps people to prioritise the email. An agreed way of changing the title so that it reflects the updated email trail is a great help even though the search function is utilised.

You do not need to be the project leader to initiate practices that benefit everyone.

SAY WHAT WE DO, DO WHAT WE SAY

The old saying that our word is our bond is very apt here. If we make promises and commitments nonchalantly, it is very likely we will get the same in return. The moving of deadlines, an inability to close actions, changing appointments etc.

These have causal effects on all those involved and are a major waste in many processes. To eliminate these wasteful, unnecessary wastes, but very real time robbers, we need to start first and start now.

Many will be nodding in agreement as we recognise this at work, where we are besieged with time robbers when we are trying to make a living. But do we notice how often this happens at home too? And we are more OK with it? We are not doing anyone any favours by being so accepting, especially at home.

BEING LATE

Once we first allow meetings, visits, dates etc. to start late, everyone will get the message that we are OK with wasting each other's time. You associate individuals, teams, groups with how lax they are and you start reciprocating.

Not only will you decide to de-prioritise them and deem it OK to "steal" 5 minutes by turning up late, it will most probably be the one you de-prioritise and be OK about not turning up to i.e., you miss a meeting or two. Misbehaviour will start breeding misbehaviours.

So try "harder" not to be late no matter what. I find it particularly strange that we try harder not to be late with customers and clients who are more of a stranger to us than we do with our own colleagues, friends and family.

Is the time of our nearest and dearest, who we supposedly know better and cherish more, less precious than that of our acquaintances and near-strangers because we do not earn money from them? We need to be more consistent with our values, behaviour and habits.

IT'S OK AND I DON'T MIND

To me, the phrases "It's OK" and "I don't mind" are synonymous with a Swedish word "Björntjänst". The direct translation means "Bear Service (Favour)". It is a well-meaning action with adverse or even catastrophic consequences. It comes from a folklore tale where a farmer makes friends with a bear.

The bear does the farmer a favour by keeping flies away while he takes a nap, but stomps around trying so hard to swat some persistent flies that he finally crushed the flies AND the farmer.

This is the ultimate description of doing a disservice, however good the intention or motive is. The equivalent term in Russian is medvezhya usluga, German is der bärendienst and the French expression le pavé de l'ours, but there is nothing similar in English.

The "It's OK" and "I don't mind" attitude is a nod to bad quality (whatever the causes) and an unconscious signal to each other that it will always be OK to blame it on circumstances and there's

little to nothing we can do about it (see the section on mirror effect and Covey's Circles). We are creating and contributing to a society that condones and accepts bad behaviour, bad service, mediocrity and excuse-making.

> "Sorry, I'm late" – "Oh, it's OK."
> "Huge apologies, I forgot to..." – "Oh, it's OK."
> "I must have mistaken..." – "It's OK."
> "Oh, I thought I did..." – "It's OK."
> "I don't know what happened, it usually works but..." – It's OK, it happens."
> "It's OK, I'll drive around and I'll find it."
> "It's OK, I'll ask when I see her."
> "It's OK, I'll let you know if it doesn't work."
> "It's OK, the second one will be better".
> "I don't mind, I'll wipe it off myself."
> "I don't mind, I'm sure it'll fit."
> "I don't mind, I'll drop by on the way again tomorrow."
> "I don't mind, I can kill time watching an episode on Netflix while..."
> "I don't mind, I can just quickly double-check."
> "I don't mind as long as it's no more than a day or two delayed."

We may not realise it but accepting this behaviour is death by a thousand cuts (see the Boiling Frog section). Five minutes here, 10 minutes there. Every revisit or rework (doing something again, every extra 40 mins of unplanned Netflix, every phone call we have to make to chase something, every repeated request, all adds up.

For every "we don't mind" and "It's OK", we all pay. We, ALL the parties involved, pay something, be it indirect costs or effort, but ALWAYS, we will ALWAYS pay in time.

PART 2
SUMMARY

Part 2 of this book introduces some key complementary thinking tools from a lean thinking perspective plus a few concepts based on some lean hard tools and techniques to optimise lean application in everyday life. This section helps readers with:

Lean Time Management

- Differentiating between random time management, where we may try to be efficient with wasting time on wasteful activities i.e., finding time to be more ineffective, and the structured approach to lean time management, which advocates a waste eliminating approach to time management i.e., making time to do what is important and useful.

- Understanding the need to be proactive to bring more situations within our control through Stephen Covey's Circle of Influence and Concern and how, from a lean perspective, to go about doing that.

- Prioritise activities using Stephen Covey's 4-Quadrants populated with the 3 lean elements of work i.e., value adding, non-value adding and waste activities through some personal examples.

Flexibility and Agility to Meet the Changing World

- Recognising the importance of flexibility and agility, not just in the mind but in processes, solutions and things.

- Appreciating how the applied concepts of modular and consolidation can contribute to agile and the customisation of solutions to meet changing circumstances and surroundings

- Grasping that smaller batch sizes of activities give faster process feedback for quicker learning, which, in turn, allows swift changes that meet changing customer needs.

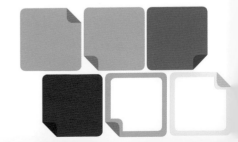

Mistake Proofing

- Comprehending that mistake proofing is all about adopting a preventative stance to help achieve consistency of quality and minimise the chances of known wastes occurring.

- Realising that mistake proofing is most effective when the people in the investigation process are involved.

- Knowing that the brain and will power are finite and the best way to get around relying on them is to engineer and design surroundings that induce correct thinking, automate actions and reduce decision making.

- Accepting through some personal examples that one of the strategies to getting things done is to do a little bit of something rather than nothing at all.

Changing the World Around Us

- Challenging ourselves with regards to how helpless we think we are in our ability to influence the world by taking on board Covey's teachings on how we are responsible (response-able) for our own quality of life.

- Valuing the importance of leading by example, as behaviour and actions are often mirrored through holding yourself to a high standard, recognising and being less condoning of socially accepted wastes.

Lean

TOOLS &

TECHNIQUES

The official qualification required to achieve lean credentials in the UK is the National Vocational Qualification, NVQ Diploma Level 2 - 4 in Business Improvement Techniques (BIT). There are almost 40 mandatory plus optional units in the qualification to choose from, dependent on which NVQ level and pathway is preferred. Suffice to say, there are enough tools in the bag to play with wherever you are on your Being Lean journey. Here are a few foundation ones, plus a few I have found invaluable which I keep reaching for in my standard modular tool bag.

WASTE **GLASSES**

What is waste? Waste is anything that is excessive and does not contribute to supporting or physically forming what customers (we) want. It must be in relation to what is of value to the customer. Wastes are any activities that do not contribute to creating value.

To put it simply, wastes are like hiccups in processes – annoying and easily recognisable as anything that irritates and frustrates you. However, I say this with care as many don't mind waste and are used to this state of turmoil. They never get frustrated with having to do the same thing twice. This may be in the guise of being "laid-back" but in reality, and understandably, many do not feel the effort is being wasted when they do not recognise that it is waste.

To me, being able to "see" wastes came as a revelation, as it has made me realise how short-sighted I was and still am. Only when you know what you are looking for can you see it. I still do a routine waste eye-check to make sure I get better glasses to match my sight as I up my waste identifying game.

"The most dangerous kind of waste is the waste we do not see."
Shigeo Shingo

8 WASTES IDENTIFICATION

There are 8 lean wastes. To remember them, we use the mnemonic TIM P. WOOD.

Transport

Inventory

Motion

People Potential

TIM P WOOD

Waiting

Overprocessing

Overproduction

Defects

TRANSPORT

Transportation waste, in a macro view, involves moving things and people. In a micro view, moving items and people (body parts) movements. The waste arises when the movements occur more often or at a greater rate than is absolutely necessary. There is a debate in the lean community that things belong under transport waste and people under motion waste. I am happy to just spot them whichever category they are in.

Some examples of this waste include:

▶ Moving products or information from one place to another more and further than necessary

▷ The frequent unplanned need to reshuffle stock (products, food in the fridge, clothes in the wardrobe etc.) or information/data to make space

▶ Moving code from one server to another

▷ Handling items (bills, documents, emails, information etc) more times than is necessary to complete a task

▶ Walking and moving (throwing away) food in the bin

INVENTORY

Inventory arises when you have too much of something, with **too much** being the key words, turning it from NVA to Waste. For physical things take up space and the money is tied up. For a more abstract inventory, it is more about distraction and stress-inducing.

Clutter is a layman word for inventory waste. Clutter suggests "messy," however, it doesn't mean that you can just tidy away your clutter into neat piles and remove the label of inventory waste. Inventory means having more than is required or beneficial.

Some examples include:

▶ Too many things, e.g. buying extra "just in case" items bought at the grocery store that you forget you have, such as clothes, stock, utensils, stationery, toys, tools etc. in our refrigerators, cupboards, and storage systems etc. Too many apps on your phone, too many emails in your inbox

▷ Too much body fat that is of no benefit to the body with the potential to cause defect wastes

▶ Too many unused things, e.g. unused furniture (chairs, hooks, candle holders etc.) in the living room, pots and pans in the kitchen, electronics and equipment in the study or office

▷ Too much stored information, e.g. long to-do lists, unread emails, downloaded movies, historic back-ups, old useless correspondences, vinyl not converted to digital format which could otherwise be used/enjoyed (more frequently)

▶ Too many tasks and activities in the pipeline, e.g. work duties, chores, to-dos etc.

Some less obvious examples, but just as prevalent:

- Clutter of the mind using up too much space e.g., too many menial decisions to make, too many things to remember

- Network and people i.e., too many non-meaningful or even negative relations and acquaintances to keep up with

- Engagements e.g., too many activities in your life or diary. Taking on more than you can deal with or compromise the quality of the outputs

- Social media i.e., too many less meaningful contents that do not contribute to the health and wealth of you

- Digital clutter. Many of us turn physical inventory e.g., photos, CDs, video, documents etc., into digital data but just because you don't see them or they do not occupy physical space does not mean they are not inventory wastes

MOTION

As mentioned in Transport Waste, motion waste is about people and people parts. Ergonomics to be precise. Like all the other wastes, this waste arises with excessiveness and the non-necessity of movement. But it also includes awkward and ergonomically wrong (uncomfortable) movements that lead to pain and injuries.

- From a micro view:
  Too many scrolls and clicks of a mouse
  Too much reaching over to change tools, the colour of pens, etc.
  Too many lifts of cutlery to the mouth when we eat too much

- Any types of awkward bending, stretching and trying to see in the dark will more often than not be motion waste

- Searching and finding things or information will often involve excessive, unnecessary movements

- Poorly structured or disorganised spaces will always cause excessive, unnecessary and uncomfortable movements

- Unnecessary, unproductive meetings and gatherings with no output that are wasted trips with unnecessary form-filling

- Refer to Lean at Home section for some motion wastes to consider when remote working from home.

PEOPLE POTENTIAL

During my time as a lean consultant, most senior management have been mainly interested in changing and improving (short- term) processes. They are 80% process focused and 20% people-focused, even if they say otherwise. The 20% involve and ask the people, leveraging their expertise and experience and then pick and choose what is most convenient and easier to accomplish or what they think will make the best process that suits their current hiccup System. This is typical of making the people Do lean.

This is why lean can be such a chore for most people who are applying it at work. In fact, this is what gives lean a bad name and a lot of lean consultants try not to use the terminologies/jargon so as not to turn people off instantly.

It is a tough chicken or the egg type choice. Should we do lean to induce lean culture or create the culture so that people voluntarily do lean? Doing lean, as described above, without the culture leads to many wastes, especially in the people waste category. Making people improve something important to you is forcing the culture and very short-term.

Allowing people to choose their improvements usually means eliminating waste within their own processes that affect them, which means they will gladly do it and it will inevitably benefit the System. According to Charles Duhigg, habits are formed through the reward system, in this case, improvements efforts will yield direct benefits to the people doing it in their own choice of area, making people want to do it again. We all love anything that makes life easier for us. People like feeling better about themselves and they are jazzed when they start getting more accomplished with less effort.

Changing the thinking and culture of people and leveraging that minimises people potential waste. I know many companies (and/or projects) who give incentives for doing lean. However, for a lean culture, you hire people for their brainpower, not just their skills or craft alone, as with brainpower, they become proactive. People's value is in their heads. With a lean culture, you get buy-in at an entirely different level.

From a home perspective, I started out incentivising my family with homemade coupons, which tailed off about a decade ago. Once you've started incentivising, it is difficult to reverse that culture but it's still absolutely doable. To wean my family off incentives, I started associating the thinking, tools and techniques relevant to my "naggings". Like all continuous improvement, old wastes fall off only to be replaced by newer ones to combat. To be fair, when I hear "this thing is not at home!" shouted at me, I am not sure whether to be happy they are Being Lean or not. Do you use incentivisation as a reward system? If so, please rethink, it can be a waste!

Some examples include:

▶ Insisting that people keep doing things they have identified as NVA and wasteful Insisting on "dumbing down" people into doing multi-roles, in the guise of being flexible and multiskill, to cover gaps or whatever the System currently needs

▶ Not leveraging existing expertise

▶ Not facilitating improvements to stretch and challenge potential

▶ No career development

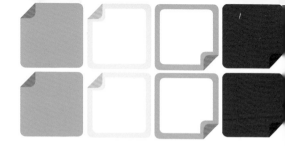

WAITING

Waiting happens when a process is not ready to accommodate them. The aim here is to satisfy the NEXT customer in the process. The inputs of a process i.e., man, material, machine or messages, are ready for the next step but cannot proceed. Think what these inputs could be.

Man – This speaks for itself as it is limited to any relevant living being, be it people or pets who are waiting and ready for something but cannot proceed. We can be waiting to be served food or any kind of service, waiting for information, attention etc.

Material – Anything waiting to be used in some way or another; and because they are things, it doubles up as inventory waste too. This area is large and can stretch the imagination a bit as you get better at seeing this waste.

Some examples include:

▶ Obvious physical material – chores waiting for us to get done, e.g. a car waiting to be washed, data/software waiting to be used or in a quality assessment/check queue, uncapitalised vertical high-up spaces (as opposed to the more obvious floor and wall space), e.g. hanging shelves, mezzanines etc.

▶ Less obvious physical material – potholes waiting to be filled (it's obvious they need filling in but not obvious they are waiting to be filled), your body waiting for you to start treating it better through healthier living

Machine – Machinery, electronics, pots/pans, tools, and other clutter not fully utilised to the maximum and waiting to be used.

Message – this is more abstract, like ideas waiting to be expanded on, information waiting to be used/applied, music/entertainment waiting to be enjoyed etc.

I get challenged a lot by people who insist that waiting is not a waste if they are doing something during that time. So, is waiting time a waste when we are productive during it?

Planned waiting time is non-value adding if, under current circumstances, nothing can be done about it. For example, paint takes the time it takes to dry so waiting for this is something necessary and there's nothing we can do about it. But if there is a fast-drying paint out there that can do it in half the time then waiting time is a waste. All waiting time, whether you play candy crush or do productive value adding work, is waste. By doing productive work while waiting minimises your waste in the whole process.

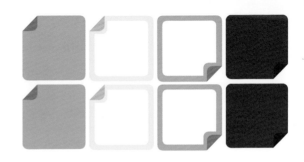

OVERPRODUCTION

Overproduction is producing more of something that can or should be expended at the time, which, and in turn, creates further waste or exacerbates existing wastes. A quick and obvious analogy is when we make too much food, more than currently necessary, which creates the need to throw it away or store it. This must be eaten at some time, whether you want to or not.

To most people overproducing makes intuitive good sense as it hedges against just-in-case scenarios, such as making more parts just in case we get a few defects, making more food just in case more people turn up etc. These are excuses galore that most people will identify with and justify. But this can be one of the costliest wastes as overproduction directly wastes time, money and effort and is compounded by the need to store it, wasting further time, money, effort and space. Overproduction waste is created almost always when you think just in case, hedge your bets or have to "cover your arse", as they say. This arises from uncertainties and unpreparedness. It also happens when there is no science or planning behind production.

Besides making too much of something, overproduction waste can mean you have made it too early, creating other types of waste. As opposed to waiting waste, you produce too early before the next stage in the process is ready, causing waiting and inventory waste.

Some less obvious examples in line with the Taguchi Lost Function where more is not necessarily better, include:

▶ Giving someone a dozen roses when one will give the same return

▶ Doing more pull-ups than necessary to get the bicep to bulge due to diminishing returns

▶ Giving a customer two watches when they only asked for one. Presumably, you still profit from doing this. So, either you could have profited more or you've made the customer pay more than necessary

▶ Planning and reprogramming in volatile situations when things will change anyway. It may be against your instinct but sometimes it is better to wait until the last minute to make decisions

▶ Signalling while turning in a car when no one is on the road to benefit from it, unless it is a planned action for mistake proofing and habit building

OVER-PROCESSING

Over-processing simply means doing something more than is necessary; being excessive by using a hammer to crack a nut. Over-processing usually leads to the above-mentioned over-production waste.

▶ Excess consumption in general, e.g. the use of social media, gaming, eating, training etc.

▶ Excessive, unnecessary information/details you are not required to understand or do the task

▶ Over doing or doing too much of, e.g., too much planning and not enough doing. Procrastination can be a sign of overprocessing; when you over-do something to avoid something else. When you don't want to do something but start organising your home office or worse, start cleaning out the shed

▶ Exceeding the customer's expectations, e.g. cutting the crusts off sandwiches to make them look nice when no one minds eating the crusts

▶ Planning and prepping a month's activities when only one week is required and knowing things will change (similar to overproduction)

DEFECT

This is an output waste easily identified by dissatisfaction about it. Some obvious examples include:

- Broken parts or things that don't work
- Software bugs
- Being given the wrong dish in a restaurant
- Failed relationships
- Ill health

Looking at defect waste from the consequence point of view, it is a waste arising from the time, money and effort spent doing something of lesser quality (resulting in defects) and later having to fix it or abandon it altogether.

This waste is synonymous with what we call "Not Right First Time" (NRFT), where the aim is to do it right first time without any error that causes a break in finishing the task, resulting in rework and/or revisits. For laxer people without waste glasses out there, this can dangerously mean doing it right the first visit.

Less obvious output examples include:

▶ Not leading by example and projecting a defective view of how it is contributing to the replication of sub-optimum (defective) behaviours

▶ Our health is an output of our body and bad health is a defect. We need to try to do it right first time by giving it good inputs of healthy living to minimise the need to revisit to put things right when we caused illnesses (defects), e.g. high blood pressure, bad heart, indigestion etc., due to inactivity or bad nutrition

DIAGNOSTICS –
COMBATING SELF-DECEPTION

We all think of ourselves as being good at what we do. We know we have weaknesses and vices but we think we mostly do well. Fair enough, but a check is never wrong.

I have always been slim-ish, well within the lower end of the healthy BMI range and I train regularly. Everyone around me thought I was all-round fit and ate well, naturally I thought the same too. At work, I work hard according to the hours I put in but I didn't know how productive I was during those times. Looking back, with a moderate approach to all aspects of my life, I obviously had no clue what work hard, eat well or train wisely meant. I did not deliberately start looking into these aspects just because I encountered lean, but the approach and thinking made me start taking note and questioning how good I really am at living my life.

At some point along my journey of Being Lean, I started monitoring some aspects of my life with deliberateness followed inevitably by intensity once I had got some concrete qualitative and quantitative data. Once I knew where I was, I was able to decide the best course of action towards where I wanted to be and where I was now. That was a diagnostic of my life and there are many different ways to conduct one.

DOING THE MATHS – BUSINESS CASES

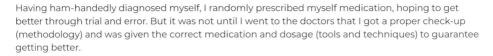

Having ham-handedly diagnosed myself, I randomly prescribed myself medication, hoping to get better through trial and error. But it was not until I went to the doctors that I got a proper check-up (methodology) and was given the correct medication and dosage (tools and techniques) to guarantee getting better.

As mentioned before, making waste more efficient is not the best use of time, effort and resources. What should we improve? Should we improve something in particular or not? How much effort should we allocate to eliminating this waste? To answer these questions, we need business cases or cost-benefit analysis. Call it whatever you want but we have to do the maths. The maths of pitting the inputs of man, material, machines and messages against the outputs of rewards, benefits and savings to be gained i.e., return of investment (ROI).

Let's use a very broad example of "taking the long way around". Physically or metaphorically, this is both overprocessing and overproducing waste, contributing to creating other wastes. But if you take the long way around with intent and plan, e.g. gain valuable experience along the way, then it is not waste but a necessary NVA. To know for sure, so that we can make sound decisions to take the long way around or not and if so, we need to do the business case, and ask ourselves how long will it take and what's the route, etc?

There are many different ways of doing the maths, with different tools to use for different situations. For example, less official "fag pack" calculations can work if we have a lot of waste in our processes (or are just getting started) because any improvements at all will be beneficial and obviously felt. For example, if we have a lot of weight to lose, just noting roughly the type and amount of food we eat is enough to help with a plan of action for a before and after story.

But if you only have the last kilo of fat to lose, every little bit counts. You may need to start serious spreadsheet type logging, weighing your food and counting every calorie to see why you are plateauing and where you can most effectively improve. Business cases can also help you decide which waste is the lesser evil. Some wastes in the process are inevitable and not within our control. Knowing which one can and should be tolerated will allow us to not dwell or whine about it and focus our effort on something else instead.

Blindly going forth to get whatever improvements we can is not optimum. Another aspect to consider from a business case is how much improvement we need. There is no point in taking minutes or hours if they cannot then be utilised productively. For example, if you free up half an hour but it is not enough to do a follow-on task, then what is the point? You don't want to end up "killing" time you've freed up. If the next task requires one hour, then you can check (using lean tools) to see if there is 1 hr of improvements to gain, making it worth doing.

DATA

In order to get a diagnosis of where we are, and what we need, plus a business case to show us which way is best, we need data (qualitative and/or quantitative). There are many different lean tools we can use to conduct investigative diagnostics. Here, we talk about hard data.

Data logging, collection, and analysis are very off-putting to a lot of people, and in many real-life experiences, a complete waste of time. However, when done correctly and for the right reasons, you greatly increase your

chances of success because they remove the pretext and misrepresentation of facts which we may not want to face. I might have been a bit harsh when I used the words self-deception in this section's title. I wasn't knowingly deceiving myself when I thought I was healthier and fitter than I really was. Nevertheless, I was under that illusion. I knew I ate too much occasionally. I knew I made excuses not to train some... quite a bit, but I did try to be active.

> "In God we trust, all others must bring data."
> — Edward Deming

I finally got some proper numbers, rather than just weight and BMI, which are not the best measures to use. Needless to say, I was a little bit surprised. The figures were not bad but those that mattered to me were not as good as I thought. Most surprising was my body fat percentage. I am not disclosing the figure in this book but looking at me, you would not have guessed that percentage.

I am in no way skinny but looking slim plus that number scarily means I'm "skinny fat" i.e., have fat around my vital organs. Another important measure (performance indicators) includes resting heart rate, which was also not as good as I expected. I was officially average in both categories. Body fat table:

BODY FAT PERCENTAGE	Women	Men
Description	Women	Men
Essential fat	10-13%	2-5%
Athletes	14-20%	6-13%
Fitness	21-24%	14-17%
Average	25-31%	18-24%
Obese	32%+	25%+

Resting Heart Rates

MEN						
AGE	18-25	26-35	36-45	46-55	56-65	65+
ATHLETE	49-55	49-54	50-56	50-57	57-56	50-55
EXCEL'T	56-61	55-61	57-62	58-63	57-61	56-67
GOOD	62-65	52-65	63-66	64-67	62-67	62-65
ABOVE AV	66-69	66-70	67-70	68-71	68-71	66-67
AVERAGE	70-73	71-74	71-75	72-76	72-75	70-73
BELOW AV	74-81	75-81	76-82	77-83	76-81	74-79
POOR	82+	82+	83+	84+	82+	80+

WOMEN						
AGE	18-25	26-35	36-45	46-55	56-65	65+
ATHLETE	54-60	54-59	54-59	54-60	54-59	54-59
EXCEL'T	61-65	60-64	60-64	61-65	60-64	60-64
GOOD	66-67	65-68	65-67	66-67	65-68	65-68
ABOVE AV	70-73	69-72	70-73	70-73	69-73	69-72
AVERAGE	74-78	73-76	74-78	74-77	74-77	73-76
BELOW AV	79-84	77-82	79-84	78-83	78-83	77-84
POOR	85+	83+	85+	84+	84+	84+

All this time I had the notion that I was in the Fitness category for body fat and Good for heart rate. To be brutally honest, I narcissistically expected to at least touch Excellent in resting heart rate.

Health and fitness was one of the better performing aspects of my life, which was in my full control and still I wasn't as good as I thought I was.

It was uncomfortable contemplating this and definitely a humbling moment for me. Being humanly superficial, my next thought was to worry about being fraudulent, because those around me still thought I was an above average fit and healthy person. Most people (or organisations I know of) would be happy to carry on with that perception and receive praise but the lean me needed to live up to expectations and deliver the quality people were expecting.

I would never have considered having a food diary, but those two sets of indicators spurred me into wanting to collect other relevant data that could help me in my quest to do better. Knowing what and how much I actually ate and drank as opposed to what I thought I did was another huge surprise.

I've researched a set of measures suitable for my needs and it helped to induce action. As I saw my figures improve, I became more ambitious. Data collection, types of indicators, frequencies of check and rigour etc., all chopped and changed in accordance with my change in circumstances, surroundings, improvements and benchmark figures as I wandered round the PDCA cycle. I believe the results speak for themselves as I have achieved my personal target for both body fat and heart rate.

This brings me to how important it is to measure the correct things to induce the correct actions and behaviours. In this case, BMI and weight tell me I am as "good" as I thought but the correct indicators told me I was most definitely not. My BMI and weight are currently the same as they were 15 years ago but I look, feel and am much better outside and in.

MEASURES AND BENCHMARKS

Another important aspect is something that I have always preached to my construction sector customers – do not get crazy benchmarking against others. This will make you use their performance indicators or industry standard and drive you to do crazy things that might not be good for the System. I love the one about call centres measuring the number of calls that each member of staff takes. The more calls the more rewards. As a result, this drove staff to take many calls without actually solving customer issues!

Even in the same industry, different organisations will be different. Like individuals, we are all human but are different in colour, creed, capabilities etc. Conduct your diagnostics and choose your measures wisely. They should drive behaviour towards the System's (you, your surroundings, an organisation etc.) goal. If you benchmark against yourself, you are guaranteed to be moving consistently forward, leaving your competition in the wake of your dust. Don't behave to look good, behave to be effective. If you behave effective for long enough, you will look good anyway.

On the other side of the coin, those less narcissistic should most definitely not benchmark against others as this will only give you excuses for what you cannot or do not need to do. So, how does one measure quality of life? As discussed, value is subjective to the individual.

Examples of the changing and the different quality of life measures I use to drive my behaviour include:

- Number of days in a week I get 7.5hrs of sleep
- Number of times I feel stressed (my own definition ranking between 1-4) per week plus the root causes
- Number of times I did not fulfil my Vital 1,2,3s
- Number of times in a week I wish I had more time to do something
- Number of times per week I feel dissatisfied with my day plus the reasons for that dis-satisfaction

I would like to introduce SMART Measures that are **Reloaded** in line with the lean approach and attitudes.

Meaningful
for us, not just for
the organization

Rewarding
actual reflection of
good performance

Stretching
to drive us beyond
the comfort zone into
real achievement

Aspirational
drive us to deliver
and not comply

Trust
that processes are
being tested first
before people

This is very much in line with the lean principle of leveraging human potential (one of the 8 lean wastes when unharvested), with inclusiveness and empowerment being the key. Very often, people are randomly reprimanded or rewarded for their work, based on the System's capabilities. This can be morale draining and make the workforce despondent and world-weary. There is currently no trust that processes are being tested before people. There is very little reward in line with an actual good performance but rather working harder is emphasised instead of being leaner and smarter.

SOMETHING'S BETTER THAN NOTHING – "FAG" PACK CALCULATIONS

Fag pack or back of envelope calculations are figures arising quickly from little analysis or investigation. Some die-hard lean or six sigma advocates will turn their nose up at this but personally, I am not averse to using fag pack business cases myself when they're needed and the situation arises. Like whether to change from a 2-piece toaster to a 4-piece toaster.

I jest and trivialise. However, I always have one rule to help me validate this data for use. When fag pack calculations are required or done for a process that involves more than myself, I make sure that I get the relevant parties' own fag pack calculations on the subject to get an average. For example, how long does it take to walk to Tesco? One person is opinion, a few opinions become credible hard data.

80/20 RULE

There are a couple of tools I use frequently to help in my fag pack calculations. There is the 80/20 rule, where the theory says that 80% of your wastes stem from 20% of your activities. So, to get a bang for your buck, find out what that 20% is and make your effort there, as getting rid of this 20% means 80% of your problems will melt away.

There is no need to take the percentage split too literally for fag pack calculating. For example, when learning a new language, start with the 100 most frequently used words as it's said they make up about 50% of everyday speech. I am not sure how true this is but it helps in my 80/20 explanation.

So, if you are looking to improve your economy, find out what your top 20% spend is and work on that rather than pinching pennies everywhere. Bear in mind that the 20% waste may have big wins when it's fixed but fixing may be difficult and longer term, while the 80% smaller irritants may be easier to fix with smaller wins but may also be recurring issues due to that 20% waste. You'll have to make your own business case to decide.

I have used this concept consistently. At home, I have a standardised waste minimisation protocol I call my Top 3 Wastes of The Month. I started out jotting down (collecting data) everything that annoyed me, estimated how often and how troublesome they were to deal with and ranked them. I then gave myself 3 to sort out a month. I kept adding and re-ranking them each month and that's been going on for a decade. The list is still long but there is a continuous improvement cycle. I challenge you to give it try.

RUNNERS, REPEATERS AND STRANGERS

Not dissimilar to the 80/20 rule is the "Runners, Repeaters and Strangers" concept. I use this extremely often in my fag pack business cases. In the manufacturing industry, it is very helpful when it comes to planning, scheduling, inventory and layout. This is applied to physical things, but nothing stops us from applying this concept to more abstract problems in our daily lives.

Runners are the items demanded or the process carried out most frequently – say around 80% of the time. Repeaters are the items demanded or the process carried out less often, but recurring enough to be familiar. Strangers are items or tasks that happen but not often.

We can look at Runner processes/activities in our daily lives to focus our improvement efforts or look at Runner wastes i.e., frequently occurring issues in our daily lives we wish to get rid of. We can have Plan Bs in place for Repeaters ready for when it does happen. And we can make a business case on whether to combat any Strangers' issues, to see if they are worth the effort as they do not happen often.

WORKPLACE
ORGANISATION-5S

Workplace organisation is more than just organising. It is a structured methodology and technique to help you organise, stay organised and BE organised.

So why do we need to be organised? A neat and clean environment facilitates higher productivity and allows us to do more at home or at work. Higher productivity means less effort to do more i.e., less motion (ergonomic) waste in finding and locating things, less inventory waste in less clutter and buying more when you can't see or find what you need etc. Being organised also means a safer environment to live in. A neat and clean environment also induces correct behaviour and improves morale.

Whenever I start a 5S workshop and ask delegates where their workplace is, I get locality or environment. Regardless of whether we have desk-bound or site-based work, many of us think of the workplace from a geographic and immediate surrounding point of view. That is in line with the macro view. Having familiarised ourselves with the process cycle, we know waste identification opportunities arise when we "see" and consider both macro and micro views. There will inevitably be realisation and an "of course..." moment when I challenge everyone and suggest that everything we use, touch and need in order to accomplish tasks for our work is our workplace.

WHERE IS YOUR WORKPLACE?

ARE YOU SURPRISED BY SOME OF THE EXAMPLES GIVEN HERE?	
· Office area (org & personal)	· Emails
· Servers	· Drawings
· Work desk	· Spreadsheets
· Cars (boot)	· Calendars
· Meeting rooms	· Application forms
· Mobile phones	· Agendas
· Desk	· Supplier list
· Desktops	· Checklists
· Bags	· Personal to-do list
· Etc...	· Etc...

Since we are not only talking about lean at work but also at home and play, we are talking about all of our surroundings. This includes everything! Smartphones, living room drawers, sports bag, wallets, fridge/freezer, sock drawer, toy box, toiletries bag, lunch boxes, larder, shed, wine stands etc.

This is why we say continuous improvement is infinite, there will always be something to work on.

THE 5S

I usually discourage judging books by the cover or wines by their labels, but I can always gauge the kind of team I will be working with as soon as I drive onto a construction site. I am seldom wrong. To be fair, people who engage lean consultants in the first place often genuinely want improvements, unless it is a tick in the box requirement by the client. Most groups I work with do not usually fall into the lax group, who are generally not too fussed, as construction is messy. They are usually very organised in their thinking and hard-working teams who are trying very hard to keep the site in-check but have difficulties getting on top of things due to project circumstances.

As mentioned in the Structured Approach section, improving without a structured approach is haphazard and random with little, one-off or short-term results. That is why most of us have to re-organise our shed, our wardrobe, our fridge/freezer, our DIY toolbox etc., every so often, again and again.

This is where 5S can help. Many organisations are quick to adopt 5S to achieve good workplace organisation. Unfortunately, most stop short on the first 3Ss as they are easier to do. The first 3S helps deal with the current situation but the last 2Ss help maintain and induce the Being Lean culture.

Workplace Organisation is the ethos and 5S is the tool that's been widely adopted. Its original Japanese language was translated into English for easy understanding in the Western world. Cs are used in the Construction industry instead, as there was a need to differentiate from the manufacturing industry for the purpose of uptake. The Americans, being their categorically positive selves, came up with CANDO, which I personally love.

SUMMARY OF DIFFERENT 5Ss

5S Japanese Version	5S English Version	5S English Adaptation	CANDO American Adaptation	Basic Meaning
Seiri	Sort	Clear out	Clearing up	Separating the essential from the non-essential
Seiton	Set (or Straighten or Simplify)	Configure	Arranging	A place for everything and everything in it's place
Seiso	Shine (or Scrup or Sweep)	Clean & Check	Neatness	Keep things clean and in good working order
Seiketsu	Standardise	Conformity	Discipline	Set the 5S / 5C standard and sustain
Shitsuke	Sustain (or Self Discipline)	Custom & Practice	On-going improvement	Consistent application, training, everyday routine and advancing the 5S /5C standard

The 5S are:

▶ Sort – Get rid of the clutter through purposeful identification of what is needed in a space, and what isn't

▶ Set – Find a home and address for your things, taking the guesswork out of finding items

▶ Shine – Maintain and enable pro-activeness, minimising the chances of re-clutter

▶ Standardise – Setting and maintenance of a set standard

▶ Sustain – Inducing the culture of improvement by all involved

1ST S – SORT

To make the below explanations more meaningful, try choosing or visualising an example area to work on. It can be anything from informational, e.g. smartphones, email inbox, bills etc to physical drawers, car boot, outside shed etc.

▶ Sorting starts with removing anything not bolted down to the ground in your chosen area of improvement. Why do we insist on that? Imagine when you're given a bag of M&Ms or a box of Lego. When asked to sort them into their colours and shape, what do you do first? You tip over the whole bag or box and then sort them outside their container as it is easier to "see" before sorting. By doing it this way, you get it done correctly the very first try. When cleaning out your wardrobe or drawers, we tend to move things around within that space. That in itself will reduce the quality of the sorting activity as we might not "catch" everything in the first place.

▶ When sorting, designate 3 piles and everything that's removed should be designated to one of these piles.

1. Keep – things we know we definitely want and need

2. Quarantine – things we do not need but are in good working order to sell or give away and anything that is to be kept but needs to be fixed in some way or another. Selling items that you don't use anymore can incentivise you to get rid of things or donate them to charity, e.g. used, old blankets to animal shelters as this benefits all parties

3. Throw (in a recycling bin, where possible) – things of no use or value to anyone or anything, not reusable or up-cyclable

This is sorting physical things but can be difficult when it comes to more sentimental things e.g., things that invoke memories. To help, e.g., digitising photographs may help, or taking photos of things before discarding as sometimes, just the sight of them is enough to do the job you need it to do. Stretching it a bit, Sort also applies to saying yes or no to things. Imagine that your time is a finite space with your activities in it. You need to decide your own rules and guidelines for sorting (yes or no) out what is to be kept, quarantined or throw.

2ND S – SET

Once you have sorted out your piles and have a definitive keep pile, it is time to Set. The strapline for Set is "A home for everything and everything in its home". This step is about allocating homes for all essentials, as well as easy identification and access without over-processing. The idea is to give an address to all our things. People have an address because we need to be found, it should be the same for our things. Think of it as homelessness – it's a bad thing for people and things too.

When something does not have a home, especially things we don't use as often, we tend to have difficulties deciding where to put them. This usually means they end up where they shouldn't be, leading to cluttered drawers, sheds, shelves etc. putting us back to messy square one.

Anything we use often usually already has allocated homes, but unfortunately, may have two or more homes. This is as bad as you'll end up going through the different homes looking for them and the panic starts setting in when they cannot be found in any of these homes. You start doubting and wondering if you left them somewhere or if they're lost. Hence, one address and one address only.

Depending on what, where and how large the area we are focusing on, not everything can have a home. The 80/20 rule and "Runners, Repeaters, and Strangers" concept can come into play here to help us choose what to prioritise.

When you choose a home, you will have your own personal criteria whatever it is, e.g. a garden, two parking spaces, near public transport etc. These are some criteria you can use to help with the effective allocation of homes for your things.

FINDING A HOME

Science behind finding a "home":

1) Physically
2) Convenience
   - Location
   - Frequency
   - Ease of use
     - Workflow
     - Mobility

- **One step Rule:**
  Ideally nothing stored more than a step away. Improve efficiency by eliminating time lost looking for items.

- **30 Second Rule:**
  Organise workplace to allow any tool, information or material to be located and retrieved within 30 seconds. This includes computer files!

- **45 Degree Rule:**
  Immediate work area layout to minimise twisting.

- **Strike Zone Rule:**
  Store things above the knees and below the chest..

- **Higher the Pounds – Closer to Knuckles:**
  Locate heavy items to eliminate bending, stooping or unnecessary arm movements during lifting.

From a physical point of view, the key thing is to eliminate motion waste. From a convenience point of view, we think of the location (where – the address), frequency (how often do we use them) and ease (as few steps as possible).

A guideline to use is the "1-step, 30 seconds, get what you need when you need it" rule. This is guidance only, and there is no need to literally stick to the step and seconds. Locations should flow and fit the process pattern, e.g. car keys situated along the way in and out of the house, towards the car and not upstairs where you have to do detours to get to them.

The point of this rule helps us make improvements, e.g. if it takes me 5 clicks, 7 scrolls and 8 seconds to get an email, how can I do better, e.g. fewer clicks, fewer scrolls hence fewer seconds. Or, it takes me 40 steps 30 seconds to replenish toilet rolls in my bathroom, can I do it in fewer steps and fewer seconds if I relocate the toilet rolls to the point of use in the bathroom? etc.

The location of homes should be as near to the point of use as possible. For example, a business case for toilet rolls. Where possible, store all your toilet rolls in the bathroom/toilet, but where that is impossible, consider using vertical space, e.g. 3-roll pull system on a stand or on the wall where a visible last roll induces the correct behaviour of replenishing before they run out, hence the importance of space utilisation.

However, do not force the issue for the sake of it, making waste more efficient. If there really is no space, it is not necessarily a better home just because it is nearer the point of use. For example, by opening cupboard doors and moving things around or out of the way to access the toilet rolls stored in the bathroom may be more time-consuming and defeat the purpose.

LESS OBVIOUS APPLICATIONS

A more abstract way of allocating homes is scheduling and creating timeslots for activities. My time is the thing I need to do the work. The calendar is the point of use and the time-slots are addresses. Slotting tasks into their homes of appropriate timeslots and durations helps me get access to my time at the correct time to get things done.

Allocating an address to things is great in helping us get to it quickly in 1-step, 30s, but it can also work the other way around i.e., help us make it difficult to get to something.

Naughty foods are a good example. To deter you or the family members from temptations, banishing them totally is best. This is mistake proofing and total prevention, unless you go get them, because you suddenly really want what you don't have. I find having some temptations in the house makes them accessible enough in my mind, but my laziness might stop me from physically going to get them.

I may also put something I use frequently out of the way (usually upstairs) on purpose, so that I have to make the effort to climb some stairs to contribute to my Fitbit targets. So, leverage this second S and make it work according to your circumstance.

Once everything has an address and a home, we just need to ensure we put everything back in its proper homes. So, before you leave soiled clothes in the bathroom after a shower, throw your bag on the couch when you get home or take your shoes off just anywhere, think about how you will have to make another trip to pick them up. Put them away where they actually go instead.

I have spoken to a huge number of people to try to understand the Set logic behind the logistics of their mobile, if there is any. It is very common for many organised people to use category folders, e.g. news, social media, music, travel etc. This gives the visual satisfaction of being organised but as they use a chat app or another, e.g. WhatsApp, Viber, Snapchat very frequently, having them in a folder means extra unnecessary taps. You should have folders but your 20% most frequently used individual apps should be accessible within one tap on the front page.

We will touch on visual management in the relevant section but it is worth a very quick mention here as it is a great communications tool providing information most efficiently. It is very good to have an address but it is even better to have this prominently displayed, e.g. the house number at the front gate.

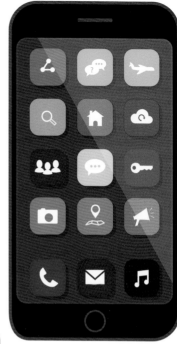

3RD S – SHINE

Shine means being neat and tidy, always. Make sure essentials are returned to their allocated homes, as suggested in the above Set step. On top of that, make sure they are returned home in good order and get replenished where necessary. The main purpose of Shine is to facilitate things going back in their home without the need to constantly tidy up all the time. This is a key step to not allowing things to slip back into the mess we sorted out before.

This step is purpose-driven and is for discovering where things are going wrong and building in mistake proofing mechanisms that make it difficult to put things in the wrong place. It facilitates prevention or in the worst-case scenario, quickly tidying along the way instead of accumulation for a bigger tidy up later.

This is very much a clean and check step in line with meeting the NEXT customer's needs by ensuring all is in order and ready for the next step in the process.

Load items into the dishwasher directly into their allocated addresses, e.g. load the same cutlery in each basket so that when they are washed, you can just take the whole bunch of spoons, forks or knives and place directly back into the cutlery drawer without needing to sort them. It's the same idea with laundry baskets – have a basket for each coloured, whites and blacks sorted at source.

Shine from a preventative perspective – you can contain chaos (mess) by reducing and limit the spread or creep disease. "Creep" happens in various forms, physically and more abstract. We all know that disease from work, where project scope creep, responsibilities creep (you end up taking on 2 people's work supposedly temporarily while the company looks for someone to take over the person that left) etc.

From a physical point, limited space can be used for visual inventory control to prevent creep. If it spills over the given limited space, it means you've got too much. This applies to clothes, food, bottles of wines, emails (e.g. if there are more than 20 emails, it should trigger action to deal with it ASAP).

Boxes and dividers in your wardrobe act as "limiters". When they start to fill up or clothes start getting tightly squeezed, that's an alarm or trigger for no more buying as the inventory is rising. Dividers also prevent encroachment in homes and are not limited just to books on shelves.

I have a drawer especially for naughty foods which I limit, and in that drawer is a 7-compartment box for my daily ration of rewards, each week. I eat all of them at once or spread them out over the week. It doesn't matter. The ration is what it is. No creeps allowed. This is great mistake proofing (prevention) countermeasure. By the way, there is no such thing as naughty food. All food consumed in moderation is good, overconsumption is the naughty part. More in the Food and Fitness section.

Shine – Mistake Proofing Example 2

I keep a designated donation bag in my closet year-round so I can easily add items to it. When I put on a piece of clothing and take it off without wearing it, whatever the reason – either it doesn't fit right or I just don't like it – more than three times, it goes into the charity bag.

Preventative S-Shine should include not putting "defective" (not fit for use) things back to be picked up for use again. A classic experience I have in Construction is when out-of-order generators are put back on the shelf. Guess what happens when the NEXT customer picks it up and puts it in their van for a long drive out to the site? Where prevention is not possible, allow and facilitate easy maintenance of the standard by building in small tasks that prevent often bigger tasks instead, e.g. use a carpet sweeper or mini cordless vacuum daily instead of a big clean with a cord vacuum.

We end up avoiding cleaning and accumulating mess partly because it is a big time-consuming task to take out the vacuum, get an extension cord and plug it in (batch size reduction).

Having relevant clean-up tools near the point of need is likely to induce action as you can just reach down and grab what you need when you need it, rather than having to walk to the other end of the house, which makes it less likely it will be done.

For example, leave a bottle of cleaning spray by the shower so you can clean it before it gets too bad. Or have wipes strategically placed so that family members are more likely to use them. Make sure that working pens are attached to the family scheduling board and not removable at the point of use or the board will not be utilised and the pen will go-a-walking.

Another batch size reduction way for keeping things tidy and in good working order is by having quarantine systems in the form of zones, areas or containers.

Cleaning out a small box of homeless things each day is less effort than taking out large chunks of time to tidy up the whole room or house. Also, specified quarantine areas give us contained chaos and specified limits and boundaries. This helps me keep the spartan Scandinavian look. I am partial to this look as less decorative clutter means fewer purchases and fewer things to wipe, ergo less time cleaning and tidying.

Remember we talked in 1S - Sort about having personal rules & guidelines to make decisions on Keep, Quarantine or Throw? Having these set guidelines established falls here in Shine. This is preventative decision on everything to prevent clutter & maintaining good standards. Having a clear "max. 3 all-purpose screwdrivers" rule means a clear "No" in decision making even when it is on 50% discount. Having a clear guideline on number of times you agree to help Tom on Saturdays means a definite "No", the next time he asks.

4TH S - STANDARDISATION

Standardisation can only happen if it is common knowledge and an understanding of some defined standard in place to adhere to. We need to get our expectations and definitions in line with everyone else's. By doing it regularly, it becomes standardised and a habit.

The standardise step involves the process of setting the 5S standards and making them easy to maintain by using simple systems and processes. Important things to consider include who does what, how often and to what standard, i.e., individual perceptions of what good looks like can differ vastly. In essence, this is where you take the first three S's and make rules for how and when these tasks will be performed.

This has to be effectively communicated to the people involved. It embarrasses me at this point to call out the flaw in my process

as my husband sometimes still leaves packaging on the kitchen table after opening up his parcels. Obviously, there is not a good enough process to induce the correct behaviour of putting it straight in the correct recycling bin immediately, even if this only happens occasionally.

There is a common misunderstanding that standardisation means rigid systems and processes. This stems from organisations that are not committed to Being Lean (all 5S) and instead have a mandate to lean specific processes (first 3S).

Generally, dictating how personal desks should be organised in the same manner or all personal filing systems done in a specific "standardised" way introduces more waste into each person's process as we all work differently hile doing different types of work and activities. The whole 5S set-up has to be flexible and adaptable in line with individual needs to facilitate the "want" to improve and maintain the system in place. Imposing a rigid and strict set of processes tends to create unnecessary resistance and, on many occasions, resentment.

An example of the application of standardisation with flexibility while conducting 5S is that you stipulate the application of 5S by all, but that does not include your T-shirts being in the drawer or trousers being hung and not folded, for standardisation. You could say every drawer and space must be 5Sed. As long as everyone gets everything they need in one step 3 sec, it doesn't matter where they put their T-shirts or trousers.

To raise the bar for perfection, it is not good enough to just be the only one who is able to get what you want when you need it, especially in shared territory and not individual spaces. It is good for the owner to know where everything is if they are to be organised, although it is not uncommon to hear people say that in their mess, there is method behind the mayhem and they know where to look for whatever they need. That, in lean terms, is not acceptable. It is great that you can find everything but it is perfect if any Tom, Dick or Harry can find anything because it is a high-level visual "workplace".

I have my own standardisation routine. I allocate 10-15 mins each week to restock and rehome (first 3Ss). I need to be very flexible with my system, dependent on the needs. For example, my fridge is always in need of space so I will prioritise rehoming things to make space, e.g. rehome pickles in the original big pickle jar to a smaller jar. I'll use the Runners, Repeaters and Strangers technique to help allocate addresses in the fridge. The more frequently used, the more central the address is, i.e., front of the fridge. That needs to be flexible too as, in my household, the taste in cuisine trends is rather like the attention span of a millennial.

The flexibility of moving and changing homes is fundamental to matching changing circumstances as we move round the PDCA continuous improvement cycle. This is why continuous improvement is infinite, it never ends.

Another standardisation procedure is allocating time for my mini 5S, according to need. It is done daily for my inbox, once a week for the kitchen, once every 2-3 weeks for my home office and it's seasonal for my wardrobe etc. These frequent miniature 5S allows for more flexibility and the ability to better meet the changes of my daily life, making it much easier and less time-consuming without a huge effort. It also helps to maintain and sustain the system. It has since become a habit that I can do without schedules and reminders. Although it's seasonal for my wardrobe, it somehow happens automatically in smaller cycles when I "see" wastes.

The point of my mini 5S examples is that the 4th S – Standardisation – means everyone in the household does mini 5Ss and completes all 5Ss. We all chose our own areas to be responsible for and contribute to helping each other make the last 4th and 5th S possible. From a macro view, whether this is in a household or workplace, it inevitably benefits the whole system and helps individuals encroach into the circle of concern, widening our influence.

5TH S – SUSTAIN

The Sustain bit is the ultimate in achieving the lean culture and is done through an understanding of, and adherence to, the principles of lean and 5S. It occurs when the household or organisation can attain a cultural shift in its behaviour to self-maintain the process. This is the way the previous four S's can be continued over a sustained period. This is achieved by developing a sense of self-discipline in individuals that make up the system.

Enforcement and adherence are required by all and all are responsible for sustaining new practices and maintain discipline. Individuals need to lead by example to empower others in their surroundings to do the same by keeping the routine and enhancing the mindset.

Facilitation of habit and the frequent usage of tools for improving skills and sustaining outcomes is vital. This is a form of flexing the lean muscle like flexing the discipline muscle. The more you are encouraged to use it, the better you get at it. Lean and 5S need to be a commitment and not one of many mandates.

5S SUMMARY

5S	Activities
Sort	Out with clutter, only essentials required
Set	A place for everything, everything in it's place. Science behind a home • Frequency • Geography • Work sequence • Ease of use
Shine	• Be up to date. • Mistake proof/prevention • Adopting process with easy built-in clean and check
Standardise	• Standardisation • Maintain the standard by having a system in place to adhere to • SOPs for training & auditing
Sustainability	• Achieved through understanding and adherence to the principles of 5C. • Organization attains a cultural shift in behaviour to self maintain the process • Routine way of doing things

VISUAL MANAGEMENT
SYSTEM

The strapline for Visual Management (VM) is "Good visual management, needs no interpretation and provokes the correct reaction." Think traffic lights. There is absolutely no ambiguity and it provokes us to stop at red, go on green and slow to a stop (or step on it) at amber.

Visual management facilitates the quick identification of items instead of rummaging and searching. For example, the ability to see what items are in the bag. Good visual management will allow us to immediately know how many pairs of clean underwear are left, and the correct reaction is to either do some laundry or not. It draws your attention to "problem areas" and provokes the implementation of "corrective" actions. For example, do you need to replenish shampoo in the 100ml container for the next trip? Situation assessment: used/unused, clean/soiled, charged/uncharged etc., then do.

One hardly gives credit to good VM because it is the simplest kind. This is one of the reasons why people sneer at shadow boarding and think it is overkill. Shadow boarding is simple, obvious, helpful and powerful.

This cartoon slide is one I use when we teach VM. It is just a square but if we did not take the time to mark out that square where would the concrete panel go? *Anywhere but where it should be is the answer.* That is just one thing. Imagine the accumulated activities associated with having to right wrongly placed items or give instructions. There is no such thing as overkill if the correct action is induced on the very first attempt and consistently every single time, and it is invaluable for people who deem their time to be precious.

The retail and car industries spend billions each year in advertising, seducing us to buy, buy, buy, and it obviously works. I've bought those special edition mini-6-pack magnum ice-creams in the coldest February. I couldn't resist them. The seductive close-up visuals of the differently flavoured hardened cream on a stick plus that crunch did it for me. I didn't eat them until later that summer though, when they were freezer burnt with ice crystals and all. They weren't as sexy looking as the ads by then but did taste good.

Visual management is used prolifically in our surroundings, especially in marketing, because it is recognised as a powerful tool to invoke an unconscious and automated reaction. There is no argument about that so why not consciously apply it more at both work and home?

VISUAL MANAGEMENT SYSTEMS

There are two aspects that make up a full VM Systems. The Visual Control part prevents abnormalities from occurring or immediately indicates that something is wrong. It looks at the current situation "now". There is a direct link here to Mistake Proofing where the ultimate level is to prevent an abnormality from even occurring, but when this is impossible have a method whereby the non-conformity is flagged up so that actions can be taken for mitigation and prevention purposes.

Visual Control is any communication means that is used to tell us the current state at a glance, e.g. how, what things are done, where things go, when we should replenish and how many are needed etc.

A very good everyday VM example of visual control is an egg carton. Before purchase, you would open up one to make sure that all is as it should be, 12 in a dozen, and none are broken.

We would see in a fraction of a second if there are missing or broken eggs. That would immediately prompt us to take it or replace it with a full proper carton of good quality eggs.

The other part of a VM System is Visual Display. It is the monitoring of processes to show performance over the longer term. It covers a period up to the current situation. The display aspect allows you to assess the results of actions taken, understand the current level of performance and provide information to guide and measure further improvement, e.g. the number of coloured stars on the children's reward star chart. Or a run chart of 6 months of a weight loss programme.

USING THE PROCESS CYCLE AS PROMPT FOR VM

We use the process cycle systematically as a structured approach to help give us prompts on what VMs to adopt. We use visual controls to manage and control the inputs of man, material, machine, message and the method of the process.

The key Is to identify which bits of the inputs and method we need or would benefit from using VM to help us to be in control and come up with a suitably good VM to put in place.

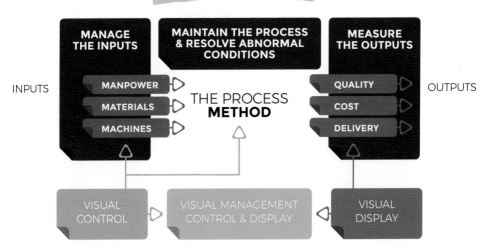

The Process View

MANAGE THE INPUTS — MANPOWER, MATERIALS, MACHINES

MAINTAIN THE PROCESS & RESOLVE ABNORMAL CONDITIONS

THE PROCESS METHOD

MEASURE THE OUTPUTS — QUALITY, COST, DELIVERY

INPUTS — OUTPUTS

VISUAL CONTROL

VISUAL MANAGEMENT CONTROL & DISPLAY

VISUAL DISPLAY

Visual aids and the mistake proofing concept are types of visual control used to prevent abnormalities occurring by promoting the right action at the right time and to indicate immediately should anything go wrong by allowing visual assessment and comparison.

Think about the inputs as controlling what and the quantities of things while the method controls how things are done, where, when and for how long (timelines and durations). There are some overlaps here but there is no need to get fixated with it as the objectives and desired outcomes are the same.

With VM you sometimes don't have to even know anything about the process to easily see if things are as they should be. One glance from afar should let you know if we are in or out of control. For example, the ways of VM includes outlines or footprints to help show if we are in or out of place, such as car parking spaces.

Range lets us know at a glance if it's within range of the control limits, e.g. an occasional check on boiler pressure lets us know if it's OK or needs topping up. Colour coding is a fast, easy way to separate different items and visually determine if something is misplaced etc.

Visual documents of Standard Operations that capture the best current method can be used to communicate processes or stipulate standards. They can be used to mistake proof and avoid bad quality and rework.

I have a good personal example of this which I hugely benefited from. I travel, and am out and about a lot, so I am always in need of house and pet sitters. I rely plenty on family and friends to help me keep house.

Remember my Top 3 Waste of the Month I mentioned in the fag pack calculation section? What wound up on that list was how much time I spend explaining how things in the house work before I leave, as well as numerous calls I get to clarify or reiterate. I created a visual standard operating procedure (SOP) document for things like how the TV boxset works upstairs and downstairs, how to get hot water, what the Wi-Fi password is, where the outside shed key is, how and when to water my plants, when/what/how often the pets/kids need feeding etc. Everything I have been asked and anything else I can imagine my sitter (customer of information) will need.

I conducted process mapping and a walk-through the whole house and its vicinity to trace a day in the life of a person at home and noted at each step if there was anything I needed to communicate clearly to my house sitter. I kept in mind the 5S mantra of "Get what you need when you need it in 1 step 3 seconds". This is very good but it's even better when a stranger who doesn't know my "workplace" can do the same. I even put Post-it notes on all the cupboards in the kitchen to give an inkling of what's behind those cupboards. This works very well for me, especially on family or group holidays in Airbnbs.

With each point noted, I consider if there is anything I can do visually to convey my wants and needs, as a photo can speak a thousand words on my behalf. The 3M Company claims human beings process visuals 60,000 times faster than text. In addition, the average person remembers 20% of what they read compared to 37% of visual images.

I now have a folder of visual aids to pull from, dependent on who and what season it is when I need house sitting help. This is standardisation but with flexibility. My house sitters are always amused at how "organised" I am and always very pleased. I, in turn, have saved myself accumulative time from each house sitting plus I've facilitated my sitters to do a good job so they give me great (help) service.

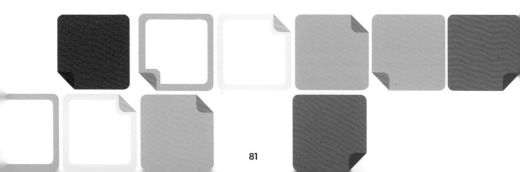

Input, Method, Outputs

Examples of visual controls to **manage outputs** include:

Labelling kitchen drawers and cupboards, ready-made food in the fridge

Trigger lines or areas for replenishment

We can always improve, e.g. there's good VM (photo of e.g., marker lines on wine glasses (125ml or 175ml) to control the amount of wine you drink

Label sections inside the washing machine, so all forks, all knives, all spoons are segregated to enable 1- step, 1-move to get them "home"

Examples of visual controls to **control methods**:

Map of where the nearest supermarket and corner shop is

How to use the remote control

Include directions/maps on all invites

Examples of visual displays to **monitor performance** include:

No. of times packaging is left on the table

Percentage no. of times someone had to wait more than 5 mins before we are all ready to leave in the car

Percentage planned dinner together missed

Involving everyone in the system (at home) so they understand where you are and are monitoring process performance over the longer term will define the focus and targets for improvement activities and track the impact of the behaviour/improvement. This is an inclusive way of inducing lean culture, contributing to betterment and self-maintenance of the system/household.

STANDARDISATION
HABIT AND ROUTINE

Ask anyone in my circle of friends and acquaintances to describe me and they will say that I am very disciplined. Every time I hear that I wonder if I really am above average? The more I think about it, the more I realise that maybe, maybe not? I realise that we all have some discipline but I, particularly, have been training and flexing my discipline muscle through standardisation i.e., building habits and routines. Without my good (desired) habits and routine would I be as disciplined? Probably no more than anyone else.

Standardisation is about routine and habits, with flexibility built-in. In the daily life of work or home, a routine that supports the organisation and consistency are essential to a smooth and efficient flow of activities. It is about being prepared for the days ahead with little surprises (Taguchi Lost Function).

In this section, I use the nouns standardisation and habit synonymously with regards to regularity and consistency. I see standardisation as the habits of individuals of two or more people who are trying to achieve an agreed standard of an activity.

Remember that lean is about achieving flow in the process. Remove anything that stands in the way of flow through standardisation and habituate your process.

Standardisation aims to define the best current method to achieve consistency in the quality of outputs, costs and time taken to conduct the activity. Naturally, tasks should always be performed safely above all else. We want individuals and everyone involved to work to the best method with minimal waste. To achieve that we need to have defined processes to train with, work to and audit against.

Standardised systems are key to waste elimination. If everyone goes and does things in their own unique way, we will be guaranteed inconsistent results varying in the quality, cost and time taken. Not only that but it will also contribute to creating waste in each other's processes. Something as simple as agreeing to have family dinners together every Sunday. Not having standard operating information and procedures, e.g. a schedule of who's home during which week, at what time, how many are turning up, who doesn't eat what etc. Chaos pursues!

What do we currently do? The steps could be, for example:

- o Calls to each other asking where you will meet this Sunday
- o Calls to find out if you need to bring anything, if you are not the hosting party this week
- o Calls by the host to request RSVPs
- o Arrival of people
- o Etc.

What are the key points?

- o Agreeing what everyone wants for dinner
- o Knowing what foods to avoid

Why are the key points Important? To achieve a consistently good quality family Sunday meal, where everyone is happy and gets what they want. This makes sure family dinners matter to individuals and they will always turn up.

Photos and sketches for visual illustration, e.g. recipes for different dishes.

FACILITATING STANDARDISATION & HABITS

To facilitate standardisation and build good habits we need to get rid of all that stops us from making bad decisions. We want to cut out the use of willpower. Never rely on will alone, as constancy diminishes when we rely on humans wanting to do something.

Motivation drives willpower and is often overvalued and exaggerated. This is very evident at work where thousands of pounds are spent on motivating people in a waste-filled system. Especially as we humans naturally have a negative bias. We have a predisposition to only remember things that go wrong rather than things that go right.

One adverse event can take over our minds. Like they say, you are always remembered for your latest work, no matter how much good you did before. We seldom get credit for going beyond and doing extra, but make a mistake and it never gets forgotten. That is also why research indicates that most of us are only happy with our pay raises for about circa 3 months. If we are unhappy with the system we work in, after 3 months we will revert to being the dis-gruntled employee feeling like we are not paid enough to (do the job) and wade through all that waste again.

Hence, we want the total opposite of mind over matter from standardisation to exclude the use of motivation and willpower. Motivation and willpower often tend to lose out to your environment, circumstances and surroundings in the long run. In which case, it is a lost challenge to make things happen with just will alone. To increase the statistical chance of success, you need to operate in an environment that facilitates and accelerates your results rather than obstructs and hinders them.

Some say that roughly 40% of our daily activities are habitual. Which means we humans spend a significant portion of our existence on autopilot with no awareness of when or what it is we are doing. We want more of that.
Automate good decisions and banish bad ones. Whether you know it or not, automation eliminates decision fatigue and allows us to concentrate on more important tasks. Decision fatigue is when you are no longer able to make decisions effectively after a long bout of decision making. Imagine wasting your decision-making ration on mundane and unimportant things. Reducing decision making is another important benefit of standardisation as indecision contributes to the waste arising. Standardisation facilitates automation.

I mentioned having a standard procedure where I keep a jar of noted mini-chores to utilise waiting time. If I have 10 minutes to wait for my ride to the airport, instead of playing Candy Crush, I set the timer to 8 minutes and pick a chore, e.g. label the new spelt flour poured into an old jar, or move that few lonely pickles from the original humongous jar
in the fridge to a small Tupperware etc. You can use this method to reduce decision making for what food to eat, exercise activities, black or coloured laundry, which room to clean first etc.

Other examples of reducing mundane decision making include standardising your environment to automate, e.g. healthy eating. Find a standard suite of 5 or 10 healthy recipes you enjoy and use them consistently as an integral part of your daily routine. Use 80/20 to prioritise improvements and actions to create habits.

Like willpower, or decision making, never rely on brainpower alone to remember things. Relying on humans to remember everything is flawed and leads to inconsistent outcomes. Always make notes. I always think I will remember but the memory fades. Hence the importance of relying on standard operating procedures and the standardisation of as many processes as possible, e.g. recipes, to-do lists, schedules etc. This is why, as I mentioned earlier, I set alarms, counters and timers around me all the time.

I would even say that I overprocess with alerts and reminders in my calendar if I didn't find them so invaluable. I set multiple alerts and reminders daily, weekly, monthly and recurring activities throughout the year. As mentioned, I can have up to three reminders as it draws nearer the task. Being spoilt and free from needing to keep so many things in my brain is true freedom, a stress reducer and a huge release for me.

A big plus is that it helps me keep my "say what you do, do what you say" promises and live up to them. Remember how people have a negative bias? They will remember when you break promises but not when you over-deliver. Like Covey said, it's easier to withdraw from the emotional bank than to bank in savings.

FLEXIBILITY OF STANDARDISATION

We have discussed flexibility in standardisation, 3rd S – Shine of the 5S. Flexibility allows your process to respond to specific demands, be agile, and use human decision-making that is necessary in so many decisions.

The standardisation of work and information processes can take many forms. Most people will understand and know standardisation from a micro view, where the processes have exactly the same process steps, same sequence, same resources etc. At an even more rigorous level, standardisation can mean there's absolutely no variability at any one time. This is an important aspect to achieve that repeatability and consistency in outputs.

From a macro view, standardisation has to include flexibility in order to respond to the changing needs of the surrounding world and markets. To build-in flexibility into macro processes, there is a need to consider the ability of the system to "chop and change" and "pick and choose" micro view processes to meet customers ever-changing needs: i.e., the concept of going modular

Self-service meals are a good analogy to explain flexible standardisation, such as tacos or burritos, where you have a standard set of ingredients on the table. You need standard recipes of the ingredients and methods to achieve a quality standard, and to produce that quality consistently time and again. No one changes anything with the dishes (micro processes) of guacamole, salsa or type of cheese and taco shells used.

The flexibility of the process comes in the choices of dishes that make up the table. The variety of dishes enables the making of different kinds of tacos that appeal to different people, meet diverse trends and a variety of tastes; vegan, vegetarian, dairy-free, keto etc.

Also, making and eating one taco at a time lets you try different tacos each time, allowing a change of mind, plus it offers opportunities for improvement if your first taco combi isn't as good as you thought it would be, e.g. too much cheese, too little onion etc. You learn from it and make a better one the next time. This can be added-value for your customers, as you work with them to meet their needs.

PROCESS **MAPPING**

You cannot fix what you cannot "see". This tool breaks the process down, providing an easily understood visual overview allowing you to visualise an entire process from start to finish. This can be used to identify bottlenecks and waste within the process and determine the current duration or lead time.

I've used process mapping at work very often but in a more formalised and time-consuming way due to necessity. As mentioned before, everything in theory sounds a bit dry, formal and orchestrated. I thought this tool might be too contrived and elaborate for occasions

outside of work but was very surprised when I realised I actually use it extremely often, albeit less formally.

Like all lean doing, process experts must be involved by using this diagnostic tool to visually represent the process by identifying who does what, when, why and how. The more detailed the level, the more opportunities you find or rather the more waste you find. Doing it this way gives a common understanding of how the process works in reality as it compares everyone's understanding of what actually happens, not what we think should happen or how we think things work.

You'll be surprised at how many different process maps (views) you get if you get everyone in the household for their version of it, e.g. the morning ritual in the house. As people within the process are being explored, they will be the best to identify the areas of risk associated with the way the process is carried out and the opportunities for improvement. They can make the complex information and communication flow understandable. We also get to understand the logic of the decision making behind the process, plus the information required to enable subsequent process steps to be carried out. You will be able to tease out the NEXT customer requirements to form an improved process going forward, i.e., a future state map.

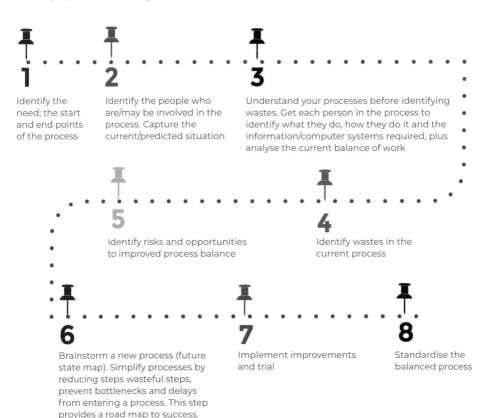

1 Identify the need; the start and end points of the process

2 Identify the people who are/may be involved in the process. Capture the current/predicted situation

3 Understand your processes before identifying wastes. Get each person in the process to identify what they do, how they do it and the information/computer systems required, plus analyse the current balance of work

5 Identify risks and opportunities to improved process balance

4 Identify wastes in the current process

6 Brainstorm a new process (future state map). Simplify processes by reducing steps wasteful steps, prevent bottlenecks and delays from entering a process. This step provides a road map to success.

7 Implement improvements and trial

8 Standardise the balanced process

There are many different kinds of mapping, the above steps run through the basic formal steps of this foundation tool. You can understand why I thought it to be contrived and formal for use at home or personally. But then again, my personal processes are not of the magnitude of a business that requires such rigidity and formality to get things spot on. Once I get the notion of this tool in its many different forms, it is invaluable in my understanding of all the activities surrounding me in everything I do. You just start seeing things in detailed steps.

There are many different kinds of maps for different purposes, and for personal use, I have found the lean mapping tools – Value Stream Map and Failure Mode and Effects Analysis (FMEA) – to be the most valuable and frequently used. They form the basis for all my new and improved processes (future state map) and all my everyday checklists, standard operating documents, decision matrices, risk assessments etc.

APPLICATIONS OF MAPPING TO OURSELVES

The description in the above section pertains to general and more macro and complex processes, but from a personal development or home perspective, we can use it on us individuals in a more micro view. We can process map to get a higher level of self-awareness.

Identifying wastes at work allows us to put organisational measures in place to overcome them. The same can be said for ourselves, where we can visualise and "see" our weaknesses and weak spots before creating processes in our life that we can easily follow.

Lean and highly productive people like ourselves are usually quite self-reflective and very aware of how our processes look. It doesn't matter what the weakness and wastes are, as long as we deploy the appropriate tools and techniques to combat those weaknesses and eliminate the wastes. If we know that we tend to be late, we set alarms and reminders. If we know we tend to be too passionate and talk too much, drawing out meetings, we set loud timers to shut ourselves up. If we know we may skip lunch because a certain meeting will run late, we bring our own lunchbox. The important part is recognising these weaknesses and waste and doing something about it.

PROCESS MAP TO ACHIEVE FLOW IN ALL WE DO

We mentioned the lean need to get flow into our processes. I have adopted process mapping in many ways. The value stream helps me combat procrastination by scrutinising my daily routines and designing a workable process to help me get my priorities straight so that once the day starts, I am less likely to get distracted by the tyranny of the urgent that pops up and gets in the way of real priorities. The maps also let me see which steps are the hardest and recognise my derailers, e.g. moods, timings, dependencies etc., allowing me to build-in ways to combat them, reducing their chances of happening.

I love going on holiday and try to do this frequently. These events are so precious that I feel I cannot leave anything to chance. I need to make sure I have the best time of my life on each and every trip. I've mapped my entire holiday travel process (over a long period) and come up with detailed checklists for each hold-point from pre-travel planning to packing, to holiday activities to laundry on arrival home. The only negative side effect I get from this is that I'm always experiencing such great flow and enjoyment on all my trips that I get a bit down when they are over.

I go modular and constantly update; chopping, changing and moving categories (and product items) in my digital grocery list with the help of spaghetti mapping my route through my supermarket's constant change in their stocking process and aisle system.

I am one of those very few customers who they find are resistant to their BOGOFF and strategic product placements.

For the macro and longer-term view of my life, I use risk assessment and analysis maps (FMEA). This is my yearly PDCA cycle, allowing me to have a view of my year ahead to see what's on the horizon. I identify all the potential risks (wastes). I allocate ratings for their probability and severity. I prioritise and put preventative or management actions in place to deal with them if or when they appear so I don't need to spend unplanned time on them when they do turn up.

One of the reasons why we need to do the mapping with the relevant people involved is to identify all the risks and ensure we are all "in on it". We all know what to do if and when the time comes. There shouldn't be any surprises. The only surprise and unexpected is maybe the Covid-19 pandemic situation. But apparently, even that was not unexpected. It just is one of those low probability but high-impact risks recognised by governments who had plans and strategy to deal with it, according to Swedish State Epidemiologist Anders Tegnell. Apparently, due to cold feet and political pressure, all but Sweden stuck to the original plan. Who got the strategy right is a different book altogether. However, lean advocates that it would be a waste to totally abandon the plan after all the expertise and time has been invested in it to combat such a situation.

THE

DOING

BIT

RESISTANCE TO
CHANGE

As business owners, the motivation to excel and improve is to increase the company's bottom line. As employees, we are motivated by the usual things that keep people coming to work, such as a good job, a paycheque, personal satisfaction, and a sense of camaraderie with other employees. Naturally, with different motivations and sometimes not being aligned, it can be hard work to make any improvement programme work or sustain it.

The same goes for personal situations. The motivation to keep the whole household does

not always align with the individuals in it. Resistance always involves difficulties or impediments, whether conscious or unconscious, that hinder us from improving. This includes beliefs, emotions, and mindsets. As with personal development, wanting and needing is not the same as actually doing and achieving. Personal resistance is a huge barrier from a micro view. We tend to put up mental barriers to getting what we want and what we know will make us happy. First, we need to want to change, and then to know how to change.

NO SENSE OF URGENCY – NO STRONG REASON TO CHANGE

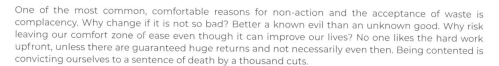

One of the most common, comfortable reasons for non-action and the acceptance of waste is complacency. Why change if it is not so bad? Better a known evil than an unknown good. Why risk leaving our comfort zone of ease even though it can improve our lives? No one likes the hard work upfront, unless there are guaranteed huge returns and not necessarily even then. Being contented is convicting ourselves to a sentence of death by a thousand cuts.

No companies go bankrupt overnight unless there's an anomaly or unusual market circumstances. They go bankrupt slowly, death by a thousand cuts, through the accumulation of inefficiencies or unhealthy cash-flow issues. Without personal growth, we are all ticking over, re-enacting Groundhog Day in different degrees.

I broached the subject of entropy in the form of the corrosion of a car without maintenance, i.e. its physical state, but that happens in life practices too. Unless it's an accident or late discovery of an illness, no one usually dies from totally unexpected ill-health but more commonly though deterioration, like bad health and bad fitness practices over a longer period.

This includes calorie creep, consuming more and more calories than we realise, if we are not conscious or aware of what we are eating. Not taking an interest causes ignorance and contributes to wastes. There's also weight creep – we get half to a full kilogram heavier each year due to lower caloric needs, lowered metabolism and loss of muscle mass as we grow older. Not knowing and not doing anything about it until

there is too much weight to shift, makes motivation to do anything at all even harder.

Finally, there's clutter creep – laid-back creep into actual laziness, procrastination creep, indecisiveness creep etc. Not being in the know or knowing but not doing anything about it is no excuse.

Don't be the boiled frog in the fable, who after slipping into comfortable warm water is unaware of the small increments in heat as it gets boiled to death.

The boiling frog is a fabel describing a frog being slowly boiled alive. The premise is that if a frog is put suddenly into boiling water, it will jump out , but if the frog is put in tepid water which is then brought to a boil slowly, it will not perceive the danger and will be cooked to death

INSUFFICIENT WHAT'S IN IT FOR US – PLAN IN REWARDS

There are many kinds of reward systems that we can put in place to motivate us to make changes. This is the part where we get the satisfaction from doing something, as long as any reward you choose does not derail your goals or habits, e.g. a calorific treat after a training pass.

We all have different values and act in different ways in the same situation, based entirely on the types of rewards that are available to us at that time. Naturally, I have a standard list of personal rewards in categories with all the things I enjoy and are of value to me. My rewards vary in size and value and I make sure that the rewards match my undertakings.

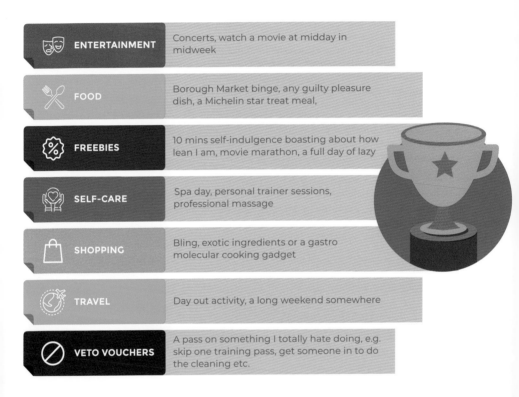

ENTERTAINMENT	Concerts, watch a movie at midday in midweek
FOOD	Borough Market binge, any guilty pleasure dish, a Michelin star treat meal,
FREEBIES	10 mins self-indulgence boasting about how lean I am, movie marathon, a full day of lazy
SELF-CARE	Spa day, personal trainer sessions, professional massage
SHOPPING	Bling, exotic ingredients or a gastro molecular cooking gadget
TRAVEL	Day out activity, a long weekend somewhere
VETO VOUCHERS	A pass on something I totally hate doing, e.g. skip one training pass, get someone in to do the cleaning etc.

As great as these micro rewards are, they are external incentives. They may or may not be sustainable, depending on how they are being dished out. In parallel to these external incentives, we need to have a more overarching internal driver. This will be different for different people. In honesty, the biggest driver and reward for me is moving away from anything detrimental to my own self-interest. This is easy as it should come naturally due to the human predisposition towards self-preservation. Making changes for a better "me, myself and I" should be of huge self-interest and appeals naturally to the "selfish" self. This, in turn, makes a better me for my surroundings and the people in it. Win-win.

Being Lean motivates me and acts as my internal driver and I complement that with external drivers. I have designed my environment and put things in place to make changes and improvements. I have improved the quality of my life tremendously and indeed, I have come a long way. However, my journey now is no easier than it was before because continuous improvement is infinite. I am on a different level to before and I feel more challenged with diminishing returns within my own competitive System. I am constantly in danger of being complacent, more so now than before.

We all have the same goals of doing and being better, happier and healthier. Benchmarking against ourselves in progress is the best for step-change and improvements. Doing something is better than nothing for us to move forward and change for the better. Find your inside reward and preferably align it with your wants as it makes change a lot easier, more fun, and more sustainable.

THE HOW-TO BIT

Even when we know that we need and want to improve, it can be a huge deterrent and de-motivator if we do not know what to prioritise or focus on and lack the skills.

As discussed in the section on having a structured methodology to work with, lean systems thinking can give us an overview of ourselves as a System. Using lean diagnostic tools like process mapping, measures, the first couple of Ss from 5S etc., can help us see the current bigger picture before prioritising what aspects of our life we want changing, with confidence for the better.

Not all tools will be applicable in your backyard but use whatever is within your grasp. Persevere as this is very important. If we want something, we shouldn't give up so easily. Nothing comes easy. With consistent practical application of the thinking and tools to everyday activities, you will start seeing movement. And for those who are more advanced in your personal development journey and have "been there, done that", we raise the bar and challenge you to come up with more advanced examples.

LEAN AT HOME

The aim and objectives of lean at home are no different from those at work. The point is to achieve the best possible quality of life (as opposed to outputs like products and services) under the current circumstances, eliminating wasteful activities in order to better meet the needs of yourself and those around you (as opposed to paying customers). As lean is a way of thinking and methodology and not some specific solutions, it will be impossible to give enough examples that will meet everyone's differing needs in this book.

I have very broadly covered a large base of the lean methodology, thinking and tools. Here, in this Chapter, I will give instances and examples of how I have practically applied lean as an individual, in my own backyard. The world is your oyster, only you can curb your own imagination and creativity. You just need to challenge yourself and allow these examples to open your mind as to how you can do similar things more relevant to you. Hopefully, these examples will give you food for thought in terms of practical application. Naturally, start with yourself but always remember to bring everyone else along with you before you get too far ahead, as this will create the waste of having to come back for them – the long way around.

We can start leaning small individual processes that contribute to a larger area and contribute to the bigger system, e.g. starting with the vegetable and fruit drawer in a fridge to the whole fridge freezer to the kitchen to the house. It can go on forever! And as the situation and circumstances change, which they do in life, the flexibility built into the system allows for change and adaptability. For example, if you turn to the Atkins or Keto diet and no longer eat as many vegetables, you can easily change your fruit and veg drawer to a protein drawer. Or, if you change projects, you can reshuffle and update your short-cut system on your mail filing system.

As stated previously, continuous improvement never ends.

15 PRACTICAL EXAMPLES

I have mentioned that some of the examples given in this section will surprisingly be the simple type of "how to breathe and walk". And there will be other examples that may seem a lot of work and overkill to many readers. This is because Being Lean does not just happen instantaneously. It is a purposeful, contrived and thought-out journey over time. Improving the quality of life is about consistency and practice. It won't happen overnight and will require constant adaption and self-awareness, as you'll go around the PDCA cycle many times round.

Don't think about it as an overwhelming hill that you have to conquer all at once. There will always be some extra "legwork" done upfront to pave the way but try to adopt a series of smaller more attainable habits that can build into something greater. You'll be surprised at how far a little step can take you.

Some examples have been briefly mentioned in the earlier parts of the book. I have endeavoured to highlight them for those who feel less inclined to delve deeper into them.

Note 1:
Depending on your skills and overlapping of thinking and waste types, the headings used are complex and absolutely debatable and to each their own. I have stated the key tools that triggered the activities for me.

Note 2:
Some of these examples are clearly replicable in one form or another for work and other circumstances so they will not be repeated in the other related chapter. For example, the kitchen can be the office, the fridge can be the laptop, the wardrobe can be the car boot, food can be emails etc.

Note 3:
As this book is written from my perspective and experience, a lot of the activities may be traditionally seen as female orientated. If so, male will need to challenge themselves and keep an open mind (see note 2) because I am confident that you will have your own "responsibilities", where the same should apply.

1) VISUAL MANAGEMENT, VERTICAL SPACE UTILISATION, PULL, INVENTORY AND WAITING WASTE:

My laundry process has evolved and gone through the continuous improvement cycle many times. I have an upright 3-tier, see-through, basket pull-out system that's sorted from source into black, white and colour. It's been on the search list for a while and was worth the wait when I found it. The size of the basket is in line with the capacity of the washing machine. When I fill, it is a perfect load, give or take. Being able to see the three baskets as we go about our usual routine tells (triggers) us without making a special effort to find out:

▶ The need to do laundry soon
▶ Which colour laundry needs doing next?
▶ Roughly how long before I can get access to my favourites because a visual of the amount of coloured laundry tells me roughly when that load will be done next
▶ When I see that the black laundry is far from its turn in the machine, I can make the decision to wear my favourite black trouser a couple more times instead of putting it in the laundry for them to just sit there
▶ Purposefully wear more black clothes (not my favourite colour) and rotate the wardrobe (inventory/waiting waste) when the coloured basket is full. We tend to wear the current favourites & newly washed

The first 3 points are quite obvious, while the last two is less evident. Going back to the title of this example, can you tell where each tool & concept comes into play?

2) MODULAR, BATCH SIZE REDUCTION, 5S AND FLEXIBILITY:

My fridge is a frequent workplace as I spend so much time in it. It is like managing a micro warehouse where the goods come in and out ever so often. You have the Runners, Repeaters and Strangers plus some homeless items. Everything, including storage, turnaround, logistics needs attention. The change in seasonal foods, individual tastes, cuisine trends and weekly BOGOFFs, require the fridge to be agile and flexible to these changing and differing needs. Not compromising on 1) customer needs, 2) the goal of minimal food waste, 3) minimal cash tied up in the inventory, 4) the need to keep everything fresh, quickly accessible with 5) never missing staples. This requires the full 5S works, including the sustainable bit. To suit my own situation, I've stuck to a few principles and tools to keep it working for my household.

My foodie crazy household is very experimental so a big inventory of "Strangers" food and ingredients is a risk. Whatever the ingredients or produce is, I try to batch them into portion size, freezing those that I can and vacuuming others to prolong their lifespan. At this point, I try to challenge fixed ideas, including what can or cannot be frozen through trial and error (squid ink CAN be frozen!), plus push the limits of sell-by-dates. I have an allocated Stranger food area for these, in the fridge and freezer, which I keep watch over to ensure they get incorporated into menus by my use-by date, and to keep experimenting and be creative with food.

I have my fridge dimensions and shelf measurements on my phone and am always on the look-out for see-through pull-out boxes (modular) of all kinds that will make the fridge serve me more effectively. This is my NEXT customer reasoning, i.e. how do I facilitate the previous step to give me quality service when I need it, whether it be man, material, machine or messages. This hunt for pull-outs is for all storage spaces, e.g. wardrobes, drawers, cabinets, cubby holes etc. just in case I come across anything that could facilitate space utilisation or organisation. Lean thinking does not advocate fixed solutions, hence, I have clothes boxes as compartments in my fridge as they fit better. There are no quality compromises by tail wagging the dog solutions. Your needs should not change to match what's available; instead, you should seek what is available to meet the needs. Look towards the home first by reusing packaging and customising old need-to-throw things before buying.

My modular system means I can do my small batch size 5S Shine to maintain and sustain order in the fridge. I can break down the tidy-up into as big or small a chore as time allows, giving me more flexibility in my schedule without procrastination and do an entire fridge clean-up while tolerating build-ups. During my daily 10 mins, I can easily pull-out modules (compartments) and do a quick 2-3 mins go-over in cleaning up and, at a glance, stock-take and logistically move cans and bottles to the front. This signals (pull & VM) the need to use according to my own categorisation of approaching the use-by date, or that I've neglected some Runners and Repeaters and risked them becoming too much of a Stranger.

3) STANDARDISATION, 5S, REMOVING DECISION MAKING AND INVENTORY:

Whatever checklist, templates or database I can create for use, I will. This combats a huge "death by a thousand cuts" waste of accumulated re-thinking time.

DISHES & RECIPES

I have many shelves of cookbooks but going through them for ideas takes up time. In small batches, I have started populating my dishes spreadsheet with (Runner & Repeater) meals. This helps with menu planning, managing food inventory, mood, events, dishes experimentations and calories etc. I can filter my spreadsheet to protein type, rotate carb usage, get lunch ideas or dinner-type meals, and if I have used up my ration for "fun/fat" meals, I can filter for slim dishes to curb my calories intake.

Protein/Dishes	Meat	Carbs	Meals	Slim/Fat	Location	Page
Fish & Seafood	F&S	F&S	F&S	F&S	F&S	F&S
Fiskgratang	F&S	Po	D	M	File	56
Smoked fish Carbonara	F&S	Po	D	S	File	26
Seafood riscotto	F&S	R	D	S	Apple Notes	
Seafood couscous	F&S	O	L	S	JO	43
Tuna Pasta	F&S	Pa	D	S	SM	101
Mussles linguine	F&S	Pa	D	S	File	8
Sashimi	F&S	R	L	F	SM	111
Terriyaki lax	F&S	R	D	S	File	26
Miso cod	F&S	R	D	S	Apple Notes	
Dry chilli lemon crab pasta	F&S	Pa	D	M	Apple Notes	
Sousvide lax & pepperot	F&S	Po	D	S	Apple Notes	
Fish bake	F&S	Po	D	S	SM	87
Smörgåstårta	F&S	B	L	F	File	22
Yellow bean sauce fish	F&S	R	D	S	File	13
Crab linguine	F&S	Pa	L	S	Apple Notes	
Saffron chilli prawn pasta	F&S	Pa	D	S	Apple Notes	
Seafood & saffron tagliatelle	F&S	Pa	D	S	Apple Notes	
Chorizo & Monkfish stew	F&S	Po	D	S	Apple Notes	

My lean take on these (check and choice) lists, is they are standardised itemised documents but the flexibility comes from the check bit. The idea is to list all the items in there and use them as prompts and checks. You get to skip those that are not relevant but never forget or miss those that are. Filtering where possible helps reduce the pool of choices, i.e. choice overload, leading to thinking and deciding time.

SLIDES & MEAL MENUS

For a more macro view, this is very much like the ISO9001 thinking of databases of standardised content. I use this similar concept at work for personal slides and presentations that are outside of company stuff. Often, I create slides to get the message across in my own way or customise it to a niche audience. I realise I spend a lot of time recreating presentations. Instead of searching and looking at full presentations to find what I need and say what I need to say, I categorise slides by using their direct and indirect message, e.g. Teamwork, Standardisation, 5S, Removing Decision Making, Inventory, Leadership, Time Management etc., and keep them in an archive to filter and pick and choose from.

At home, I have a database of weekly menus which I have created officially and digitally since 2004, a few years into my career in lean. I was travelling and away a lot for work but had to care for my home even though I was never there. Meal planning for the household was crucial especially if you want the meal process to flow automatically without being there, often for a few days in a row.

I decided the week's menu, based on many factors, including individual needs, time availability, dietary demands, inventory, prep-ability, e.g. if dishes could be frozen or ingredients kept fresh for the required duration etc. I always plan in "time-consuming" experimental dishes on Fridays. Time-consuming sounds like a waste but not in my book. When I have a glass of wine in hand, I chalk it up as quality time spent cooking with family and friends.

Veckor 2021 - 2121.doc
Veckor 2104.doc
Veckor 2105.doc
Veckor 2106.doc
Veckor 2107 - 2207.doc
Veckor 2108 - 2208.doc
Veckor 2109 - 2209.doc
Veckor 2110 - 2210.doc
Veckor 2111 - 2211.doc
Veckor 2112 - 2212.doc
Veckor 2113 - 2213.doc
Veckor 2114 - 2214.doc
Veckor 2115 - 2215.doc
Veckor 2116 - 2216.doc
Veckor 2117 - 2217.doc
Veckor 2118 - 2218.doc
Veckor 2119 - 2219.doc
Veckor 2120 - 2220.doc
Veckor 2121 - 2221.doc
Veckor 2205.doc
Veckor 2206.doc

Everyone becomes a sous chef with me curating, while I double-up by prepping Saturday's (batch size reduction) lunch. This is so we don't need to just "grab a sandwich", sacrificing the quality of that meal due to the lack of time to fix a good lunch. That is so important for our quality of life, as we have earned it, having been so hardworking all week.

The weekly menus created became data that showed my eating and spending trends over time.

GROCERY LIST

I spend a lot of time thinking about food and meal planning, and my grocery list is an extension of that, as it's my "customer of information" in the NEXT customer (Supplier) principle. Unless I get everything I need, in the correct amounts and in the least amount of time, I will not have flow in the process of meal planning, prepping and cooking, compromising customer satisfaction on all levels.

I do one big shop a week but have scheduled in a mini, mid-week shop for the sake of exercise, as I walk back with a heavy shopping load on my back. However, big shops are only recommended for relatively lean people or it'll result in a lot of food wastage. Lean household shopping is not a standalone thing, and just making a shopping list alone is not Being Lean but doing some lean. You need meal planning (according to what you have and the use-by dates) and food (portion) prepping. Buy what you need and use what you have. Hence visual management and reduced batch size are so important, i.e. you use what you know you have.

Most grocery lists are either random what you come-up-with-first lists, or categorised by food group. Using a 5S approach would suggest that we section, according to your supermarket layout, and change according to when the supermarket re-aisle. Add or remove from the list accordingly during the PDCA mini tidy-ups.

Organise the grocery list according to the aisles and layout (fruits/veggie, meat, deli, dairy etc) of the store so you can shop efficiently. Feel free to use Dairy 1 and Dairy 2, for instance, when the milk aisle comes first, then meat and then cheese. This helps as you are not running back and forth.

It also helps prevent me from wandering unplanned into aisles I shouldn't be in (such as the candy and/or junk food aisle). It takes just a few minutes to mark the list in line with my weekly menu, but it saves me a lot of time at the supermarket plus I don't get distracted by store sales/discounts. I can do my big shop and check out in less than 45 mins without falling for all the marketing tricks and buying things I don't need or aren't in the plan.

4) BUSINESS CASE, DATA AND INVENTORY:

I love curries and have tried cooking many different kinds from all over the world. To help me manage my spice purchase and inventory, I started out listing the different curry dishes I make and the spices they require. The one-off data compiled over a little bit of time started to give me a better picture of the favourites and what spices were used more often. This helped inform me what spices I should buy in bulk and which ones were needed for experimentation and other dishes, so spices do not end up unused, losing flavour and being trashed.

Marker for bulk buying ↓

CURRIES \ SPICES	Aniseed	Asafoetida	Bay leaf	Cardamom	Chillies & pwdr	Cinnamon	Cloves	Cocos/cream	Coriander	Cumin	Curry leaves	Curry powder	Fennel	Fenugreek	Fish sauce	Garam masa	Ginger	Galangal	Lemongrass	Lime leaves	Mace	Mustard seeds	Nigella seeds	Nutmeg	Paprika	pepper/corns	Poppy seeds	Shrimp paste	Tamarind	Tomato burk	Tomato paste	Tomatoes	Tumeric	Vinegar	Yoghurt	TOTALS
Pasanda				1	1	1	1		1	1						1	1																1			9
Spinach sauce		1		1	1	1	1		1	1						1	1				1									1				1	1	13
Rogan Josh			1	1	1											1	1												1	1	1		1			9
Cinnamon & fenugreek sauce				1	1	1	1			1				1		1	1													1				1	1	11
Peshawar				1	1	1	1		1	1							1													1			1		1	10
Balti				1	1	1			1	1							1							1						1			1			9
Beef rendang					1			1	1								1	1	1										1				1			8
Vindaloo				1	1	1	1		1	1	1		1			1	1					1				1				1			1			14
Burmese pork															1		1											1								3
Tomato & chilli fish					1												1													1	1	1	1			6
Penang fish curry					1												1											1	1				1			5
Goan Prawn curry					1			1	1				1				1										1			1			1			8
Madras					1				1	1							1							1									1	1		7
Bombay									1	1							1													1			1			5
Biriani				1		1	1					1				1	1																			6
Prawn Curry				1	1	1	1		1	1						1	1														1	1	1			11
North Indian Lamb Curry			1	1	1	1	1									1	1								1					1						9
Lamb wt Green Chillies					1	1	1		1				1			1	1													1			1			9
TOTALS	0	1	7	14	19	12	10	5	19	17	2	1	3	3	1	11	22	2	4	2	2	1	1	3	1	6	2	1	4	11	4	4	16	5	3	

Another simple data collection trick is putting all my clothes hangers in backwards. Then, when I wear something, I put it back the normal way, from right (more frequent) to left (less frequent). In running months, it becomes visually apparent which pieces are Runners, Repeaters and Strangers plus what I have not touched for 6 months.

Data analysis and the 80/20 rule can be very useful in home budgeting. I used online banking bill tracking to keep an eye on household spending but found it not fit for purpose and started my own very simple template instead. All bills are direct debit and trigger and alarm set for automation, but knowing what items we spend on helps to keep the budget in check. Prevention is better than cure and seeing what we spend most on (80/20), allows us to make clever decisions and targeted saving efforts.

Through my continuous improvement cycles of improving the configuration of wardrobes, I've listed some improvements points for your consideration.

I literally do exactly the same thing for my larder, freezer, stationary drawers etc., just exchange clothes for spice bottles, frozen food or staplers.

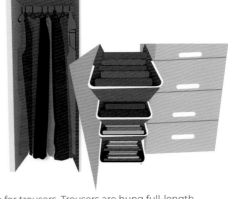

- Clothing is folded and kept vertically for easy access (while not messing up the pile) and better visual view (there's a better chance of usage if we know it's there) of all that is available. It started with just T-shirts but now includes undergarments, socks, other tops and bottoms etc.

- Further easy access and better visuals can be attained by using pull-out and see-through wire baskets instead of boxed drawers.

- Further space utilisation includes using Ikea bought boxes as pull-outs for drawers. This two-tiered system enables a quick change over of seasonal clothes.

- For space utilisation, I created a new hanging system for trousers. Trousers are hung full-length vertically, maximising usage of the whole length of the wardrobe. To further this "smart hanging", trousers are hung alternately leg up and leg down to optimise lateral space.

6) VISUAL MANAGEMENT AND 5S:

My maps are an extension to all my (choice and check) lists. They can be visual or just categorised to let me know what I have and where they are. I mentioned my dishes list, where I list the what, i.e. the dishes, protein, whether it's slim or fat and more suited for lunch or dinner, but also the where, i.e. where (which cookbook, Apple notes or file page) I can find the recipes. The same can be applied to other things and parts of the house. Go from room to room to see if there is anything "behind closed" doors that needs "seeing" without physically checking. Some of my own examples include:

- Shed logistics – A simple shed visual map showing the macro layout of the shed and the overarching category, e.g. extra kitchen stuff, paints, plaster and wallpaper, clothing and textiles etc., of what is stored in each section. I might not need this as I know where everything is, but then I have to do everything myself or take the time to explain. If I send someone to fetch extra wine glasses, this macro map will show the correct direction and area (1-step), e.g. kitchen stuff where there are 3 kitchen-related boxes. To get to the wine glasses (3 seconds) you naturally open the box labelled glassware and see photos of what is in the box. I do that for all my Repeaters and Strangers shoe boxes. This is especially good for "miscellaneous" boxes where there are too many knick-knacks to write on masking tapes.

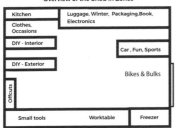

Overview of the Shed in Zones

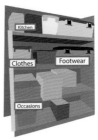

Kitchen, Clothes & Occasions

Our household has stashes of wine bottles all over the house, on top of a fully stocked wine fridge in the kitchen. To manage the what and where, a shared wine spreadsheet in Dropbox sorts this out. Like the dishes, the *what* is filterable by name, countries, region, grapes, drink-by, red/white/port/dessert etc., price, bought at and where it's kept in the house. The spreadsheet is naturally as good as the updates. The last 2Ss – Standard and Sustain – of the 5S is always harder but can be particularly difficult if only one person is dedicated to doing the "dirty job". For example, the warehouse keeper is always dedicated to cleaning out the warehouse at the end of the day. With no one needing to do the dirty work, no one bothers about prevention and keeping the warehouse clean. But if everyone who uses the warehouse takes turns to clean up daily, they would be more cautious in how they left the state of the warehouse. We take turns with the inputting into the spreadsheet of wine purchases but each is responsible for updating consumption. An occasional missing or misplaced bottle (data quality defect) here or there has been experienced, unavoidable human error, but the system seems to work well.

7) MODULAR, INVENTORY, STANDARDISATION, FLEXIBILITY AND BATCH WORK REDUCTION:

There are many benefits to meal planning and prepping. The trick is to reduce the batch size of the cooking process and do them at a suitable time for you. Do the prepping whenever you find some time, so that the quality of your meals (health) will not need to be compromised through lack of time.

I found the modular concept a great help in my meal planning and preps, just like my cleaning. Unlike the conventional way of composing dishes or prepping complete meals, I find prepping food by components more flexible and less restricting. This way, I have a buffet of carbs, veggies, proteins, sauces, and dips to choose from, depending on our needs and mood. This allows the whole family to piece together meals in exciting, imaginative ways throughout the week, so we don't get tired of eating the same things.

This leaves us with much more room for experimentation during the week. Utilise existing frozen food or cans but challenge fixed ideas! I am always amazed when friends and family don't know you can freeze rice or cheese. Some examples of my usual components for modular cooking include:
Carbohydrates – they can be in the fridge or frozen. I portion my brown rice, couscous, bulgur wheat, cold pasta etc. Any steps removed is good, e.g. it may not be the best idea to store mashed potatoes but you can always have boiled potatoes, and mash them, instead of spending 15 mins cooking them. Baked potatoes can become a side dish, and marinated beans (all kinds of cans available) can be piled on toast for lunch or even mashed and eaten as carbs or sauce.

Protein – A lot of boiled (hard and soft) eggs are in my fridge, all forms of pulled meats in different marinates are in the freezer, as well as portioned half-cooked deep-fried katsu (Japanese breaded pork or chicken) that can be thrown in the oven for 15 mins as a treat. I also have a portioned mixture of preferred seafood or shellfish for lavish warm salads or lush pastas. I freeze individual chicken breasts for either myself or many others. I take as much or as little as I need, when I need them.Vegetables – I love fresh salad but it can get boring fast. Roasted vegetables can be used in salads or sandwiches to "fancy them up". I love half-cooked vegs, e.g. mangetouts, beans, asparagus, broccoli, carrots etc. They give my lunch salad crunch and I can pop them in the microwave for a warm lunch. I have pods of roasted full garlic in the freezer that can be easily thawed and squeezed into creme fraiche, kvarg or yoghurt to make lovely dressing, sauce, dip or filling.

Sauces and Dips – I have all sorts of stocks I freeze in muffin tins and then clingfilm to give me a puck-sized portion to make sauces, like red wine sauce, or boost stews. I treat sauces and dips like jam. I put my favourites in jars and pick and choose from them, such as chimichurri, tahini-based, salsa verde, gochujang/tomato mixture etc. They can be used as they are or I scoop a tablespoon into yoghurt, and you can get access to a variety of lovely dressings, sauces or dips. I top-up a ¾ mayonnaise filled squeeze bottle with sriracha (or mustard, honey, garlic etc) and use that for anything and everything.

Reduced batch size – modular cooking gives you standardisation of the process along with the flexibility to meet changing circumstances and needs without waste, and it promotes creativity in meals. The more you do it, the more challenging and fun it can be!

I mentioned in the process mapping section about mapping ourselves. That refers to us self-reflecting, and identifying our "risks". On many other occasions in the book, I accentuated the importance of "knowing" the situation, "knowing" the circumstances. This is in essence a value stream map (VSM) where we identify our strengths (VA) and weaknesses (NVA & Waste) and come up with a plan of attack to get flow in our life. By knowing how "we (the process) look", we can use the same tools, techniques and thinking, the same way we remove hiccups along any process to facilitate more VA (strengths) and reduce NVA and Waste (weaknesses).

Very often I have sat down to start work, attack household chores for the day or time for the day's exercise, and I just don't feel like it. It may be a difficult task, an energy problem, or that I'm just not in the mood. But until you "know", or can "see" the value stream, can you put things in place to counter them.

I avoid counterproductive activities through designing my environment and create standardised processes. I try to do the right task at the right time, where I can. Choose a day, a time, a place, people that suits that activity. Some examples:

- At work (remote or in the office), I am not the kind that needs to spend half an hour browsing the web or checking out BBC online before starting value adding work. But knowing that you are that kind, then you need to plan that into the schedule instead of it eating into your value adding time. However, if I do not have my Vital 1, 2s & 3s for the day planned, I WILL start checking what I bought most recently from eBay that is still not here yet. While I'm at it, I'd have a gander at my watchlist while I'm at it.

Never abuse the flexibility of remote working

- Flexibility (physically and mentally) is key to a better quality of (productive) life. One of the benefits of working from home is the flexibility to accomplish what you have to accomplish in your own time within that day. How many times have I been grateful, I can pop out for my dentist appointment, leave my desk to accept a parcel from the postman or have a longer lunch because I have errands to run. This can be abused reducing productivity of course, but more often than not, most people like me end up stretching "work hours" and working more, compensating because there no longer are clear boundaries when to stop work. As mentioned with procrastinator types. Knowing which type(s) we are helps us better combat that. In this instance, ike chess players, I have a stop-clock to help me keep (work) time, accompanied by my daily Vital 1, 2s & 3s list. The days of working hard and not smart are over!

Simple engineer my surrounding success examples:

▶ Right place; I hate waiting for weights and self-conscious training among lots of sweaty huffing and puffing people so going to the gym is a no-go and non-motivator. The risk of me not training is high. So, I did my business case and invested in my own weights and a treadmill at home. At home, better motivated but still remnant chances of not training, so I set-up a folding shelf on the wall, where I pull out my treadmill, to accommodate my laptop so I can get pleasurably distracted and get through the painful ordeal quicker. Keep a lookout for an article on subjective time dilation from a lean perspective on our website.

▶ Right day & time; I fast every Mondays. Why? I always over-indulge in the weekend and have so much stored energy that I actually look forward to it and get through it easily. I always put on a couple of kilos and they take forever to (or never) get rid of plus I get quite depressed after a holiday. With the holiday ahead of me, it is easier for me to lose the holiday weight before the holiday, plus I never schedule a home journey to start a full work week the next day. And I always plan a party weekend to look forward to when I get back.

▶ Right people; Whether going to the gym or learning a language, doing it together with like-interest someone else will always facilitate it being done. For me, most crucially to my quality of life is having the right people that will facilitate the health, wealth and growth of ourselves and those around us. I absolutely love living the most boring and predictive lifestyle. I hate drama in my life and however much I love my dramatic sister, I only allow myself to speak with her once a month. Believe me, I am most definitely not being mean, but lean.

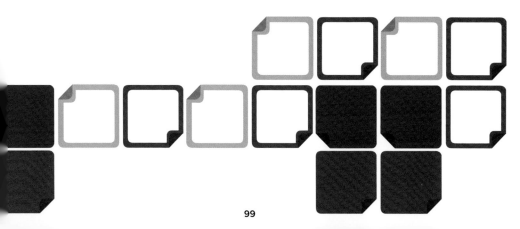

The most common lean visual management example but needs mentioning because it is indeed a great communications tool. Visual boards of any form can help you and yours stay organised. Hang hooks for everyone's keys, cascading (visual) filing systems for various category documents, like mail and bills for actioning plus coupons, takeaway menus for quick access. There is also a wipeable joint household calendar with a marker for appointments and events, a Notes/Action section for communication with allocated colour markers for the attention of the relevant person.

Visual management is extremely helpful in communicating and conveying information and practically very useful as it helps reduce inventory and waiting waste.

Create your own relevant board & flexibly change according to the events of your life

I've ended up with a collection of many sets of measuring spoons. Throughout the years, I've shuffled and reshuffled them in the utensils drawers to become more organised and make space for new stuff. But in the end, they were inventory sitting in the kitchen drawers, waiting patiently to be used. Recognising that, I've put them to use as scoops in all sorts of containers, e.g. coffee, flour, spices, sugar, oat etc. Card list of spices

I have A4 cards with a list of spices and cans/staple food in my spice and food larder. This gives me a better view of what I have so that I can use them and control my stock. By reducing the inventory, having cash tied up and food waste, these lists contribute to my meal planning and menus. I label stored spices on the top so I do not have to pick them up to see what they are. Portioned fresh or frozen food gets labelled. With 1 step – 1 glance, you get what you need when you need it. top labelled spices

Masking tape is a good friend for labelling many things when I find the opportunities to do so. Anything in opaque containers of all forms, shapes and sizes. It's not pretty but it helps me to identify what is in these containers without having to check.

The same can be applied to other things and parts of the house. I go from room to room to see if there is anything "behind closed" doors that needs "seeing" without physically checking.

I have a PDF document of all my clothes on my phone categorised by tops and bottoms. Being able to see them all gives me a better chance of them being used. Also, this allows me to be productive in planning my work and weekend clothes while tackling the Time Robbers.

This is a classic standardisation but with the agile ability to customise and adapt to constant changes. I mentioned earlier modular compartment pull-out boxes in my fridge. They are allocated to separate longer and shorter duration perishables, plus frequency of use, e.g. they are accessed a few times a day and potentially need binning by end of the day, daily use or less frequently needed. The reason for areas instead of specific homes for these perishables is space utilisation. The size of containers changes with the different brands of products bought that come in different sizes, e.g. original big jars of pickles and mustard get downsized to smaller jars to make space as they are being consumed.

Also, shopping lists change with the seasons, product availability, diets and taste preference changes etc. Hence the need to have a flexible fridge system to meet these changes, with allocated areas (mansions instead of flats) and not specific addresses.

Once we've allocated a home for our material, machine, messages, we tend to leave them there even when circumstances changes. The same concept can be applied to the need to change energy suppliers, insurances, banks etc. This is witnessed through our static storage of digital data and information. Once we find a "home" for folders, apps. etc., they never get deleted, moved or relocated even though circumstances have changed i.e., completed projects, apps no longer of use etc.

Like a lot of women, I own many pairs of shoes taking up too much space. Having too many pairs is a waste (inventory). Having just enough is when you know your Runners, Repeaters and Strangers are all being used and in rotation. For more frequently used ones, I hang a cascading 6 pair shoe shelf and change the set according to the season (with the flexibility to meet changes in need). Hence, there's only "too many" if you don't use them and have them for "just-in-case" situations. The same goes for most things, e.g. playlists, tools, toys, clothes, food, stationery, wines etc.

This thinking can also be applied to more specialist (Repeaters & Strangers) and non-standard requirements.

I mentioned before about being a huge foodie and an aspiring experimental cook. Buying unusual, infrequently used ingredients can be costly and wasteful. I have a plastic filing box in which I keep portioned ingredients plus bits and bobs in the freezer for my experimentations, e.g. squid ink, nduja, truffles, black pudding, micro leaves and other herbs etc. Going modular, breaking up the food/ingredients into smaller portions, and freezing what can be frozen reduces food waste and also allows flexibility in my food experimentation without food waste or inventory.

Optimise use of vertical space on freezer door

Home for "tall" things for optimum use of vertical Space

Reuse of part of an old folder to contain smaller things to utilize vertical space

Experimental food box with visual labelling of portioned contents

Nduja Squid ink

Smoked garlics

3 x Black pudding

Bottarga

I used to have a notepad hanging at the entrance of each main room for making notes whenever I think of something. I have since evolved to using self-adhesive wipeable whiteboard vinyl wall stickers.

For my study room, I have plastered half my desktop with this vinyl wall sticker and use it for my daily Vital 1, 2s and 3s, my to-do list, and frequently used information, e.g. my credit card numbers and space for taking notes when on the phone so I don't waste paper.

In the kitchen, I have this wall sticker on one side of my fridge freezer to plan and communicate menus for every day of the week. We have a To-Buy section and a Notes/Action section for communications. There is also a removable magnet board of inventory of what is in the outside shed freezer. This can be removed to bring out to the shed where necessary (flexible point of use) and it does the same as the inside freezer board so I don't have to make trips outside, especially in the winter. Note that the 3 sections represent the 3 drawers, so I know which drawer to go for straight away.

There is a mirror in the entrance hallway,for a final check before leaving the house, whithout waling to a mirror a distance away, half-taped with a vinyl wall sticker for general notes. It is being used for inspirational quotes, mini messages and quick reminders.

It was a battle at first to combat my own inflexibility and having this illogical need to put a good chunk of time (a few hours, i.e. large batch size) into cleaning and tidying or any other tasks. I knew it was a psychological deterrent but never realised how big a deterrent it was. Once I freed myself of that mentality and replicated the thinking, I was set free from procrastinating and made so many more changes and improvements to save time but still got things done.

Having a good quality wireless handheld vacuum has prompted me to vacuum small things more frequently because I don't have to go through the hassle of lugging out the full size one and deal with the cord, especially if pushed for time. Smaller batch size activities and point-of-use things induce the correct behaviour. I stash a pack of biodegradable cleaning wipes in the bathroom wall magazine stand and swab things whenever there is a free minute so I am never forced to do a proper clean-up due to accumulated build-ups.

Reflecting on my activities and seeing where I can reduce the batch sizes has helped to miraculously free up so much of my time. My daily small batch 10-mins tidy-up, not even 10 consecutive minutes, is a great way to keep the little daily things from piling up. 5 mins in one room, 5 mins in another one day and another 5 mins in 2 other rooms the next day rotating around etc. Most mini-tasks take only 2-3 minutes, and it's easy to make that time. I may have encroached into some TV time, so it's a better use of time with no negative effects. This actually means I am moving in the same direction as Covey's ultimate Quadrant of personal leadership.

This gives my diary the flexibility to manage Time Robbers and other inevitable urgent and important tasks. I am more flexible with a greater ability to chop and change short chunks of timed activities. If I have to cancel or postpone the hour slot allocated to my once a month deep-clean in one room, I am perfectly OK with that as the daily tidy-ups have ensured it's not urgent or important and it will not turn into a dump before the next scheduled slot comes around. In line with the 3rd S-Shine, this prevents build-ups.

This is replicated in most aspects of my life, including my work diary, where I am in control of dealing with emails, meetings, phone calls and other piecemeal work activities.

Create a system that ensures you regularly get rid of things so mess and clutter doesn't accumulate over time. Whether it is a macro or micro-environment, I allocate containers or areas for things with no home. As discussed in the 5S section, it is usually the homeless with no fixed abode that contribute to clutter and mess accumulation.

Shed – a black bin and an allocated area with a large box by the door is allocated for trash and as a quarantine area. The black binbag facilitates quick binning, which prevents "putting it somewhere first" until it's convenient. Anything that you cannot decide what to do with or where to keep goes in the box. This way, the bin and box can be dealt with very quickly in 10 minutes each week, maintaining the clean and tidy standard (4th S – Standardisation) of the shed. Everyone who uses the shed does it (5th S – Sustain).

Kitchen – There is a couple of areas in the fridge allocated to ever-changing frequent Repeaters that disappears too quickly to have a home. The same goes for the fruit and veg drawer. Separate from the staple carrots and cabbage is a section apportioned to the quick turnaround Repeaters, so they never encroach on the other's homes.

13) SPACE UTILISATION:

Vertical spaces are very underrated and under-used, which is why it is usually floor space people talk about when they complain about lack of space. There is no floor or vertical space left for any extras in every room of my home, without it looking cluttered and messy.

I have specifically got some extra tall wardrobes so I don't waste the useless space on top of the wardrobe and use it inside the wardrobe instead.

Available upright storages are the simplest form of upright against the wall storage, e.g. hanging organisers for shoes, bags, scarves, accessories, caddies for bathroom toiletries, cascading file organisers for the office or hanging car backseat organisers, or peg-boards for tools or kitchen pots and pans, floating shelves etc. Where permanent fixtures are not possible on "wall" spaces, I use all sorts, e.g. stick-ons, magnets, suckers etc., on tiles, mirror, windows etc.

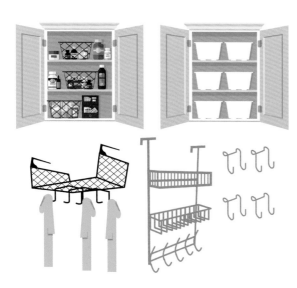

Stackable bins and shelves utilising vertical "wall-less" upward space in fridge and cupboards that can act as dividers, quarantines areas etc. are also invaluable vertical space utilisations. Door hanging caddies and pull-outs give easy access and are great space utilisers in drawerless cupboards.

Ceiling hanging is a great method of the downward use of vertical space, e.g. hanging grids and rails for tools, pots/pans, baskets or any decorative containers for use. Rails, basket and shelves inserts on floating shelves are a double whammy of ideas. Thin storage shelves to use up otherwise useless narrow spaces also help to free up countertop space, making the place look tidier & less cluttered

Wheels are a huge facilitator of flexible space utilisation. For all flexible temporary storage space utilisation, consider wheels whenever possible. Anything that does not need to be a permanent fixture or piece of furniture should consider wheels. Mobile countertops, quarantine (clutter) boxes, toy boxes, beds, under bed storages, mobile cupboards, tables etc. Movable and mobile furniture also help with easy access for cleaning.

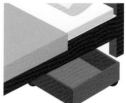

I have attached wheels to a large wardrobe drawer for under the guest room bed. It functions as huge, hidden temporary storage, and acts as a quarantine and "overflow" area for bulky homeless things I cannot find space for but use frequently, so the turnover in the "drawer" is quick, e.g. bulk buys like BOGOFFs, cat sand, toilet rolls etc.

14) MOTION (ERGONOMICS) WASTE:

Whenever you're walking to a different room, don't go empty-handed. Decide to never leave a room empty-handed. Always grab something you can put away. We keep one nice looking basket each on each end of the stairs. We fill it up with things that need to be taken upstairs (newly-bought soaps and shampoos) or downstairs (like empties, e.g. mouthwash bottle, for recycling). When one of us makes a trip up or down, we just pick up the whole basket or things within the basket on the way. This way, we don't have to make the unnecessary extra trips up or down.

Not being able to see in bad lighting is a classic ergonomic waste we don't pay attention to, as we waste time and effort looking for clothes in the closet. First, I added two cordless battery powered lights, which shaved off some searching time and reduced the squinting. Then I decided to install proper wardrobe lighting and it is now a pleasure to open my wardrobe doors as I can truly see!

I started to see where else such a simple light solution could help, such as the space under the stairs to access my toolbox or get a bottle of wine.

For home office, consider ridding some Motion Waste to induce work productivity when working remotely e.g., :

▶ Comfort; An ergonomic chair, sturdy table, your own and not family shared computer, keyboard and mouse as oppose to trackpad. Consider your reach to necessary and frequented things with regards to inputs of Man, Material, Machine and Messages e.g., printer, scanner, double screens, shredders, microphones etc. Have things to hand, e.g., inventory like stationary or data.

▶ Lighting. Natural light sources are preferable or at least at source e.g., ceiling light is in the middle of the room but your desk is situated far corner with least light reach. Whatever the case your workspace should never be dark or dinghy.

▶ Noise when working remotely at home, noisy Starbucks or satellite cubicle. Strict closed-door policy or/and use noise cancelling earphones, invest in triple glazing etc.

▶ Clutter (can also be inventory waste). Distractions e.g., water/tea/snacks runs, clicking on adverts/notifications are all physical and digital clutter that are conducive to procrastination and not doing the actual work. Any amount of time you spend clicking around trying to find, access information or browse, is time you could be spending on value adding work. It adds up throughout the year. How you set up and use your digital or brain workspace is just as important as how you set up your physical workspace.

We don't see digital clutter. I have spoken to a huge number of people to try to understand the logic behind the logistics of their mobile, if there is any. It is very common for many organised people to use category folders, e.g. news, social media, music, travel etc. This gives the visual satisfaction of being organised but as they use a chat app or another, e.g. WhatsApp, Viber, Snapchat very frequently, having them in a folder means extra unnecessary taps. I sort by swipes or touches. If you don't use the app everyday, it shouldn't be on your homescreen. Your 20% most frequently used individual apps should be accessible within one tap on the home screen.

Strictly adhering to what the 5S tool say about Sort; remove anything not bolted to the ground (see analogy about the box of Legos in that section) i.e., delete or remove all apps on your mobile or if you go crazy just thinking about that, move them all to the next screen to create an empty home screen. Sort it into Keep, Quarantine or Throw and Set by giving it an address (home) i.e., over a week's time, let the apps earn their prime locations on the home screen. The more frequently they are used the better location they deserve. Even within the home screen, I have my tiers of hot property prime locations. My first-tier prime locations are areas on the right, left & bottom edge of the home screen, where my thumbs can easily reach.

The unused ones, by a month I bravely remove totally. Experience has led me to be ruthless, no "just -in-cases". Whenever I get an idea of a new function I need, I never check if I have anything suitable hidden away anyway, I go look and install a new one, hence the accumulation. I had a few measuring apps, a few heart-rate counters, a few scanning & photo-to-text converters, need I say more?

The same can be done for tablets and laptops. Don't forget the digital photo albums, different criteria but nevertheless, they are the worst.

Tier 1 prime location for my thumbs, within the prime location of being on the home screen.

LEAN WHEN
TRAVELLING

Travelling for fun is a luxury I enjoy and treasure tremendously, so letting the quality of my hard-earned holiday be compromised by self-inflicted waste is an absolutely appalling thought. So, it is important that I do whatever I can to maximise my pleasure and minimise waste, through prevention or planned management.

I have process mapped the process from cradle to grave and gone through the continuous improvement cycle many times over the years. It is still not perfect but I have not had a so-so holiday for as long as I remember. On the contrary, I love my holidays so much and am on such a high when I get home that I have to take a day to recover and come back down to normality.

Considering the NEXT customer principle is very important to my own happiness. A lot of the time, our actions and attitude can dictate the level of flow we attain in our processes. As I have preached repeatedly, everything is a macro or micro process, from pre-prep, duration, and post-process to getting a ride to the airport, boarding the plane and going through security etc. We need to anticipate all 4 lean customer needs to make the process smoother. For example, don't make it difficult for people to clear you through the gate, security, or customs. Have everything that's required ready, e.g. belt, shoes, coat already removed, filled-out documents, destination address readily available etc., and properly orientate your paperwork, document or zoomed-in (readable) info on your mobile. Even if these people do not appreciate your lean effort, you will. The process map will let you identify where such efforts can/should be replicated and benefited from, e.g. hotel arrival, car hire, ticket purchases etc.

My process map starts from the moment I decide to take a holiday, with or without the dates or duration in mind, to coming home and acclimatising to work life. The map has naturally evolved in the form of checklists, templates, decision-making matrices etc. All these are developed as a result of the identified waste in the "cradle-to-grave" process, to eliminate waste and induce the correct behaviour. This includes how to deal with my "coming down" emotional dip on being home again. Some risk mitigation actions for this include:

- coming home midweek so I don't have a full work week to deal with,

- having only minimal unpacking to do and unclean clothes so there are not piles of laundry and chores to do,

- a prepared fancy meal with minimal prep required waiting for me that day I land,

- planned happy activities I can look forward to,

- making sure I lose the holiday weight before going on holiday so there is no need to "be good", and many more.

I've brought my holiday blues adjustment time down to just the day I come home compared to a full week in the old days. Can it be that one of the "side effects" of Being Lean is that you're "too happy" and "spoilt" by the good flowing processes? A hypothesis to be investigated.

In this chapter, I share some snippets of doing and Being Lean for my travels through my perspectives, experience and practical applications. I find these applicable not only for holidays or travels but for some everyday situations too.

7 HABITS OF HIGHLY-EFFECTIVE LEAN TRAVELLERS

I would like to think that I am a lean, highly effective traveller with a range of ever-evolving tried and tested habits and procedures that ensure I am prepared for anything. Most of my travels are independent and I often visit less-modern destinations, so most processes do not work as they do at home or as planned. To identify waste in this process, I had to conduct a detailed process map to "see" where my risks (wastes) are and based my original macro travel process map on this scenario. If I cover the most difficult scenario, then all-inclusive, package holidays and work travel with fewer micro processes, will be easier.

BE PATIENT – DON'T COMPLAIN

Before I get into fully-fledged lean applications to pave the way for enjoying precious travels to the fullest, I need to emphasise the need to be patient and not complain. When things don't go as expected, don't waste time complaining. A more effective use of time is dealing with the situation instead of getting all worked up. We need to realise how lucky we are to be where we are and do what we are doing. When it looks like things are going to take a while, I find a nearby craft beer joint, wine bar or roadside juice hawker to try the local brew, watch the world go by and see how I can send a photo message to make my posse at home jealous.

DECISION MATRIX FOR BEST VALUE

This is one example of a prioritisation tool I created to help with the business case for making decisions while planning my travels.

It is not uncommon for me, and those I travel with, to be plagued by indecision when planning holidays or activities. This can be worse if there are too many cooks when travelling in a group. This prioritisation template is very flexible and suits my circumstances. It allows me to personalise the matrix and use it to make decisions for a multitude of areas. The benefit is it's a standard operating procedure for me to utilise repeatedly, changing the categories and/or criteria to suit. Standardisation but with flexibility.

For example, I have used the matrix to help plan and make decisions regarding:

- Which cities to visit?
- Which accommodation gives the best value?
- Which package tour to take?
- Which activities to prioritise?
- Which restaurants to line up for the trip?

I have used this for travelling alone as well as a group. When travelling in a group, just agree the criteria and a rating system. It will help to give some objectivity and consensus before the trip. It is actually part of the fun of group travelling coming up with the ratings. You understand each other better and thrash out all that needs thrashing out before the actual trip, e.g. which restaurants to choose without being awkward once you're out there, as different groups have different budgets. This is a great way to understand all the customers' needs and to ensure everyone enjoys the holiday and gets whatever they want from it.

Decision Matrix

Example criteria and rating system (5 – 1, with 5 being best)

Example 1 – Choosing Accommodation:

Accom. ID	Lodging A	R	Lodging B	R	Hotel C	R	Hotel D	R	Lodging E	R
Cost	£300	5	£375	3	£450	2	£380	3	£350	4
Location	OK (15 mins walk into town)	4	OK (10 mins walk into town)	4	Very central	5	Central	4	Central	4
Space	-Spacious -Lovely terrace	5	-Spacious -No outside space	4	-Medium -Small balcony	4	-Smalish -No outside space	2	-Spacious -Big Kitchen -No outside	4
Interior	Dated	2	Cosy	4	Minimalist & bright	5	Cosy	4	OK	3
Surroundings (e.g. supermarket, restaurants, bus-tops)	-Bus & tube -Supermarket 10 mins walk	4	-Bus -Supermarket 2 mins	4	Very good	5	Good	4	Good	4
Amenities (e.g. WiFi, late check-out)	No TV or WiFi	1	OK	3	Free gym	3	OK	3	OK	3
Facilities (e.g. parking, pool)	-Nice big pool -Free parking	5	-Nice big pool -Free parking	5	Pray parking No pool Free breakfast	3	-Pray parking -No pool Free -breakfast	3	-Pray parking -Tiny pool	1
Notes (additional plus or minuses)	Nice ground level flat	5	Dodgey looking street	2	Not self-catering	3	Not self-catering	3	OK	3
Total Points	31		29		30		26		26	
Rank	1		3		2		4		4	

Example 2 – Choosing Tour Packages:

Tour Package ID	Costs Adeje (Thomes Cook)	R	Costs Rica (TUI)	R	Package 3	R	Package 4	R	Package 5	R
Cost	£500	4	£1,200	5						
Transfers	Included	5	Included	5						
Board Basis	All-inclusive	5	Half-board	3						
Activities (Spa, scuba, day trips)	Good – beach orientated	4	Very Good – beach & wildlife tours	5						
Flight timings (am/pm/late/early)	Morning there Evening back	3	Afternoon there Afternoon back	3						
Hotel & Amenities (pools/bars, entertainment)	5 restaurants, 8 bars, daily kid's club	4	Very good + big balcony	5						
Distance to town	Walkable 30 mins	3	Shuttle available	5						
Reviews	3.7 out of 5 (400 reviews)	4	4.5 out of 5 (799 reviews)	5						
Notes (add itonal pluses or minuses)		0	£100 off £1500 spend	1						
Total Points	32		37		0		0		0	
Rank	2		1							

RISK ASSESSMENTS

To have good quality time on my holidays I constantly ask myself what is important to the customers, i.e. my travel group and I. Comfort? Cost? Time? Adventure? Plan, prep and optimise accordingly. This is where my detailed process map comes into play. For a start, do a basic risk assessment, at least. I do a very detailed one following the map and consider all the what's and their probability of it going wrong. This is the typical legwork upfront that you can build on once you've done it. It will be a bit of work if you are just embarking on this activity. But having gone through the map hundreds of times – from slightly unreliable public transport to changeable weather – there are no longer any surprises. I just go through the lists.

It's the same for plans B, C and D that have been collated throughout time, albeit there's a bit of extra effort when customisation for the situation is required. This helps me think ahead and be prepared. There is nothing worse than having to stress and waste time thinking of how to combat a situation, and then arranging for that to happen when this identified risk does happen. Instead of utilising precious time during the holiday, it is savvier to use less time upfront before the holiday to do the legwork in your own good time minus the stress.

While doing the risk assessment I never fail to be in lean (resourceful) mode, doing my research and using fag pack data analysis and business cases to get more for less wherever possible. When planning, prepping, problem-solving or decision making, I have learnt to always conduct a quick analysis based on our priorities, whether they be comfort, cost or time. The cheapest option may not be the best, the more expensive option may not be better one and free may not be bad or time-consuming. In a nutshell, be a lean, mean cost-benefit thinking machine. Good things to consider include should you get a local SIM card and will you travel by train, plane or automobile?

PACK LEAN (SMART), NOT MEAN (LIGHT)

Packing smart to streamline your packing without leaving any essential items at home makes a huge difference from conventional packing light. "He who would travel happy must travel light." Not sure whose quote this is but they are so wrong.

Why compromise on an important occasion? Lean advocates looking into how you can bring all that you and your family need and want as long as you use them all. However, you will do it wrong if you stuff your travel bags to the brim and return home without using half of the items. I always pack whatever I need without compromise for my long-awaited, hard-earned holiday. Why would I not bring my pair, or two, of heels because they take up space? Packing light for the sake of it does not contribute to the quality of my travels or my pleasure. A quick reminder that value for individuals differs, hence the blanket advice from "travel gurus" like, never pack walking boots or don't bring toiletries as you can buy at the destination, are too specific solutions that do not always work.

Like many travellers out there, I used to overpack and still ended up buying necessities on arrival. My own informal, root cause analysis shows that the main reason for my overpacking was mainly due to just-in-case packing. This means that, like many women's handbags, I wanted to have everything required for all eventualities. I thought that was a testament to my ability to plan and risk assess. I had to tackle the root cause and ask myself why I encountered so many different, unexpected "eventualities" in the first place?

The purpose and activities of my trips dictate my packing choices. The less I know about the destination and what it has to offer, the more I put myself in "spur of the moment" mode, and the more I tend to overpack. Hence, the best prevention and management actions to overcome this root cause are research, planning and decision making.

Understandably, the time and effort of planning what goes inside a bag are greater than simply throwing in whatever you feel is necessary. It is only when you are on the trip that the impact of that convenience becomes apparent. Planning is NVA (macro view) but is foresight, and is exactly what it says on the tin; investing time and effort upfront to reduce the unnecessary time and effort down the line.

Unfortunately, packing smart is not as simple as it sounds. This lean skill is a craft and acquired over time from Doing to Being Lean. It is one of those Systems thinking things where the bigger picture dictates your ability to pack smart or not. Your ability will be on par with the level of research and planning you put into your trips.

Standardised comprehensive packing checklists also enable better packing. I started off using so many different customised checklists; short breaks, different season travels, beach holidays, urban jaunts etc. They have evolved into a more flexible system I have standardised that is comprehensive by the category, e.g. travel documents, toiletries, footwear and accessories, food items, medical kit etc. The same package beach holiday can still be slightly different, rendering an earlier customised checklist defective and inferior in quality. With the specific type and duration of a specific trip in mind, I run through each checklist and extract what is applicable, never missing anything or needing to think. A standard operating packing list procedure, modular style.

On top of packing smart, it helps if you get luggage and bags that facilitate space optimisation and get what you need when you need it. Better yet, practice modular packing using suitable bags and accessories with no unpacking required.

Note: This Lean Travel section is sponsored by LeanPac.co.uk – Pack Easy. Stay Organised.

TRAVEL RESEARCH AND PLANNING

To facilitate and master lean packing, you need detailed planning. You cannot do one without the other. I have created a visual A4 daily schedule matrix template. Populating this schedule helps induce the correct behaviour of planning and prepping in detail, as in what, when, where, how long etc. The more this matrix is populated, the better I can pack and the more flow in my travels. This document is key to my happiness when travelling. Naturally, the more detailed and informed the better, but a start is a good start.

Here's an example of an early version 1-week daily schedule for a New York trip in 2017. The schedule prioritises all the must-do's, eats and sees. Daily activities are decided by logistics, place, times, occurrences etc. It is populated with any important information for the day, supermarkets I would be frequenting, what activities were planned am/pm, the time taken between destinations and mode of transport, restaurants I planned to dine in with built-in flexibility slots for free and easy off-the-cuff activities. Maps and lesser important activities are noted in the form of Plan Bs and printed on the other side of the A4 document.

This "simple" double-sided 1-page document acted as my compass for the duration of the trip. While packing and I asked myself if I should bring, e.g. yoga mats or gym clothes, teabags, how many pairs of sunglasses etc. I checked my single page and programme. A yes answer facilitated me bringing items that I would use while a no aided calculated decisions to minimise my "just in case" pile.

This is my ...A4 Single Page Travel Schedule with built-in flexibility for change and a degree of spontaneity, achieved with a list of researched to-dos and to-eats.

APRIL 2017							
Date	12-04-2017	13-04-2017	14-04-2017	15-04-2017	16-04-2017	17-04-2017	18-04-2017
	Wednesday	Thursday	Friday	Saturday	Sunday	Monday	Tuesday
INFO	Virgin Atlantic 3 LHR (T3) 09.05-JFK (T4) 11.40 (7h35m)	Midtown to Upper West Side		Visit Brooklyn		Coney Island	Virgin Atlantic 138 JFK (T4) 20.01- LHR (T3) 08.00(+1)- (6h59m)
ACTIVITY	Travel & check -into apt. 553 2nd Avenue, New York, NY 10016	· 17mins to Grand Central Station - E41st St · 18mins to Time Square Theatre	· 31mins to The High Line - 529 West 20thSt · 8mins to Chelsea Market -75 9th Avenue	· Subway to Brooklyn Bridge (20-30mins walk)	· Central Park - E65th		· Korea Town W32nd St (14mins walk from apt.)
LUNCH	Grocery Shopping: · Morten Williams – 311 E 23rd St #1 · Trader Joe's – 200 E 32nd St NY10016 · Fairways – 550 2nd Ave	Le Bernardin (12.00hrs) 155 W. 51st St. New York, NY 10019 +1 212-5541515	20 mins to Cotenna (13.00 hrs) 21 Bedford St., New York 10014	Smorgas-burg, 90 Kent Ave	Jean Georges (13.30hrs) 1 Central Park West New York, NY 10023	Katz's Delikates-sen	
ACTIVITY		· 23mins to Century 21 Dept. Store 1972 Broadway, New York, NY 10023	· Greenwich Village · 19mins to Little Italy · 6 mins to Chinatown		· Union Square Greenmar ket		
DINNER	JG Melon 1291 3rd Ave, New York, NY 10021	Hill Country Chicken 1123 Broadway (Corner of 25th) New York, NY 10010 (15mins)	Donostia (20.00hrs) 155 Ave. B, New York 10009 (30mins) http://www.donostianvc.com /memu/	Contra (20.45hrs) 138 Orchard St, New York, NY 10002		Tim Ho Wan Dim Sum 85 4th Ave, New York, NY 10003 (25mins)	
ACTIVITY		New Order Concert Radio City Music Hall	· Bohemian Hall and Beer Garden · Whiskey at The Flatiron		Comedy Store		

Trip Photo 1 – Thursday before lunch activity, a 17 minutes' walk from our accommodation to explore Grand Central Station before embarking on an 18 minutes' walk to Times Square giving us half hour to stroll around before taking the subway to a table booked for 12.00hrs for lunch.

Trip Photo 2 – Spaghetti donuts, which I've heard of and wanted to try so badly, from Smorgasburg, the largest weekly open-air food market in America; attracting 20,000-30,000 people. Only on weekends and in different locations, so pre-planning & research made this Saturday in Brooklyn possible & a fantastic experience.

I cannot appreciate enough the fact I no longer visit restaurants that end up being mediocre, or visit markets that only have a quarter of the stalls still open because they are closing. I no longer waste time doubling back as I should have visited destination C before destination B and A along the way. Or visit the same area the second day because I did not know the activity was just a few streets away. Neither do I spend time deliberating by the side of the road, especially if I'm in a group, trying to get a consensus on what to do when an activity has turned out not to be as fun or we have some extra time on our hands. Time is too precious to while away by "just" walking around unless a slot, such as "whiling away in the Italian quarters" (planned flexibility), is in the plan.

In the guise of spontaneity and flexibility, statements like "take me where the wind blows", "be spontaneous and see where it takes us" or "I prefer to be more laid-back" offer a 50%/50% chance of introducing waste into the process (they are way worse odds in my experience). An off-the-cuff restaurant or walk around may end up being the best experience, but as I'm very much lean (Taguchi Lost Function) in my preference, I would be happy not to have fantastically good surprises if I NEVER got mediocre ones.

Every trip seems to get better and better, regardless of the destinations. Having such great experiences fuels me to do more legwork upfront. It's only when you get the rewards, do you get the confidence to invest that upfront time.

TRAVEL EATING

When on holiday, especially a good long one, it is not uncommon for me to "subconsciously" adopt an "I-can-eat-whatever-as-I'm-on-vacation" attitude. The result is often holiday pudge that I will have to shift somehow or another. Food temptations and peer pressure (if travelling with company) will be the biggest lures for me falling off the wagon. The key to success is research, planning and prepping.

This will help keep the need for willpower minimal, while you are away. Then again, even the most disciplined and health-conscious travellers struggle to maintain a healthy lifestyle while travelling. To combat willpower-depleting temptations along the way, I have a few "stay somewhat on-track" eating guidelines I came up with once I had identified this recurring and troubling issue on my process map. These doable guidelines help me to reduce the urges and opportunities to over-indulge without concession or compromising the quality or pleasure of my holiday.

1. Plan Ahead and Know Where You're Going.

On my decision-making matrix, I prioritise self-catering or apartments over hotels but if it has to be hotels, I make sure they have a mini-fridge. I also look up all grocery stores and markets nearby. The closer they are, the easier it is to make a stop or two throughout your trip and stock up on healthy perishable items, like fruit, cooked meats, pre-made salads etc. This will also make it easier on "not eating out" meals/days.

Experiencing new, local cuisine is a huge highlight of my travels. As this is important to me, I do a lot of research and identify a handful of restaurants along my routes (consult my One-page travel schedule) I may or may not visit, on top of those I have already booked. Wherever possible, I look at the menus beforehand and have an idea of what suits me so I don't get caught "off-guard" and waste a precious calorie splurge for that day.

2. Splurge Strategically.

Trying new foods is one of the most important and enjoyable parts of any vacation. I allow myself treats (whether it's a meal, a dish or alcohol) but am selective and pick something unique to that destination/occasion. I try to stick to a reasonable portion of whatever I choose, and savour every bite.

3. Snack Healthily – Eat Every 2 to 3 hours.

I get extra hungry and extra often when travelling. I can fast a full 5-days at home but get "hangry" if I go too long between meals on holiday. So, I make sure the situation never arises. It doesn't have to be much; hard-boiled eggs, cold meats, yoghurt or local fresh fruits are good enough. I have since avoided any "so hungry I ate a whole packet of biscuits" before dinner situation.

4. Choose the Correct Booze – Drink Smart.

Judge if you must, but it is not a vacation for me, without a drink or two. This is another identified risk that's high in frequency and probability on my process map. Most umbrella cocktails can easily top 500 calories so I avoid them like the plague. Try smarter choices like vodka with club soda plus a splash of fruit juice or a gin and (slim) tonic. Rum or whiskey with diet coke is another slimmer option. Otherwise, if you're drinking wine, go for dry white or bubblies and lastly light beer, which I am averse to. I'd rather have a proper IPA than three light beers but that's my preference.

5. Smart Choices – Scan the Buffet/Menu/Snacks.

I choose and eat plenty of protein. It stabilises my blood sugar; preventing energy lags, enhances concentration, and keeps me lean and strong for holiday activities. I am an eating machine so I try to feed my body with high-quality, lean protein, e.g. beans, oats, broccoli, asparagus, salmon, tuna, chicken, eggs, yoghurt, cottage cheese, almonds (small handful) etc. I make smart choices most of the time and when I splurge, I do it strategically as stated above.

As much as I want to stick to my usual routine of working out as best I can, what are the chances of that happening when it is hard enough to do while at home? I am on holiday after all, so I try to give myself a break and not be too hard on myself or have too high expectations. The mantra, in this case, is that doing something's better than nothing, so I try to reduce decision making and work-in physical activities or mini passes into my planned holiday. This is perhaps the perfect occasion to adopt the 10,000 steps concept.

Among my many lists is one of the flexible routines I have adapted to my travelling circumstances. Before I go on holiday, armed with this list, the only promise I make to myself on training is not to miss "being active" for more than a day. If I spend my day lazing around the beach reading and having leisurely lunches, the next day I will do something active.

Here is an excerpt of my pick and mix (modular) activities to choose from, to get my heart rate up. I either get **one proper full workout pass OR pick 3 to fulfil throughout the day.**

▶ Do a proper full workout routine

- ▫ Bodyweight exercises in the hotel room

- ▫ Cardio or strength training in the hotel gym

- ▫ Jogging or run up the hotel stairs as quickly as you can

- ▫ A circuit pass on YouTube

- ▫ TRX or bands workout

▶ Plan and build-in a workout into the day's activity, such as:

- ▫ An active tour, e.g. hiking, walking, cycling, canoeing, golfing, snorkelling

- ▫ Walk a good stretch on soft sands

- ▫ Dancing at a nightclub or line dancing at a country and western bar etc.

- ▫ Grab a city bike and see the sights instead of public transport

- ▫ Plan your route for the day and find sections where you can walk the "blocks" or a picturesque stretch instead of grabbing public transport

▶ Pick a day when you know you are going urban, and go for the stairs every time you come across a lift or escalator. If you have to take the escalator, walk instead of standing still.

▶ Find a supermarket at least 20 mins walk away and go there for your shopping throughout your trip, even if there are nearer ones.

▶ Choose a restaurant where you'll have a half an hour walk back.

▶ Before hitting the shower and getting ready for the night out, turn on some music and dance vigorously for 10 mins to some serious tunes.

▶ Choose a suitable moment (daily) to jog on the spot for 10 min, e.g. while catching up on the daily news on the hotel TV.

▶ Your choice of exercise, e.g. push-ups, burpees, star jumps etc., to start and end the day. My go-to is invisible rope jumping for 3 minutes at the start and end of the day.

I hardly need to justify the inclusion of this chapter as a healthy lifestyle with enough physical activity and a balanced diet can help prevent bodily defects and improve the quality of life. Like all outputs of good quality products, there are requirements for good inputs and processes. From the process cycle perspective, our body is the most important customer to satisfy and our ability to perform and do what we need to or want to in life are outputs of this body.

From a macro view, what adds value to this customer and what is waste? From a micro view, what are the value adding and wasteful processes within? Leaning our health is a process like any other and if we want to improve it, we need to apply the same lean thinking, methodology and structured approach. Random acts of eating well and being active go a long way but without an overarching strategy and trips around the PDCA cycle, it's "just being organised"
and not Being Lean.

I am not a certified personal trainer or have any formal qualifications in nutrition but what I am is an expert on myself. The more I map myself, the more I know myself, in terms of what is value adding, non-value adding and waste in my own doing, willing and ability. With this, I am more able to be more effectively achieve the good health I demand from my body and mind.

I have, so far, progressed to the overall good health I seek, but I recognise that to further improve, I may soon need help from more knowledgeable sources in the field. Nevertheless, by knowing myself, I will have laid a good foundation that will let me be a good Supplier of information to my NEXT customer and facilitate good coaching from them. This both minimises the cost and maximises the value of their expertise, according to my business case.

There is so much involved in living a healthy life and to each their own. Here, I write about the fundamentals of having a lean and healthy body which will facilitate living that healthy life from a lean perspective.

ESTABLISH A PURPOSE FOR A LEAN AND HEALTHY BODY FIRST

Motivation is transitory and very fleeting, and depends on the mood, willpower and phases of our lives. A purpose on the other hand can be perpetual. When I was younger, my motivation for physical training was my strong desire to lose fat, be shapely and look attractive. Now, as I reach my five decades on Earth, my purpose has shifted to being strong and healthy so that I can live an active, disease-free, natural life for as long as my body can provide, not only for myself but my loved ones too. It helps that I have achieved my earlier more superficial goals but it now goes beyond body composition or even strength just for the sake of it.

I train because it improves me both physically and mentally for what's important to me and my priorities in life. I need to be physically able to do everything I want to and need to do in life. At the same time, or rather in turn, my fitness creates the life I need to and want to lead. But it the consistency of my purpose that makes these priorities possible. Being Lean has made it quicker and easier for me to shift from my motivations of wanting to be physically fit and attractive to the bigger picture and longer-term purpose of living a more meaningful and better-quality happy life.

A lot of fitness discussion is focused on either changing body composition (losing fat, gaining muscle) or performance benefits (more strength/endurance). They are all important attributes, but they are just a part of being able to move your body well. Health, appearance, and fitness means more than strength and endurance as body control and awareness are important factors as well. Balance and agility will come into play as we grow older and need to have better body control. Your purpose may change over time, but to make it sustainable, you need to have a meaningful one that drives you on because we do not take vacations from living healthy. **Quality of life comes first, there's no compromise.**

IMPROVEMENT OR MAINTENANCE MODE?

Your purpose of wanting a lean and healthy body will coincide with the mode you are in. This could be an improvement mode or maintenance mode. It is important to state this because the mindset and level of lean application will be different for different modes.

You are in improvement mode when you want to change your body composition, whether that be to lose fat or tone up by increasing muscle mass, or improve athletic performance or have targeted wants, e.g. run faster and longer, do an L-sit from the ground or do more pull-ups etc. This requires more stringent application and discipline.

What Training Mode are You in?

Improvement Mode:

If you want to change your body, lose fat, get leaner and toner.

If you want to change performance or capabilities for physical progress, e.g. run longer, do more push-ups, manage 1 pull-up etc.

Changing for the better or desired equals improvement, which is your goal?

Maintenance Mode:

You are content and comfortable with your current body size and shape.

You are satisfied with your current level of effort and state as you have reached goals you have set yourself regardless of what they are.

You need to maintain but at the same time prevent back-sliding or natural deterioration.

The maintenance mode is more relaxed. This is when you are happy and contented with where you are. It's different for different people, but a set of limits act as thresholds for backsliding triggers. In this mode, there is more leeway to splurge or deviate from your scheduled, plan or programme. With the improvement mode, less deviation from compliance is allowed as there is a need to stick to your programme at least 90% of the time and make marked progress.

Knowing what mode you are in is vital in the adoption of the different examples and thinking in this chapter. If you are in improvement mode BUT adopting the maintenance habits of eating and training, you will not progress or gain the improvements you expect to get.

A good example of this is the use of "get it done, something is better than nothing". When on maintenance mode, your training programme might be to train 3 full pass a week. But instead, you do only 1 full pass and 2 "get it done" reduced passes over a period of time. This will probably not result in very notable consequences. However, if you are in improvement mode and do this, your progress will most definitely be hampered. A reality check will tell you that you may only be "entitled" to one such occasion in a fixed period, making that your 10% leeway deviation from the plan. In such cases, please do not claim that lean does not work as the correct level of application is required.

TRACKING WITH DATA AND VISUAL MANAGEMENT

When you embark on a journey to achieve a lean and healthy body, your body will change from the effort you put in. These changes are necessary for fat loss, improved body function and improved performance, but it's hard to get excited or motivated about changes that we can't see and feel. It is especially hard when we cannot tell if the time and effort we put in are taking effect or not. And if not, what went wrong, what do we have to do less of, and what went well that we want more of?

ACCOUNTABILITY

All that time and effort is needed to produce results. To achieve them, we need to increase your awareness and make you more conscious of your eating and training patterns to enable the creation of a strategic fat-loss or healthy living programme that can hold you accountable. This is very much in line with the mapping done to see where the wastes are and to come up with an improvement plan to eliminate them.

REALITY CHECKS AND SELF-AWARENESS

Food and fitness are favourite topics of mine. In my many exchanges with people, it is not uncommon to hear their complaints of a strong dedication to training, including full passes 5-7 days a week without them, making any progress in fat loss. This is more often than not because we are training with improvement mode stringent discipline but eating with maintenance mode habits. Without data, unbeknownst to most of us, you can't change what you're unaware of.

I had a couple of "aha" moments myself. I found out through my 80/20 analysis that my top two wasteful calorie inputs were mindless munching and eating with company. I knew I was snacking a bit here and there but surprised how much mindless munching calories they truly add up to and I'm too embarrassed to disclose it here.

Eating just because I have company was also a big discovery. It is a big thing in the family to dine together at mealtimes. I was eating just because it was mealtime, whether I was hungry or not. I'd snack and have tea whenever I had company or a second "light" lunch when I was with someone having a late lunch. Just knowing that helped me focus on reducing those occasions without the need to deprive myself of any particular foods.

Another crazy revelation. I supposedly don't make many poor food choices often but the data says I do it more often than I thought. I knew that emotional experiences can lead many people to make poor food choices. My eating trends show that I don't make bad food choices due to sad or stressful experiences like most people. On the contrary, I eat when I am happy and I am happy a lot of the time. Does this mean I need to be less happy?

KNOWING YOUR BODY

There is a myriad of advice out there. We all know by now that fat loss and fitness programmes are most effective when tailored to the individuals as our bodies work, feel and are motivated differently. Logging our improvement activities and progress lets us know what works for us and what doesn't. I definitely learnt more about my eating habits and how they have evolved and are still evolving. Logging keeps the subject in the forefront of your mind. In the beginning, just logging led to weight (not necessarily fat) loss just because it gave me awareness. That fuelled my interest and more voluntary data collection.

The same-ish situation happened with regards to the household's alcohol intake. I knew the middle-age alcoholic drinks-creep was happening. I needed a reality check. Data collection doesn't need to be elaborate. Using visual management, I placed a 6-wine carton next to the wine fridge for empties, but ended up needing another for the many bottles that we'd consumed in a week. I was not shocked but was absolutely not happy about being confronted by it.

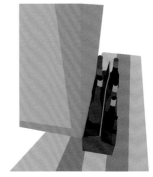

We had a family meeting to discuss. We all had different ideas about who drank how much but nevertheless agreed that there was a need to drink less. And we did for the next few weeks just because we spoke about it. After that, I had to nag whenever the number of empty bottles tripped over to the second 6-wine carton got too many.

This was a constant fixture on my Top 3 weekly-to-deal-with waste list. It sat there for ages. Finally, I lead by example and created a wine log for myself as an individual. It started off as an 1111 slash thing but the template evolved a few times as I didn't include the beer I had with lunch, the whiskey with chocolate or the dessert wine with my French tart. I gave myself "freebies" (the last splashes in a bottle) but I have since learnt that I'm the one that looks at the numbers and acts on them, so who am I lying to?

Like the food log, it has raised our awareness and helped prevent further creeps. Everyone who drinks has a column on the family wine log now. We all log our own consumption. It sits visibly on the kitchen board. I'm responsible for entering the monthly data into my spreadsheet. Visuals and figures show that we are doing well and keeping to our allotted rations, according to gender and age, with a bit of leeway for the summer and holidays. Yes, I do keep logging while on holiday as appalling as the numbers are.

Among other types of data collection, I've kept a daily weight log since 2012-2015 and progressed to a weekly weight and body composition log from 2015 to-date. It is amazing how much I've learnt about my body from that.

I give my weight in a range within 3-4kgs because that's what weight does. It fluctuates by so much, depending if I am fasted or fed. Even when I am feeding, there is the weekend and the weekday weight. I used to get upset when I was on the upper end of that range. But now, I know pretty much what to expect. For every fluctuation of however many grams, I know what to attribute that to, whether it is carbs from the pizza or soya for the sushi.

I know roughly how much I fluctuate when I deviate from my usual brown rice to fried rice with my Chinese instead. I even know how much fluctuation to expect when I've pushed myself on a weight pass and got muscle ache that week, due to water retention in the muscles during repair.

DAILY REMINDER AND HABIT BUILDING

I know how crazy the above and some parts of this book might sound to normal ears but I reiterate the effects of Being Lean. I did not actively seek to be an expert on own my body but knowledge and habits just develop and evolve throughout the consistent application of the structured lean approach to my processes. It is amazingly empowering.

Keeping daily food and exercise logs has been my way of establishing healthy habits. It started as a reminder and guide for me to eat healthy foods and exercise, but has since been effortlessly automated. Over time, I just did these things without even thinking about them. I just know my calorie allowances. Meal calories became easier to calculate. Good food choices are easier to make and by choice. "Bad" calories during my improvement mode became acceptable calories in my maintenance mode. I've learnt how and when to switch between modes so that I never need to compromise my quality of life or deprive myself of the food I love. All of this is only possible through knowing where we are first and letting the data show us the most effective way to go around the continuous improvement cycle.

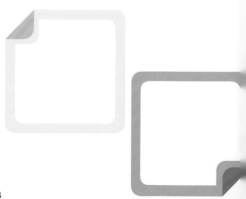

MEASURE THE CORRECT THINGS

Whatever your health goals, you need to measure the correct things to induce the correct behaviour to get the correct results. If you are just embarking on your food and fitness journey, your main objective is fat loss and you have a way to go. It will be more effective to focus 80% of your initial efforts on food and 20% on fitness. It is not uncommon when you find motivation to start that you go all out on the fitness bit. However, you get less win from that plus you will run out of steam pretty quickly with fast diminishing effect. Leverage your beginner's wind and reap the beginner's reward over a longer period by taking it slow and steady.

Food logs are almost always a must and the key to successful fat loss. How in-depth the log or journal needs to be depends not only on where you are on your fat-loss journey and how much fat you have to lose but also on how much effort you are willing to put in.

There are a lot of apps out there to choose from but they can be quite time-consuming and overwhelming if you are a beginner. I am still not fond of apps and prefer my own spreadsheets as they are specifically tailored and evolved for me and my circumstances as an individual.

SOME MEANINGFUL PHYSICAL FITNESS MEASURES

As I am not a certified personal trainer, I will not recommend any particular measures for you. As a lean practitioner, I will introduce a few measures I have used myself over time that have been meaningful in monitoring my progress and at the same time induced my correct behaviour plus fuelled and motivated me.

Percentage body fat is a great measure as the objective is to lose excess fat, not just weight. Similarly, centimetre losses in body measurements at set points is a great way to let you know that you are losing fat even if you are not losing weight. This was particularly motivating and "enjoyable" in the beginning when there was movement to be seen; however, once the margins began to decrease, it became less useful but it is still something worth keeping an eye on.

A weight log is necessary, although normal bathroom scales when used in isolation to just track weight can be misleading. I am not sure if anyone buys these scales anymore, but when they are used, paired with fats and mass measures, they can provide good indicators. There are currently multi-measure scales that provide all sorts of metrics, including body composition, that do not cost much more. I would recommend one of those if you are going to start a weight log.

Photos are a good visual gauge to help you see real progress over time. I have photos taken on different occasions. Looking back at them has shown me how different I have looked over time. But when I check them against my weight log, I am surprised when my seemingly slimmer self weighs more than my less slim looking self. It would have been fun and motivating to have gathered a complete picture of my progress over the years. I would advise anyone to deliberately take photos from the front, side and back, and repeat this regularly. Relish your progress, admire your results and visualise your goal.

Resting heart rate, the number of times your heart beats per minute while at rest, is my favourite. In my opinion, it is the most effective overall gauge of fitness. The number of heartbeats per minute while you're at rest is a real-time snapshot of how your heart muscle is performing. A lower resting heart rate can mean a higher degree of physical fitness with better cardiovascular fitness and functional capacity.

I keep an activity log for my different kinds of activities. I have 3 categories: strength training, cardio and all other activities. Smartwatches contribute to this too but I use them mainly for the "other activities" just to make sure I keep active on non-training times.

There are many ways to track progress: pen on paper, spreadsheets, electronic apps etc. Whatever keeps you tracking, just get it done, something is better than nothing. Choosing a few from the above will give you a thorough overview of true progress, allowing you to gauge success, stay motivated, and make positive decisions to move you forward.

BENCHMARKING

Body type, or somatotype, refers to the three generalised body compositions that people are predetermined to have. That, more or less, dictates your body shape thereafter.

We all have different body types, body shapes and different body fat distributions, while age also makes a difference in subcutaneous body fat measurement. Sometimes we just need to be resigned to certain physiology realities and the way we are built, e.g. you cannot get taller; women store pockets of fats in their tummy, thighs and bum while men mainly in their belly.

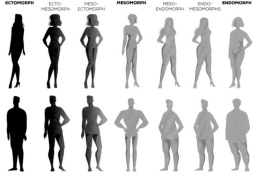

If you are a bell shape, it will be impossible, no matter what your body fat percentage is, to be a waif-like Twiggy.

One of the biggest wastes of time that contributes to a negative mindset, wrong behaviour and goalsetting is benchmarking or comparing yourself against someone else. "Oh, if only my stomach, arms, legs, bum, look like hers/his." In doing so you will probably compare what feels like your worst parts to someone else's best parts. Free yourself from comparisons.

THIS IS HOW DIFFERENT 150LBS (68 KG) CAN LOOK! depending on different body types & different fat percentage

Instead, visualise how you want to look and work towards that. The best benchmark is yourself. Similarly, do not wish for a flatter tummy, smaller thighs or bigger biceps etc. Go for skills and the desired results will happen. Focus on being able to do a push-up or weighted deadlift etc. Benchmark against improving your numbers and increasing skills that will get you on your way to your visualised shapely self.

I have never felt pleased with myself for having a body as toned or more toned than someone else, but I do secretly want to shout from the top of my lungs that I bet I got there easier, in less time and with less effort. I can probably splurge on calories more and exert less effort in maintaining it too.

According to Roy Taylor, a Professor of medicine and metabolism at Newcastle University, you should aim to be as near your body weight at around 21 years old, as that is when your body is set up for life with regards to organ and skeletal maturity. Any weight you gain after that will be body fat.

A large percentage of us will have deviated from that ideal and need to lose the accumulated fats. if so, consider making changes to your eating habits first before training. This is a leaner, more efficiently effective way to do it with regards to effort and returns, and should be prioritised.

Let's face it, most of us start on food and fitness because we want to look good, achieve our ideal weight and shape. We can work our hardest to build the leanest, meanest set of muscles, but that will only make us look bigger under a good layer of subcutaneous fat. But if we work on reducing that layer of fat, with just a little bit of muscle work, they will "bulge" through.

In lean, our body is the customer that deserves the good quality inputs required to thrive and be satisfied. Waste is defined as anything the customer does not need or is not willing to pay for, even though we pay for it in one way or another. What materials we put ini.e., eat or drink, whether that be overfeeding or poor quality, will dictate the type of performance we achieve as outputs (refer to the Process Cycle).

There is so much that can be done in this field but, in this section, I have chosen a few foci I feel are the 20% areas that can contribute to 80% results for your efforts.

WHY IS FASTING LEAN?

I would like to be politically correct and say fasting (abstaining from eating) is not for everyone. But I cannot. Maybe there are special cases for those with an underlying health or medical condition that rules out fasting. However, please do consult your doctor or do your own research before deciding to take on this practice.

I have read up on this subject extensively and my two steadfast sources of data and advice come from the pioneering experts Dr Jason Fung, a diabetes expert and author of many books, among them The Obesity Code, and Brad Pilon, a pioneer in modern-day fasting and author of Eat, Stop, Eat.

Our body is like a fat bank. All surplus glycogen and dietary fat get transferred from our current account into the fat savings account. While there is always surplus glycogen and fat coming into the current account, there is never any need to dip into the savings account, allowing it to keep accruing year on year. In our fast, convenient and foodie society, normal functioning adults like us need to give our bodies a much-needed occasional break to use up some of the stored fats for energy instead of busily processing incoming food all the time.

Fasting is a practice that dates back centuries and plays a central role in many cultures and religions. It was always thought to be an important natural part of the recovery process and has since been used as a complementary method in combating illnesses, including diabetes and other diseases. It was during these instances that the beneficial side-effect of fat loss was discovered and popularized by the Michael Mosley BBC documentary on the 5/2 diet.

I have been fasting since 2012 and have an extensive weight log to prove its success. My dalliance with fasting started with fat loss as the goal but it has since become a lifestyle with the aim of a long, good quality of life. I have highly recommended this practice to all around me and in my experience, fasting is one of the most efficient diets for many reasons.

I was never fat and have always been within the healthy recommended BMI. However, we have our individual ideal weight and body shape, and like many people, I have tried all sorts of diets. Some work better than others but your "body thermostat" will always defend your body's set weight and ensure it maintains the status quo. This is why hard-lost weight always comes back, sometimes with a vengeance.

Let us not forget that, on many occasions, weight losses are exactly that; water weight loss. Once I started eating "normally" again, the water weight always came back as it was never truly fat loss. And even when I do lose fat, that last 2 – 3kg is like the holy grail, impossible to attain.
The closest I ever came to my ideal weight (shape) and the longest duration I have been able to sustain it was through low-carb diets and Atkins. But these diets never last as they are exactly that, diets. They demand a lot of willpower and it played havoc with my moods.

Fasting was the most incredible thing to ask of me. I, who gets extremely "hangry" if I don't put anything in my mouth within 2 hours from my last morsel. I suffered from gastritis and was constantly drinking milk to counter my acidic tummy. I would never consider not eating for even a short period.

Unlike other diets, they sound easy but they are hard to do, while fasting, in contrast, is really hard to contemplate but extremely simple to do as well as stick to. Once I overcame the initial apprehension (flexibility of mind), it was simple, straightforward and my tummy troubles became a fading memory.

From an overarching lean and effectivity point of view, fasting allows the body to use its stored energy by burning off excess body fat. That in itself is a winning business case for guaranteed results.

To put it simply, if you are fasting you are not eating. You will be in a fasted state of burning stored energyi.e., you're depleting stores or withdrawing from the fat bank.

The opposite happens if you are eating. You are then in a fed statei.e., you're increasing the stores or making deposits.

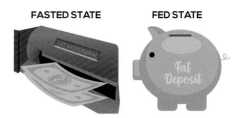

FASTED STATE   **FED STATE**

There are many different types of fasting protocols and ways of fasting. You just have to choose the balance between your fed and fasted state that suits you and your circumstances, and will help you to achieve your fat loss goals at a safe and comfortable pace. This could be as little as extending your fasted state (while sleeping) for a few extra hours after waking up or extending to up to a few days.

Not only did that last 2-3kg of fats quickly melt away, I also moved the goalposts and managed to reset my body thermostat and lower my stubborn body set weight even further. The process was highly motivating and beneficial in more ways than just fat loss as it initiated a lot more improvements in other aspects of my life.

More specifically, fasting is also lean in terms of its waste elimination capabilities resulting in time and money savings. By not eating, not only do you get direct cost savings from groceries but also indirect cost savings from petrol to go shopping and soap for doing the dishes.

As for time savings, you save time and reduce decision fatigue from not needing to think, plan, shop, cook and clean up after meals. Not forgetting the cost and time savings from not taking sick days and trips saved from not needing to see the doctor from improved health.

I used to travel a lot for work mostly driving and flying. Eating well those days can be a trial. All those workshop sandwiches and meeting cakes and cookies. Fasting was a very lean solution for those days as it simplified my eating process and I didn't offend anyone when I said it was my fasting day and not touched any sandwiches or cakes. I could have said that anyway and not touch those sandwiches but I did not have enough willpower to resist the guilty pleasure on an eating day.

Fasting as a lifestyle is my choice. I am very attuned with my body and have never felt or looked better. I am no longer as weight orientated and obsessed over the size of my thighs, which have been the bane of my life since I was 15 years old. Regular fasting helps me keep my body fat percentage in-check but more importantly, the improvements in my yearly check-ups and blood work show that my feeling and looking better than ever is NOT an opinion or perspective but evidence through numbers. This has convinced me that the benefits of fasting include longevity and the reduction of the risks of illnesses, like cancer and cardiovascular disease, to be true.

A small confession though. I don't want to live longer starving, but live life to the fullest. I no longer fast for fat loss but use it to maintain my lavish eating habits. For example, I still do a stringent improvement mode of fasting and training regime to shed a kilo fat to earn a fore coming holiday. I love the flexibility of fasting and play around with the different (modular) fasting protocols for different purposes. Plus, it is a great tool to train and flex my discipline muscles.

KNOWING AND ENGINEERING YOUR ENVIRONMENT

Do I get tempted to eat some not-so-good food every once in a while? The truth is, most definitely, but as a lean food and fitness practitioner, I am tempted less often. I believe I have successfully deployed lean thinking and techniques to combat the need to use will power to "be good". Like all fine-tuned high-performance cars, you run low on fuel. When I am well fuelled, a piece of chocolate fudge cake is perfect and enough. But when low on fuel (tired and stressed), only a whole cake will do!

With lean tools and techniques in a well-designed environment, I make sure I am never low or out of fuel first and foremost, and when those very few inevitable occasions it happens, I make sure there is no whole cake to be had.

This is my unique set of circumstances i.e., maintenance mode. The food that was not so good for me before, like cake, is not bad now, but for those that aren't there yet, even one piece of chocolate fudge may not be a good idea. However, regardless of the circumstances, the same lean applications apply.

My risk assessment maps tell me that my tendency to "fall off the wagon", make poor choices and eat badly has gone from high frequency, high probability and high impact to

low probability and medium impact. And the root cause and data analysis tell me those occasions when I am worn down, stressed, tired or distracted. Since I've known who, when, why, what, where and how, I have done many 5S activities in different parts of my house and workplaces to design my surroundings and environment to combat the different risks i.e., eating, skipping workouts, procrastinating on tasks etc. This mistake proofing activity is a big reason why the probability of me making bad eating choices has reduced tremendously since I started making good choices, engineering them into good convenient fast food, instead of bad convenient fast food. This has reduced the probability of me falling off the wagon but the impact of it happening remained high as I still had access to real calorie bombs and processed stuff.

A further improvement I have made since is to get the impact downgraded from high impact to medium by planning for these inevitable moments. When preventative measures don't work, I now recognise the triggers and make sure I manage the problem by having alluring but acceptable "not too bad" foods available for those occasions. Why wouldn't I, when I know it will happen?

A handful of mixed nuts on the left is 30g, while the one on the right is 55g i.e., 55% (ca.150kcals) more.

Visual Control   **No Visual Control**

Draw a circle on the palm of your hands. This gives you a handful of nuts. This prevents food creep. A lot of us either think we eat less than we do or we know we eat a lot but not how much. Not knowing is obviously not enough to motivate us into action

Some examples of recognising triggers and engineering environments:

▶ Don't walk down the supermarket aisle of bad and processed foods that you do not want to buy or eat.

▶ Design your week so there is no need for deprivation and you are not giving up anything. Work-in an indulgence or two in the form of healthier options, e.g. better versions of homemade pizza, burgers, curries or bubblies instead of sweet cocktails etc.

▶ Configure and create flow and establish pull in all your food larders and storage areas to facilitate good food choices.

▶ Avoid being near food or doing food prep on fasting or diet days. Have family meals prepared and automated for them and do not eat with them to avoid making it harder for yourself. I do not think you will be missed by the family for a meal or two in a week, in support of your endeavour.

▶ Do the opposite of 1-step-3-seconds. Store "bad foods" a distance away from you according to their "badness" so they are difficult to access. The worse the food, the more steps to get them, e.g. you need a chair to get to the cupboard's top-shelf plus you need to pull stuff out to get to it. Make it also more difficult to access them by tightening screw jars, putting a box within a box, lock and key etc. Better yet, avoid having them at home altogether.

▶ Always have the things you want eaten displayed prominently along a frequented corridor or walkway. This works well for encouraging healthy snacking as you're more likely to grab the first thing you see when you're hungry and in a rush. That's why "bad foods" are called convenient food. This can be fruit if you want to encourage more fruit-eating or a bowl of seeds or chickpeas for snacking. Prep and display anything near its sell-by-date that needs to be eaten, e.g. boil old eggs and leave them out in their shell, and put out carrot sticks from old carrots.

▶ Meal prep is essential to successfully engineering your environment. The reason we often reach for unhealthy options is convenience. If we make healthy, filling meals convenient that are easily accessible, we will eat them. Cooking twice as much food doesn't take twice the time and change the definition of convenient foods. Try meal prepping one day of the week so you can spend the rest of the week doing something besides cooking or figuring out what to cook. Better still, try reduced batch size, modular meal prepping as discussed before. If meticulous meal prep's not for you, write a weekly menu of what you want to have for lunch and dinner each night.

▶ Invest in food vacuuming and sealing apparatus for reducing portion and batch sizes. I portion and repack everything I can for many reasons. When it comes to food, repack "naughty" food into a smaller portion size so you eat a reasonable portion if you fall off the wagon, instead of overindulging. For example, eating 3 – 4 cookies instead of ¾ of a pack. I love cheese and port. If I lay out the different cheeses as it is, there is no accounting for how much will get eaten. I do French boards, portion up the different cheeses and then vacuum seal them into per person portions and freeze them. Whenever I feel like cheese or have guests, I take out whatever I need and thaw them in the fridge. This mistake proofs that I never over-indulge in is calorie-bomb food, which also helps me to manage what everyone else in the household eats.

▶ To a large extent, my wardrobe has been designed to induce my correct behaviour. By using the quarantine concept of the 3rd S – Shine, I no longer have baggy clothes that allow me to hide the consequences of long-term unhealthy living or bad choices, whether this is food, fitness or the mental confidence to rock an outfit. Practically, this means wearing snug clothes to restrict the amount I can indulge in. At the same time, it visually displays quickly and obviously when I have been lax over a longer period and it triggers me to rein things back.

With snug clothes, you cannot hide

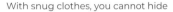

▶ Have a Plan B for out of the norm environments, e.g. try volumetric eating which emphasise eating low-energy-dense, high-nutrient-dense food, like fruits, vegetables, whole grains and low-fat dairy to fill you up first. This is a great trick/habit when travelling and faced with a breakfast buffet table. "Binge" on fruit and vegetables first, then fill up on meats and then carbs. Closer to home, I have a bowl of sprouts or chickpeas to pick on while cooking, which helps "ruin" dinner. For "naughty" food, choose popcorn or cheese puffs over crisps. They are NOT necessarily lower in calories or healthier but from a "hand to mouth" frequency, you get a bigger bang for your buck, prolonging the pleasure (unless you shovel them in!).

FOOD AS REWARDS

A combination of very palatable fats, carbs, flavours and salt pushes up your reward boundaries and you need more and more to get satisfied or you'll keep thinking about it. Foods affect the brain in the same way that drugs do. Dopamine, a major role in the motivational component of reward-motivated behaviour, equals motivation for any kinds of pleasure.

Works the same for sex, drugs, risks, training (for some) and my holiday highs. Anything that gives you pleasure; you seek out more and more. This is one good reason why food rewards for someone trying to lose fat may not be a good idea.

It's the same reason why moving to healthy eating from a fast food, processed food diet is difficult as it doesn't provide the pleasure reward hit. Stick with it for a lifestyle change until your palate changes and your sense of pleasure and rewards change too. Who would have thought that one of my "bad" foods was fruits? This is good food for most of us but I eat too much. It is not uncommon for me to eat a whole honey melon AND a huge carton of grapes all by myself. I eat fruits like others eat a bag of crisps in front of the TV. Human nature means we always find ways to be "up to no good" in some way or another. This is why we need to consider why we eat the way we do and not just what it is that we eat.

GOOD AND BAD CALORIES

I use the words good and bad (naughty) food but this needs clarifying. Each unit of calorie has the same amount of energy. One dietary calorie contains 4,184 Joules of energy. From a process point of view, a calorie is indeed a calorie, as an input into the body. Whether you put 100 calories of chocolate or 100 calories of broccoli into your body, they will both give you 41,840 Joules of energy.

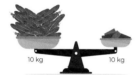

10 kg   10 kg

Just like ten kilogramme of feathers or ten kilogramme of bricks, they both weigh ten kilogramme when you weigh them. However, the machinery used to weigh them needs to be different, their volume is different, the uses of the materials i.e., the feathers or bricks is different and the rate they fall from a height is different.

This is similar to calories as a unit. Let's just look at calories and ignore the metabolic effects of each calorie plus how the body digests it and how you retrieve energy from it. Ultimately, it matters where those calories come from. It's more important than counting the number of calories you ingest. In this context, some calories are – like chocolates – more fattening than broccoli calories. Calories derived from protein, fats and carbohydrates all stimulate a different hormonal response from our body. They also solicit different effects on the brain centres that control our hunger and eating behaviour.

From a weight gain or fat-loss point of view, excess input of calories, wherever the source happens to be, is naturally bad. Good calories will normally be calories derived from foods and nutrients that do not have a negative effect on hormones, our appetite and metabolic health. Calories from protein have always been referred to as good calories as they require more energy to metabolise, are more satiating and reduce our overall appetite, hence they're less fattening than carbohydrates, whereas refined carbohydrates lead to faster, bigger blood sugar spikes, which lead to cravings and increased food intake, hence they are often referred to as bad calories. The body requires all these three macronutrients to function well. From a maintenance mode perspective, if we understand the effects of different macronutrients on the body and with that, there's a moderate and balanced intake of calories, there are no good or bad calories.

From a lean point of view, we can reduce a lot of wasted time and effort in the process of trying to lose fat and build mass if we understand what good and bad calories really mean. Just making small changes to your food selection can lead to much better results than simply restricting your calorie intake, depending on how much fat you have to lose and where you are in the improvement mode. With chocolate and broccoli, it may be obvious which is good and which is bad. However, fructose and glucose provide the same number of calories but which is good and which is bad? Take interest now, and go find out!

PRACTICAL APPLICATION - TRAINING

The health components of fitness are universally important. There are many components to fitness but a complete fitness and exercise program should incorporate the three basics of aerobic endurance, strength and flexibility. The skill-related fitness components are more relevant to certain athletes or more advanced trainers, while everyone can benefit from daily walks. We all want to get the heart pumping but it isn't necessary to develop the speed necessary to run a five-minute mile.

Having the right progression goal is important. Diagnostics will show that you can't start doing pull-ups if you have weak wrists or a weak core. You'll have to strengthen those first before trying to do them. Imagine the wasted effort of trying to do it the long way around and keep pulling yourself up. It's a sure way to not succeed and a motivation drainer.

The next lean, smart move is to find an exercise that doubles up to give you wrist and core strength, e.g. a hanging leg raise. But before that, if you are overweight and a bit too heavy overall, it's leaner and smarter to focus on fat loss through diet first, even if that feels like a total diversion from your fitness goals. See how having a big picture methodology can give guidance on how to do and choose the right cause of action, even if the heart is more impulsive and unwilling?

Wherever you are in your journey, meaningful progression goals are important to the sustainability of the programme. I have been right through the range from a beginner to where I am currently; here's an idea of the things I took into consideration from my lean "do less to get more" fitness journey.

Do Less, Get More

Training Goals for Beginners - My first short-term goal was to exercise consistently, making training a habit. Just showing up and doing the work, whether it is cardio or strength training, was the main aim no matter what. I started out very gung-ho once I got the idea I wanted to be fit. I burnt out quite quickly skipping passes, not necessarily making excuses but I was really weakened. It was more important that I did any bit of training consistently according to schedule than a lot sporadically.

Training Goals for more Intermediate and Advance Training – Once you've passed the beginner's stage (which is usually at least 6 months of consistent application), your goals should progress and be different from a beginner's. Most people have the vague goal of "getting in shape" and carry on doing more, longer and harder versions of random exercises or workouts that they have been doing as beginners. However, you want to improve and become more advanced in your fitness, not become an advanced beginner.

I was paying attention to my food and doing various forms of cardio. I was diligently and consistently doing my hour, 4-5 times a week: treadmill, spinning, circuits, Pilates etc., to achieve my weight goal but with diminishing returns. I just kept eating less, cutting out carbohydrates and training more. Plateaus will see me push myself harder and eat even less. I would blame my own weak self-discipline

when I fell off the wagon. I would despair after putting on some holiday weight which I had worked so hard and suffered for, as I was back to square one. I would get so disappointed with my weekly weigh-ins when the numbers didn't reflect my effort. This went on for at least a decade and my weight log showed the ups and downs within my fixed body set weight range.
Training Goals for Beginners - My first short-term goal was to exercise consistently, making training a habit. Just showing up and doing the work, whether it is cardio or strength training, was the main aim no matter what. I started out very gung-ho once I got the idea I wanted to be fit. I burnt out quite quickly skipping passes, not necessarily making excuses but I was really weakened.

It was more important that I did any bit of training consistently according to schedule than a lot sporadically.

I created a visual skill-related fitness component single-page plan as my guide, which I'm still using and evolving. Having a plan allowed me to see and celebrate every time I passed the many major milestones and goals I achieved. Unlike before, I was able to see and savour my efforts, which added up to new skills or attributes I'd never had before. From not being able to do a single wide arm push-up and having to start from a wall push-up, I progressed step-wise to a stair push-up, and a knee push-up to a wide arm one and finally, to my ultimate goal of triceps push-ups. It was the same for chin-ups, pistol squats, L-sits etc. It was motivating and exhilarating and memorable to finally achieved the first of these major wants of mine.

Training Goals Around Stress and Life Events – The multitude of risks assessments and process mapping have taught me that there is nothing more consistent than spanners in the works. It may be that as one grows older and life gets more complicated, the statistical chances of spanners in the works increases. Very lucky for me, I don't have much stress in my life nor have I encountered too many life disrupting events requiring substantial change or readjustments. However, I have had enough life disruptions causing non-compliance to my healthy food and fitness quest.

A root cause analysis of my weight (body composition) log against my plan showed me that these occasions, which were stressful enough to register hikes in my body fat percentage and dips in performance, have been due to: 1) training injuries (physical), 2) changes in circumstances (psychological) and 3) long-duration travelling (circumstantial). Getting back on track is a must and is good, but prevention is better. Having training goals for such circumstances help maintain your progress, especially if you have no idea how long it will be before you can get back to the norm. This could be months and years.

Do not let circumstances derail all you have achieved, even though you are going through something major. You can do this by simplifying your training by using the time to entrench and maintain your habit of training rather than working to your plan in achieving or improving. Now use the Something's Better Than Nothing section examples to help set your goals and life event programme. A few minutes is better than no training at all. Make sure that whatever you decide to put in your plan is flexible, so you can pick and choose according to mood. Make sure it is manageable, e.g. a minimum of 10 mins. And lastly, it doesn't have to be official or written down, just make sure you have a plan and never play it by ear or wing it.

LESS FOR MORE – BIGGEST BANG FOR YOUR BUCK

The leanness in the training regime is propagated by my dislike for it. So much so that I cannot even bear the thought of wasting more minutes on it than necessary. However, if there were ever any areas of my life that I am in utter control of, this is it.

A full Systems thinking analysis was warranted to make sure all value and wastes were identified with the waste eliminated to optimise the processes for maximum value. Doing less to get more has never been so crucial or apt. In this instance, I am the System and doing as little as possible to get more is the System's goal.

From a personal preference point of view, I am not a fan of time-based training. As I am trying to go for less is more, I want more performance outputs in less time. Time-based training is getting more performance out of a fixed amount of time. A minute's plank is a minute no matter what. To increase your performance outputs, you have to work harder by either increasing the number of minutes or doing more difficult variations.

That in itself is no reward for me as it is still 1 minute of torture. I prefer repetition-based exercises where there are time-saving incentives. For example, I may be able to do 10 push-ups in a minute but I will be incentivised to do 10, without sacrificing form (quality), in less time. From a macro view, I can potentially reduce (improve) my 45 minutes strength training pass to 35 minutes over time.

I do balance my training with time-based short cardio passes and being as active as I can in my daily life. However, strength training is the key lean vehicle to continuously improve my effective training that ups the game and my outputs, but never encroaches on my time. The improvement window comes from being able to do more repetitions or tougher variations in less time.

FULL BODY COMPOUND EXERCISES

Your body is designed to work as a system of integrated parts so your exercise selections should be based on the integrated function of your body. Reach out for a glass of wine at the kitchen table and you're recruiting muscles at the shoulder, elbow, wrist joints and fingers.

Compound full-body strength training works multiple muscles at a time, incorporating movement across many joints. Isolation exercises emphasise movement at one joint, dividing the body into parts, training one muscle group at a time. The body isn't designed to work that way and it is very inefficient from a time-management perspective.

I have found, from my lean training point of view, that isolation exercises like ab exercises are a waste of my time. Compared to compound exercises like squats, deadlifts, push-ups, rows, overhead presses, chin-ups, and dips. Doing any one of the above will give you a free set of 20 crunches each plus more, so why do sets of 20 crunches when that is all you will get? The same goes for bicep curls. You won't have to add 5-10 different types of biceps exercises to your workout when chin-ups and rows alone will overload your biceps, give you the result plus "freebies" on other parts of your body and more.

TIME SAVINGS AND ADDED CARDIO

As I am a huge proponent of proper research upfront to reap the benefits down the line, I have spent a reasonable amount of time looking into what workout suits my fitness objectives and goals. There are many reasons why compound strength training is my lean choice of workouts but the business case that won me over, on top of the maximum performance outputs criteria, is the time savings and added benefits of cardio without actually doing cardio workouts.

The fact that multi-joint exercises involving multiple large muscle groups contribute to more time-efficient training session is indisputable. You can cut your training time in half by focusing on compound exercises as they are like doing two exercises in one. In addition, you can further optimise your effort by targeting multiple major muscle groups to get even more out of it. One compound large muscle mass exercise, such as deadlifts or squats, can exercise as many muscle groups as eight small muscle group isolation lifts.

Targeting major muscle groups that work with every major muscle group in your body efficiently. From a macro view, your largest muscle groups include your legs, bum, back and chest. Your gluteus maximus (bum) muscles are the largest in your body. Always choose compound moves that involve two or more from these groups. From a micro view, within one muscle group, e.g. your arms, most people work on their biceps to build mass or tone up when the more effectively efficient way is to target your triceps instead, as they make up about 2/3 of the upper arm (80/20 rule).

By training compound lifts involving a combination of multiple major muscle groups, you train the whole body in one training session. This reduces not only the training time required for one workout pass but the number of workouts you need to do per week. To demonstrate how much more you can derive from the compound training model, there are Complexes. These are exercises that can be done separately but are combined and transitioned smoothly in good form from one to another without a rest in between. They are time-efficient exercise bombs.

EXAMPLE COMPOUND EXERCISES

They are far from easy but are so efficient and effective that once or twice a week can be good enough to maintain if not build strength and mass. Reps can range from 1-5 with intensity varying from 50% – 85%. I came across this way of training while investigating further continuous improvement lean ways of doing even less (occasions not intensity) for more, improved outputs.

I mentioned how compound exercises involving major muscle groups is like doing two exercises in one and can reduce your training time and frequency by half. Consider how much more time-efficient complex lifts of 3 or more exercises in one can offer once you've earned your ability to perform them.

Like all lean tools and techniques, once you have the tools in your bag, problem solving and countermeasures are only limited by our own imagination.

The other benefit of this way of working out is that you can get cardiovascular benefits without having to do additional cardio work. Many people think that improving the ability of the heart to pump and deliver oxygenated blood to organs and working muscle can only be achieved through typical cardio activities like running or spinning. But the truth is that any exercise that raises your heart rate does that. This happens just as well when you use a significant number of muscles at a very high level of exertion whether in the form of heavy loads, high volume or short rest periods circuit style. Try doing a weighted complex and see how your heart rate accelerates and maxes out. The burst is comparable to 0 – 60mph in less than 3 seconds for a supercar!

SOMETHING'S BETTER THAN NOTHING

The lean requirement for consistency to achieve quality, like standardisation, doesn't mean you have to train exactly as you planned every time. It just means showing up consistently and doing what you can. The concept of doing something because it's better than nothing, applied to training, is in the context of getting through your week or any stressful life event period while maintaining consistency. The idea is not to progress or improve but how to "skive" when absolutely necessary, e.g. when you are at your lowest emotionally or physically, without significant consequences. Likewise, this is also the reward and luxury earned by those who have already done the hard work to reach maintenance mode as you no longer have to work as hard to keep your good health and physique as you did to build them.

Before moving on, there is a need to understand that, as with all things lean, quality should never be compromised. Hence, workout volume (how much, i.e., number of exercises or repetitions) and intensity (how hard) are as important as frequency, if not more so. Quality, not quantity is vital, which is why compound exercise strength training is great for reducing the frequency, as well as increasing volume and intensity

And to further clarify matters, I need to stress there are no days when I am happy to train, including "OK I'll do it because I have to" days, "I don't feel like it but I'll do it" days and "I really, really don't feel like it or I physically cannot" days.

Fasting days are usually good days for me. It's usually after a weekend when I have excess energy to burn. In a fasted state, I feel light and bodyweight exercises are easier the lighter I feel. Bad days can be anything from a long, hectic, stressful, late workday to an "ate too much and too many carbs that I feel bloated and very heavy and fat" day. Or, a rundown week where I feel like I'm coming down with something or I've sprained something enough to prevent me from doing proper full training passes.

I may have mentioned before that reward, even though I do use it, doesn't work as well for me as it does for some people. Pleasure is like a drug for me, I always crave more and more, pushing the boundaries, and we know we cannot always have pleasure all of the time. So, this strategy of doing something instead of nothing and just get something done is a frequent go-to for me.

I know Mondays are not good training days as I get Monday blues, not just mentally from having such enjoyable weekends but also physical withdrawal from all the good wining and dining. I fast on Mondays as I have so much surplus energy from my weekend meals and it is almost a relief to not think about eating. I always have the best intentions when it comes to training, but by the evening I'm absolutely dreading it.

Unsurprisingly, data analysis shows that most of my skipped training days are Mondays. No surprise there but it took seeing it on paper to make me actually do something about it. I have Feeling Fat Fridays too but I leverage the fact that it's the start of the weekend and I choose from the "fast and furious" routines that are brutal but short to just get me through the session.

My fitness risk assessment mapping had me investigating my minimum viable training volume, intensity and frequency, for various high probability scenarios of skipping workouts. There are many research papers out there with recommendations of how long and how often you need to train to progress and keep fit. It will be different for different individuals, especially whether you are in the improvement or maintenance mode. It got a bit complex but I aim to always do 3 full-body workouts each week to keep my body strong, powerful, mobile, flexible, and healthy. Each pass will consist of 3 sets of 6 – 10 reps of 6 exercises plus a 20-minute cardio workout of some sort.

For days or periods where I do not have the emotional or physical bandwidth to cope, a sub-optimal routine is much better than a perfect but abandoned one. I leverage and play to my good and bad days to help me get results plus maintain the consistency and habit of training.

I drive myself to exert that bit more on good days and exploit bad, lax days when something's better than nothing. Through time, I've collated a tool bag of something's better than nothing tricks I use to help me maintain my hard-earned gains without missing a training pass or jeopardising my consistency in working out.

Mapping the risks gave me the insight to engineer my circumstances and surroundings around them. I came up with the different scenarios, options and choices to eliminate bad decision making and facilitate doing something as it's better than nothing at all. Using this strategy, I cannot remember the last time I missed a single training pass. The non-decision-making help gives me the just-do-it I need to get started.

To facilitate a leaner process of applying this thinking, I have, over time, collated a standardised archive of exercises I can easily pull from, removing decision making. Also, with the number of options, there is always something to suit the degree of how badly I feel like skiving, so there are no chances for excuses.

You can find some of my more frequently utilised "something's better than nothing, just get it done" routines on the Being Lean website.

Most of the time, I start off with a "something's better than nothing" (trigger habit) routine, but more often than not, the mood improves or guilt takes over and I end up doing more than I planned or, at least, the equivalent to a normal planned pass. I will top up or combine it with one or two more "something's better than nothings".

Standardised archive of visual core exercises to choose from, on a whim:

The whole chapter, like this whole book, acts as both a prompt and food for thought. If you are compelled to start being "healthy", go do a diagnostic. Map and establish what your fitness level is, what you are able or not able to do, what hinders you, what you are willing or not willing to do, how much time you want to dedicate to it etc. Go find out.

LEAN AT **WORK**

My ability to influence, impart lean knowledge and inspire project teams and those around me, in a short span of time, is absolutely crucial to the success of my services as a lean consultant. There is a need for results, as in the classic scenario, e.g., a reduced construction programme, reduced cost of rework, percentage of bids won etc. It is easy to get results as long as the teams I work with follow my lead in the methodology, adopting tools and techniques you recommend and closing actions etc. I have a multitude of case studies I can use to market my services as results are not difficult to achieve. I simply leverage process expert's teamwork and expertise, plus raise the bar a bit and do things differently.

Naturally, it is not as easy as I make it out to be as every project has its own challenges and difficulties, but the kind of results I personally want is much harder to achieve. What I want to do is (this is going to sound very cult-like) to indoctrinate someone from Doing to Being Lean; get a lean culture going. I'd estimate it's 1-in-1000, if I am lucky, considering each project I work with can consist of an average of 10 – 20 team members. There are plenty of organised people but none will hitch-on to the lifestyle of Being Lean.

Personally, I feel that people who encounter lean at work are mostly willing to make the effort for work and leave it at that. And if they really take to the concept, some thinking and doing may spill over to random applications in their personal processes but more often than not, it's in a pick and choose way rather than a structured approach. Hence, I have formatted this Lean at Work chapter slightly differently.

The pandemic has changed the way we work and it will probably never be the same again. Looking at this from a positive point of view, we can say, we've been given some sort of a clean slate and the opportunity to rethink how we do our jobs and how we run our companies.

We don't know all the changes yet but 9-to-5 and office-centric work is definitely no longer convention. What works well now that we want more of and what bad habits and inefficient processes can we take the opportunity to discard?

Our daily experience of work will change significantly. For most of us that can work remotely, the hybrid model, in different home /office proportions will most likely be adopted. There will be need to try to balance the efficiencies gained by remote working with the benefits of social interactions which is vital to creativity and innovation.

Days not commuting will gain us an hour back on average in our day. This however, extends the work day, diffuses work-life boundaries and can reduce mental wellbeing. And even with the efficiencies of online meetings, some face-to-face interaction is required to facilitate collaboration, build relationships, solve complex challenges and generate ideas.

We are all making new choices about where we want to live, have expectations about flexibility, working conditions and life balance. More so now than ever, does Being Lean as an individual and the lean culture of an organisation come into play.

More so now will managers need to know how to manage, coach, collaborate, evaluate performance and motivate their team remotely. More and more data will be saved on cloud with applications to allow virtual collaborations without hiccups. Organisational culture will need to prioritise trust and belonging with care and intent being key to relational connections.

I believe that only a lean culture at a workplace (virtual or not) populated by many individual lean thinking practitioners can produce true meaningful outputs for the organisation.

From my own personal Being Lean point of view, nothing much has changed other than the fact that many more people will now have more insight into how important it is to live a quality lifestyle. This in turn is very important as it makes people more open to changes in life processes and open to thinking plus tools and techniques that can help us make and adapt to those changes.

I have formatted the **Lean at Home** section from the individual's and personal development perspective. I trust that Being Lean as an individual makes no difference, whether you are working remotely or not. On the contrary as there is now, more urgent need to arm ourselves with the correct thinking, tools and techniques to manage as much as you can within your control. Whether that is learning to prioritise work-life balance or learning to communicate efficiently or manage work relationships and productivity remotely, or working to ever changing circumstances.

In this chapter, instead of focusing on individuals processes or demonstrating how lean or specific tools and techniques can be used or applied to work from a project or process point of view, I have decided to use examples to highlight some key learning, thinking and messages that individuals can benefit from at work. The emphases I have chosen underpins Being Lean as individuals concentrating on things within our control to influence our surroundings. They are:

▶ NEXT Customer Principle

▶ The importance of Data

▶ Pull from Customers

▶ Macro & Micro Views

▶ 5S – Workplace Organisation

> **By constantly adopting, applying, teaching and influencing all around us with these few, key thinking tools, they should spread, influencing other individuals and their surroundings, contributing to a lean culture at work. Once the lean culture exists, starting with your immediate workplace, e.g., your project team, regardless of whoever new is joining it, will have to conform to the way "things roll" in your circle.**

I have used my own work examples as best I can to convey *the learnings* through the thinking and not necessarily the hard application of the tools. You will have to use your imagination to see how the thinking and learning can be transferred to your own backyard.

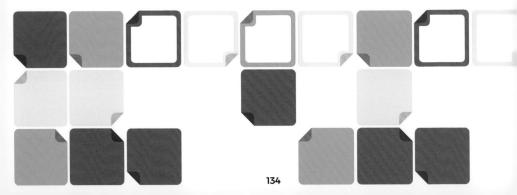

NEXT CUSTOMER PRINCIPLE

A quick recap to remind us that Lean has identified 4 customers along any one process:

1. Supplier (customer of information) – the one that comes before a process step

2. Next – the next step in the process

3. The cash customer – the person paying (monetary or otherwise)

4. End user – the final one utilising the output

From a lean point of view, it insists that we understand value from the end user's perspective. However, to ultimately achieve end-user satisfaction, there is a need to focus and satisfy the needs of the NEXT customers along the process in order to achieve flow i.e., no hiccups (wastes). For added value, by paying attention to the customer of our information (Supplier), we help them deliver good outputs to us as NEXT customers.

We may all have the same goal along the process and we all strive to do our best within our part for the end users. But without understanding the System (bigger picture), identifying who our Suppliers and NEXT customers are, doing our best by ourselves for ourselves may not be optimum for everyone involved. cro view of multi-processes is cyclical as they flow to and fro.

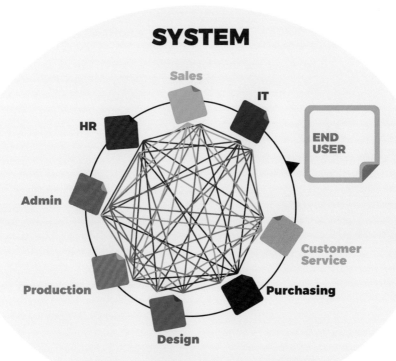

Cyclical process of NEXT customers regardless
of in-house or external services

Micro view of process steps in a linear view, extracted from the System cyclical view, where you can see the immediate NEXT customers. Note the recurrence of NEXT customers. We will always be someone's NEXT customer and vice versa.

MACRO VIEW SCENARIO: FROM DESIGN TO CONSTRUCTION

On a build project, from a traditional viewpoint, the design team and the construction site team will both have the same cash customer i.e., the client commissioning the building. The client will have a budget for the designers commissioning the building's design and a budget for building contractors to build the building. Both the designers and construction team will aim to please the client.

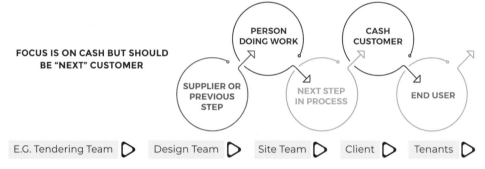

Working with the designers, their objectives will naturally be to stay within budget to deliver a quality design that exceeds the client's expectation within the planned design programme. Naturally, it will be a pre-requisite for the design team to profit from this venture. When asked how we can lean the process, the design team immediately suggests the need to process map and "streamline" the design process and minimise the drawings produced. By Doing lean, they can maintain, if not improve the quality, do it in less time, at less cost and potentially share the win with the client and secure further work down the line.

The desired output stated may be valid but the approach is lacking as it attempts to make waste more efficient. This is potentially using a plaster on a gaping wound i.e., realise a minimal win for the effort. The reason is that by focusing on pleasing the client they may not necessarily be facilitating or helping them get the building up cost-effectively as the clients are not the end user of the drawings, nor experts in putting up buildings.

Instead of the design team's immediate idea of leaning the process, we got them to focus on NEXT customer needs, in this instance, the construction team. When asked, the construction team wanted a "good handover to site". Further diagnostics defined what a good handover actually meant to the site team. NEXT customer needs measures were put in place to drive the correct behaviour towards achieving end user value.

The traditional aim of improving the designer process and reducing the number of drawings would have driven the wrong behaviour when what was important to the site team were, among others, minimal changes, clear documentation (Employer's Requirements), completed design and good buildability.

EXAMPLE OF NEXT CUSTOMER MEASURES INCLUDE:

Minimal change
- No of drawing revisions from start to end of construction project

Completed design
- Percentage achievement of plan
- No. of Request for Information (RFIs)

Good buildability and clear employer's requirements
- No. of non-buildable points
- No. of planned visits
- No. of unplanned visits and causes, e.g. design buildability
- Feedback questionnaire from site

Traditionally, the folder of Employer's Requirement, made up of different documents and drawings, was created by the designers and handed over to the site team in a format, layout and scale that is logical and convenient to the designers when it should be a pull system of information and data tailored to the needs of the site team who are the NEXT customers.

The whole design process was re-engineered with a "challenge fixed ideas" attitude. About 15% more drawings were required but they were value-adding profitable work, instead of down the line unplanned rework eating into the budget. Scales, layout and different layered drawings and documents were created outside the norm, according to how the tradesmen wanted it. A lot of the design team's work, which was usually spread out throughout the construction duration, was completed upfront before we started on site.

Based on calculations from the historical data of the Architect and Structural Engineer, and M&E's time spent on-site during construction doing rework, they reported 30% savings in time and an 80% reduction in rework. The construction team was able to deliver the project in 30% less time than programmed without leaning their processes. But the design team's willingness to "go at it" first and achieve NEXT customer satisfaction paved the way for lean improvements on-site going forward.

MICRO VIEW NEXT CUSTOMER SCENARIO: FROM PLASTERER TO JOINER

The same NEXT customer principle would apply to the construction site process. If we take the productivity of the plasterers as an example, for improved productivity and to get cash flowing, they would put up large pieces of plasterboards, move along quickly and get paid.

Whether the site manager finds the time to do a check or not, or make enough noise for the plasterers to return to finish or not, the NEXT customer turns up as planned. This is most probably the carpenters, whose biggest gripe (waste in their process) that stops them from doing the work and earning, is not being able to proceed because of the small bits and bobs left undone by the plasterers. They will abort, do something else, and come back when they have the time or when those bits are completed.

The point here is that nobody goes to work to purposely do a bad job, they might not do the best job but no one goes to work to sabotage others. *If we understood the NEXT customer principle,* we will know from the carpenters about the "bits and bobs" problem that's stopping them from doing a proper job. We know the need for the site manager to do the checks in-between and the need to "nag" each time. We then find out the plasterer does that because he gets paid per square meter, hence the rush to put up the big boards and the shirking of the small bits and bobs.

After asking the carpenter what is required and knowing the above, a change in payment method from meter square to completion of a unit *changes the behaviour and induces the correct actions.* By creating measures based on the NEXT customer requirements it reduces the large amounts of different types of wastes that opportune each time there is an interface in process steps.

There MUST be flexibility in organisational benchmarks. They must change in line with current situations. As types of wastes changes, Next customer/departmental measures should change to measure what's important or matter at that time, in order to Induce the correct behaviours.

DATA – NOT RIGHT FIRST TIME (NRFT) MEASURE

I have worked with a lot of Estates and property management teams from Councils all over the UK and whenever we discuss the measure "Not Right First Time', no one has ever gotten it correct. It may seem like a trick question but it really isn't.

These property management organisations manage properties owned by Councils. They usually have teams of men and their vans running around every day making planned and unplanned repairs and maintenance to the properties. In this scenario, the workmen are given a list of properties each day managing their own time to close 8 jobs on the list that day.

I pose this scenario in the process steps to them:

1 You start the first job, arriving at 09.00hrs as planned. The tenant was not home but lucky for you, there is a job two streets down which you can jump on to and come back after.

2 That job went smoothly. The tenant was there and ready. It was a simple double-glazing lock issue so you fixed that in 10 minutes and returned to the first job.

3 As luck would have it, the old lady had just popped out for milk and was home when you got there. She led you and your toolbox to the boiler cupboard and you see straight away that it is one of those old Worchester Borst boilers, so you probably won't have the part it needs.

4 You have a word with the tenant to get a better idea of what's wrong and open the boiler up to do your thing. The boiler was more difficult than you anticipated to deconstruct and you need a couple more tools from the van.

5 Don't have it!

It was the part you thought might be the problem with these old boilers, just as you expected. You probably don't have it with you but there might be one from an old job lying around so you walk to the van to have a look anyway, just in case.

6 Not finding what you need, you make a call to the depot to see if they have the part in stock. Luckily for the tenant, they do and you let the depot know you'll pick it up when you drop by after lunchtime.

"I'll drop by"

"I'll be back!"

7 You let the tenant know and say you'll return later when you have the part

The rest of the day is a doddle. There was a couple of no shows so you skip them and move on down the list and got a few easy pressure gauge problems, small leakages, small carpentry jobs etc. It is a good day and you easily close 10 jobs. You close the first boiler theoretically as you return with the new part but the part couldn't get the boiler working and the boiler had to be replaced. As that is a new job, you have to create a new and separate ticket for it.

After describing the scenario above, I ask the team how many NRFT instances were there? The answers I get will usually be that since more than the targeted 8 jobs were completed, there were none. Or I will get one as the answer, since the boiler job was technically not totally completed, NRFT is one. So, how many NRFT was there? Seven!

NRFT 1	– Arriving on time but not able to get in
NRFT 2	– You left for the van to get the tools required to open up the boiler
NRFT 3	– You went to the van to double-check and see if you had the part
NRFT 4	– You had to get the part from the depot
NRFT 5	– You returned with the part but that didn't work
NRFT 6 and 7	– Two no-access instances

As I run through the NRFTs, I can see how much these workmen despise me. Unfortunately, with the blame culture we live in, how can I blame them? These men took for granted that I thought they were not working hard enough or organised enough and it was their fault that the tenant was not in or they were to blame for not having the required tools in their toolbox or the required parts in their van.

> "The most dangerous kind of waste is the waste we do not see."
>
> — Shigeo Shingo

Not right first time is exactly what it says on the tin. When you cannot complete something (task, step, plan etc.) you plan to do the first time round, you have to revisit or complete the task (big or small) on the second, third, fourth or fifth try. It is not right the first time *regardless* of the causes, *regardless* of the reasons. It is NRFT *whether or not* it is within our control or not.

We tend to accept wastes and not see NRFTs when they are not within our control, and there is much need to challenge that idea. This is where data comes into play and why it's so important. It is not the individual workman's job, or within their capability, to know what and how to configure and stock their vans.

A data workshop with the Council showed that they indeed had a lot of data in the system, collected for financial purposes like most data are, but not for analysis or utilised for seeing and improving processes. Analysis threw up a lot of useful trends and information. We were able to filter the data by different types of refurbishment programmes, e.g. double-glazing, boiler replacements, kitchen upgrades etc., by dates, geographical areas etc. We were able to identify which areas had what types of boilers, how old they were and repairs by boiler types etc.

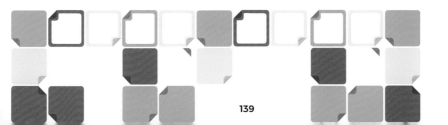

The gas engineers' vans were configured with a purpose-built modular racking system. Science was behind the calculated optimum stock and levels of Runners, Repeaters and Strangers. These were aligned in accordance with the different teams in their different areas of work

Data also threw up the different customer requests at different times of the year, prompting the van to be reconfigured according to season. This is standardisation of the System but with the flexibility to meet changing customer needs. This particular effort generated an additional 15.6/week (826 jobs/annum) gas boiler jobs with improved productivity by an average of 19% and carbon savings of approximately 10 tonnes/annum.

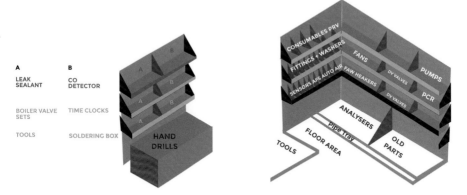

From a macro view, it is the organisation's responsibility to facilitate flow in the workmen's process by making sure they have what they need in 1 step-30s to do value adding work, as demonstrated above. From the micro view, it is the individual workmen who must then be responsible for their own NRFTs, i.e. configure their toolbox to make sure they get what they need when they need it in 1 step 3s.

This does not take care of the "no access" NRFT but that was dealt with in another improvement project where the level of no access in the trial period fell from 6.21% to 1.51% of jobs. It is only when you can see and know what the wastes are can you decide whether it is within your control or not. Case in point, the NRFT measure and the power of data.

DATA COLLECTION – FAG PACK QUICKIES

The NRFT example above was a concerted effort by the council with collaboration from different departments to make the "impossible" more possible. It is a classic example of deploying Covey's spheres to increase our circle of influence and get what we need from the sphere of concern. Here is a case in another Council Estate where the general repairs assistant manager (middle management) took things into his own hands without the support of the Council (upper management). He did not have access to any all-alluding data to play with other than the fact that his team's vans were overloaded and weighed over the legal limit. There were 5 absent days in the past 6 months specifically due to injuries in vans.

There were other productivity issues, but as usual, it is the legal and health and safety matters that trigger actions. Luckily for them, improving the quality of processes usually make those issues disappear and also contribute to increased productivity.

The manager was proud to inform me of their standardised van stock and layout and I was presented with one of their more organised vans, manned by one of their more organised workmen. The idea was that if we could find some gains with this van, the others in the fleet would be low-hanging fruit. I've done hundreds of vans, containers, portacabins, offices, desktops, drawings etc., so this was a good opportunity for me to demonstrate the difference between organised and Being Lean.

The van was in much better than average condition. Standard-sized boxes were provided and used. Some faded labelling was used but VM can be improved. The van owner will have little problems getting the standard materials and products when he needs them, although "visitors" (van share when he is not using it himself) may take a bit longer to orientate themselves. The main searching time will occur while looking for Repeaters (less used products and materials).

One will have to spend time searching through "homeless" boxes to find these products, unsure if they are in stock.

Standardised but inflexible storage boxes were provided. This allows the size of the box to dictate the content and stock level instead of the optimum stock and level dictating storage options. Regardless of productivity, the main issues with the vans were accessibility, space and weight.

The two immediate things that popped up as soon as we opened the van doors were the two large plywood boards wedged in the middle of the van. These were restricting and needed some manoeuvring to get access into the van, i.e., motion and transport waste. The other was a second ladder mounted above the shelves on one side. Both men were unable to tell me how often these two things were used but said they were necessary.

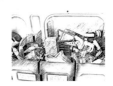

Nobody likes collecting data, but being consultants, we are experienced enough to know when to insist or not to. Knowing that I won't get anything formal out of these boys, some form of fag pack calculations will have to pave the way. For their homework, I requested they question the 10-man team "who, when, why, what, where and how often" about the two ladders and ply. Even for a fag pack calculation, one person is just an opinion, 10 become credible enough hard data.

Investigating the frequency of use of the 2 ladders showed that 3 workmen had used one of the ladders once in the last 3 months. An investigation into the frequency of use for the plywood sheets used for boarding showed they were used by 4 of the workmen, totalling 6 occasions in the last 3 months, and 5 of those occasions were on a Friday/Sat night due to vandalism. On 2 of those 5 occasions, they required more than the 2 ply sheets they were carrying but the stores were closed, so they could not complete the job anyway.In another words, the ladders were not utilised enough to warrant space in the van. The plywood sheets were occasional needed, mainly over the weekends. And when they are needed, the stocked 2 sheets are seldom enough and as it's the weekend and at night, there was no way to get more to complete the job.

From the van weight, H&S and accessibility issue, both ladders and plywood sheets were removed from the standardised van configuration. Free lock-up areas were organised for out-of-hours

access to materials. On top of the above issues, we conducted the usual 5S and from the results, easily contributed to bringing the weight over to the legal side, removing any potential H&S issues.

From the productivity side of things, the gains were recorded to be, on average, 19-man days for the team. This equated to about 40mins/day per man. Bearing in mind that if upper management found out, they would "reward" these men by making them work harder i.e., an extra job now that they had got an extra 40 minutes. The men felt that 40 mins/day might not be enough for them to comfortably complete another job. It's more likely, the job will trip over, causing them to leave work later.

But because we had confidence from the various data we had been collecting since the ply and ladders, the team was willing to do more. They were tasked to "find" another 20 mins improvement from somewhere in their process. Their improvement effort was reported in the Council newsletter and they have since been dubbed the 9-job team (as opposed to the 8-job daily target) as they've raised the bar for the whole department. Another testament to the power of data, even if it is just fag-pack

POWER OF DATA

Macro view – As an organisation, you have more data than you think. With concerted effort and a structured approach, you can extract great NEXT customer data analysis to better target improvement efforts and drive the correct behaviour.

Micro view - Even as a loner, as soon as you understand what a difference the power of data can do in a business case, you should start out alone however way you can.

PULL – WHO AND WHAT CUSTOMERS WANT

To reiterate, the idea of the lean pull principle is to produce what the customer wants and (not push what you have to give) hoping that they will take it. Even now when writing this book, after almost 2 decades of Being Lean, I introduced so much waste into my book writing process by pushing information instead of adopting the pull principle. I am such a staunch Being Lean zealot and have wanted so much to say and tell to convince and convert. I wrote this book in my own words, using my own way of thinking, with my level of lean expertise, carefully choosing the messages that I want to convey.

Against my own credence, I took the long way around. My test readers provided the bit of pull applied after the fact, near the end of the process. Not only did their feedback give me food for thought but along with it, a huge load of rework plus wasted time and effort. Hopefully, I got it right in the end.

This is important to view from a macro view of the NEXT customer principles as it concerns all 4 of the lean customers. As discussed, this helps rid most of the waste created most during the interfaces between two processes. This also allows us to apply smaller batch sizes to reduce waiting waste between these interfaces, e.g. how many parts does the next customer need.
Let's say 5 to proceed with their process instead of us making the number of parts that our circumstance is capable of, e.g. 50. Instead of proceeding after every 5 parts, the NEXT customer has to wait until you are done with 50 before moving on.

A simple example I have of seeing pull at work is when I work with site managers on building projects. They will take the extra time and effort to go through a long generic standardised list of checks to make sure each room is checked and fixed and "good" before getting the Clerk of Works (CoW) to do a final check and sign-off. However, more often than not, we all have different ideas of what "good" looks like. Instead of making everything "good", all he had to do was ask the NEXT customer what good looked like to him and come up with a shorter but targeted list.

In this particular example, all that the CoW was concerned about was that, as long as nothing jumps out, he'd just do a check around the window sills as that's where he normally finds defects. All that rework for "good" is overprocessing, where we do too much, and overproduction, where outputs are above and beyond the requirements – waste.

Whether it is products, services, construction drawings, blogs or websites, you need to know who your customers are and what they want to buy, even with lean improvement projects. You cannot sell an improvement on process X, no matter how good your sales pitch is if the customer (the people carrying out the improvements) prefers an improvement in process Y.

Selling improvement on Y process is no X process but you are selling and benefiting from it. Hence, lean systems need to be flexible to meet pull from customers.

PULL FROM CUSTOMERS ON THE INTRANET

The pre-construction Design to Construction example in the above NEXT customer principle section is a great example of pull applied.
Instead of pushing and producing an information package, in accordance with industry standard and what their current system processes are capable of, they asked the site team (NEXT customer) what, how, when and in what "chunks" (batch sizes) they needed (good) and wanted (great) it.

Another good example of this applied pull of information from customers can be found in a project where Workplace Organisation (5S) was conducted on a messy, under-utilised and not fit for purpose intranet.

Most of us may have had the experience of going into our company intranet totally frustrated by the time taken to find what we need, not forgetting the lousy search function, which is of little help. Plus, the fact that we only use the intranet when we have to, and we have to a lot because ISO (International Organisation for Standardisation) says so.

Unlike 5S on micro-projects like vans or desktops, where we know who the customers (users) are, the intranet is a bit more complex with multi-role users. We were not able to start with the usual first S – Sort. We could not sort the pages and information into Keep, Bin or Quarantine, when we had no idea which to keep, which to bin and what needs fixing.

Instead of pushing whatever existing information there was, rejuggling, reorganising and randomly minimising the pages and contents, pushing it all out there for the customers to choose from. We applied the pull principle by first identifying the customers and then finding out what they "wanted to buy".

User Group	Who?	What information?
Employees involved in the XXX programme	• Project Managers • Project Sponsor • Project Teams	• Latest updates and reports • PM Tools, templates and guidance
Employees involved in business improvement	• BI forum • BI teams	• Latest updates and reports • BI information • PM Tools, templates and guidance
Employees involved in lean, innovation and business development projects	• BI Forum • Business Development people • Innovation people • Pre-construction • Quality people	• Project information • PM Tools, templates and guidance • Contacts
Employees looking for general information	• Employee with intranet access • New starters	• What the programme is? • Who is involved? • Project information
Employees looking for specific information	• Employee with intranet access	• PM Tools, templates and guidance • Latest reports and updates • Contacts

Once we identified the different user groups, we were able to identify who they were within those user groups and what types of information they needed or used. Data analysis helped throw up user traffic numbers and patterns, high-level users, as well as what was the most sought after information and the more frequented sections, pages and information. This gave the team the pull information required to populate the intranet with what the customers needed and wanted.

Frequency
What sections and pages are most frequented?

Most popular sections	Top five popular page	Top five popular page
1- Project Management	The start (content page)	Volunteers
2- The Projects	Project date sheet	Project health checks
3- How are we doing?	Key tools	Programme Team
4- What is it?	Programme dashboard	SMT
5- Who is involved?	List of projects (incl. project managers & sponsors)	EMT

For more details, the full 5S project can be found later in this chapter.

MACRO AND MICRO VIEWS

Throughout the entire book, I have repeatedly reiterated the many thoughts, concepts and principles, and the macro (eagle) and micro (ant) views are one of them. In line with the first 2 lean points of the lean approach, the macro view lets us see the bigger picture so that we can hone in on the micro view, which is worth the time and effort when we start investigating that process in detail.

THE LEAN APPROACH TO IMPROVEMENT

- Understand **the bigger picture**
- Investigate the **process in detail**
- Use a team based approach to **identify and eliminate wastes**
- Generate **actions for sustainability**

These two views yield different results but also throw up more opportunities to choose or start from. They can definitely help you (micro) or your organisation (macro) make more informed decisions about what path to use to improve your business activities. They also help with differentiating what is within your sphere of control (micro) and what and who you need to influence (macro) to make things happen.

I could fill a book alone with just this topic, giving examples and case studies to illustrate the power of this principle and the opportunities it presents. But for simplicity, I am presenting very generic examples of how to apply 5S from the two viewpoints, in the physical location and from an informational context.

THE MACRO AND MICRO VIEW OF THE INTRANET

From a macro view, in an organisational context, the intranet is a Non-Value element of the business that is necessary to facilitate doing work the customer is paying for, e.g. a commissioned building. The intranet review project aims to improve its effectiveness making it fit for purpose to facilitate more value adding work by the business and its employees. On the next level down, you can see the intranet system itself as the Macro view, while the pages can be viewed as the Micro view. And working top-down or down-up can give different results, depending on various circumstance, as was discussed in the section above, but having both views will throw up more opportunities for improvements than we would ever have time for.

This example project had that luxury and was able to make significant improvements. But more often than not, we are individuals or small teams with little support and resources to make changes. Even so, we can put on our macro and micro glasses to see what we can do within our control for our own (NEXT) customers. In this context, the macro can be our contribution to pages or documents attachments within the intranet and the micro can be sections, part contributions or even participation in the feedback loop etc.

The 3 elements of the Intranet process from a Macro & Micro View

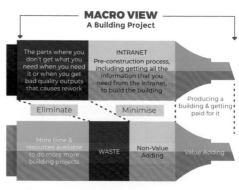

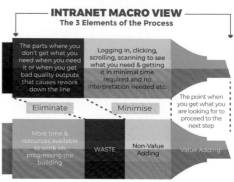

5S – WORKPLACE ORGANISATION ON THE INTRANET

This is the more comprehensive 5S project to the "Pull from customer on the Intranet" activity mention above. Before we move on, a quick reminder of what the 5S are:

Sort	A thorough clean-up by separating essentials from the non-essentials
Set	Configuration of the workplace by finding a place for everything and everything in its place
Shine	Clean, check preferably through mistake proofing to keep things in good working order
Standardise	Set a standard to conform to and sustain
Sustain	Consistency in 5S application and cultural shift in behaviour to self-maintain the process

A waste identification exercise was conducted to get a common understanding of what wastes looks like on the intranet.

8 Wastes	Examples
Transport	The site's navigation is poor and users cannot find what they are looking for
Inventory	There is too much content that is duplicated, irrelevant or out of date and/or information unfound, so unused
Motion	The user either cannot find the content or takes longer journeys to access it
Potential Under-utilised	Users not using the tools, templates and training because they can't locate the information
Waiting	Time wasted by users trying to find content. Using flash and links slows the system.
Overproduction	Producing more content to cover a topic than is needed by the user
Over Process	Additional links, scrolling and flash images causes the user to come across more barriers before accessing the information
Defects	Missing documents, out of date information and broken links.

As discussed in the previous section, having identified the different types of customers and the types of information they require, the team was able to Sort and Set existing features, pages and content of the intranet into keep, quarantine and bin.

From a micro view, war on waste was conducted on each individual "to keep" or consolidate pages, scrutinising them to see how much scrolling was required, checking for superfluous texts, duplication of information and redundant images etc. New pages, content, links and downloads were created in line with the pull from users.

From the Set (configuring the site and allocating "homes" to contents) perspective, "Point of Use" is vital in this particular case. Physically, the point of use is having things located where they are to be used, e.g. a marker pen on a whiteboard and not in a drawer somewhere. A more abstract way of looking at this is having the correct information required by the user where they will be able to find it and use it i.e., what (content) to go where (page and links) etc.

A new, more simplistic, logical and understandable process-based site map was produced to enable a high level "get what you need in 1 click, 1 second" state.

OLD SITE MAP

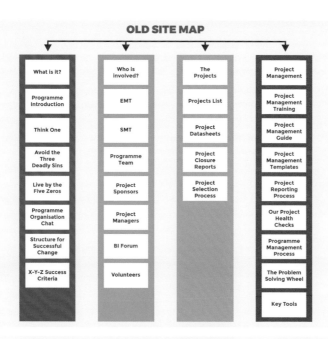

What is it?	Who is involved?	The Projects	Project Management
Programme Introduction	EMT	Projects List	Project Management Training
Think One	SMT	Project Datasheets	Project Management Guide
Avoid the Three Deadly Sins	Programme Team	Project Closure Reports	Project Management Templates
Live by the Five Zeros	Project Sponsors	Project Selection Process	Project Reporting Process
Programme Organisation Chat	Project Managers		Our Project Health Checks
Structure for Successful Change	BI Forum		Programme Management Process
X-Y-Z Success Criteria	Volunteers		The Problem Solving Wheel
			Key Tools

NEW PROCESS BASED SITE MAP

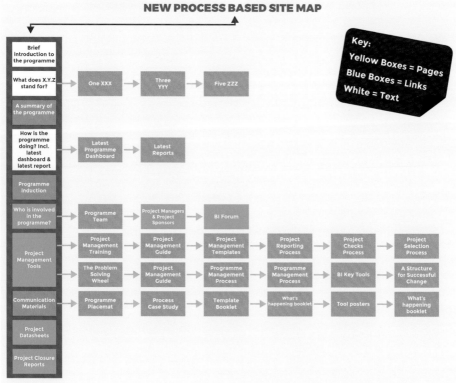

Key:
Yellow Boxes = Pages
Blue Boxes = Links
White = Text

- Brief introduction to the programme
- What does X.Y.Z stand for? → One XXX → Three YYY → Five ZZZ
- A summary of the programme
- How is the programme doing? Incl. latest dashboard & latest report → Latest Programme Dashboard → Latest Reports
- Programme Induction
- Who is involved in the programme? → Programme Team → Project Managers & Project Sponsors → BI Forum
- Project Management Tools → Project Management Training → Project Management Guide → Project Management Templates → Project Reporting Process → Project Checks Process → Project Selection Process
- → The Problem Solving Wheel → Project Management Guide → Programme Management Process → Programme Management Process → BI Key Tools → A Structure for Successful Change
- Communication Materials → Programme Placemat → Process Case Study → Template Booklet → What's happening booklet → Tool posters → What's happening booklet
- Project Datasheets
- Project Closure Reports

Here's a summary of some of the activities undertaken in the project.

5S	Activities
SORT	Remove any duplication or irrelevant information. Compact the content into less buttons & pages and reduce links & scrolling.
SET	Find a "home" for each page and/or section. Create a new clear contents page on the start page.
	Ensure the popular information is clearly visible (seen) and the not so popular is accessed via "click here" (not seen).
	Re-vamp the whole site including creating new pages, reducing text, using colours and visual management.
SHINE	Be up to date with web traffic and patterns.
	Log & deal with issues & complaint within allocated time using prioritisation tool, with timelines.
	Adopt process with easy built-in e.g. clean input requirements using go/no go.
STANDARDISE	Produce a schedule/plan for weekly/monthly maintenance checks and annual feedback questionnaire for users.
	Conduct audits on parts of the key process in order to induce correct behaviour from all parties.
	Maintaining the standard by having a system in place to adhere to.
SUSTAIN	Achieved through understanding and adherence to the principles of 5S. Create and utilisation of NEXT customer measures.

The 5S effort reduced pages and links that did not add value to the intranet by 72% and 84% respectively, and traffic increased by 33% in the 3 months after the official closing of the lean improvement project.

LEAN AND SUSTAINABILITY –
GLOBAL CITIZENSHIP

Sustainability means meeting our own needs without compromising the ability of future generations to meet their own. In addition to environmental quality, we also need social equity and a healthy economy to achieve that.

Eliminating waste serves both business and the environment and this cannot be done without taking people into consideration. It may be true that lean, from the start, achieves a level of sustainability by default, not because it is its main concern. However, the sustainability dimension is inseparable from lean, since it requires "right first times" to achieve high standard working processes, people expertise and minimal resource wastage.

The adoption of lean by the Western car manufacturing world in the late eighties was inevitable when proof of underperformance was produced and the obvious threat of further market encroachment by this superior performance was witnessed. This led to revolutionary changes to work practices and attitudes. The same is happening now with regards to sustainability. Any lean thinking and adopting company that does not incorporate sustainability into its mainstream business goals will be left behind and uncompetitive in the marketplace. The same goes for individuals, from a micro view, who make up organisations and society.

More attention has been given to the economic and environmental benefits of lean in sustainability whereas the social aspect is touched upon less. This area is not usually touched upon from the lean perspective. Note that I have time and again stressed the importance of knowing the 4 different customers of lean. As we know by now, the Customer does not comprise of the paying customer alone, but extends to the before (Supplier customer) and NEXT customer along the process, including the end-user, as well as the whole of society and anyone benefitting from the process or final product. It emphasises empowerment, teamwork and collaboration.

There is a host of what lean can contribute to sustainability from different views and perspectives. The diagram below shows some potential generic impacts on the different aspects of sustainability, which work from both the macro and micro view.

Potential Impact of Lean on Sustainability

Induce pride of self and work, getting it right first time

Reduce frustration and stress

Reduce worker motion waste

Less resources (raw material, water, energy) required due to quality processes and outputs

Right first time reduces carbon footprint & emissions

Reduced raw materials required for replacement product/materials

Reduced defective/ruined material requiring disposal

Less energy usage for extra transportation of material

Less energy required for lighting, heating etc.

Longevity of possessions reducing need for new

Reduce instances of health & safety incidences

Self-empowerment through the ethos of continuous improvement and learning

Improved relationships through consideration of NEXT customer, stress on collaborative teamwork and process expert consultations

Increase productivity

Less resources required due to quality processes and outputs

Direct & indirect cost of resources to carry out rework

Less time required to carry out rework

Reduced cost of replacement product/material

Longevity of possessions reducing need for new

Multiplication of benefits through collaborative lean supply chain and personal relationships

SOCIAL

BEARABLE **EQUITABLE**

SUSTAINABLE

ENVIRONMENT **VIABLE** **ECONOMIC**

There is so much compatibility in the vision between lean and sustainability. The holistic view of lean thinking and its principles can contribute and facilitate the achievement of sustainability through application, albeit it's quite dependent on the nature of the customers' main values and how they understand lean values.

Lean eliminates tangible and intangible wastes to increase the process efficiency to satisfy the customer. Even if it may not be possible to choose our customers (at work or people around us) currently, bear in mind that our customers (people in general) are getting more and more savvy and worldly. They are starting to identify themselves as global citizens and understand that one's identity transcends geography or political borders.

According to Oxfam, a global citizen has an understanding of how the world works economically, politically, socially, culturally, technologically, and environmentally. From a lean point of view, this is scaling up the thinking from the micro view of understanding and reacting to our immediate surroundings to the macro view of the world.

The butterfly effect is a very apt way to depict how every decision we make, every action we take, affects more than just ourselves or the here and now. Being a good citizen entails taking personal responsibility for one's decisions and actions, including respecting people and the planet, obeying rules and laws, and setting a good example to others. To achieve a good quality of life you have to consider people (social), planet (environmental) and profits (economics) to wage war on waste.

LEAN SUSTAINABILITY

To be truthful, most lean activities are not initiated for a sustainable reason, at least not the people and planet part anyway. Typically, environmental savings are not often part of the financial justification for lean improvement activities. I have embarked on my lean journey mainly in awe of the time and cost savings it has reaped. Lean Green is usually considered to pertain to the field of marketing and winning work.

However, my educational BSc background is in human ecology and geography (People), my MSc in sustainable environmental management (Planet) and my work as a Lean Consultant, qualified Lean Trainer and Assessor (Profits) makes it inevitable that Sustainability is a holistic theme that's weaved its way into my way of thinking, moulded my values and shaped the way of my life.

I continue to write this book from a personal development perspective i.e., working from what is within our control while influencing our surroundings. I believe that our values (as individuals and customers) drive our behaviour and, like lean, are applicable, whether we're at home, work or play.

From a practical application point of view, I have given some examples of how I have applied lean sustainability in the different aspects (home, travel, health and work) of my life. Like all other examples in this book, they are not meant to be replicated exactly but more as prompts to come up with things you can do within your own relevant circumstances.

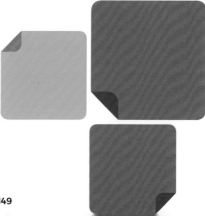

LEAN GREEN AT HOME

Two underlying conditions motivate my lean green efforts. This will be different for everyone, naturally. The first is that with my environmental background and having been lean for almost two decades, there isn't much lean green advice and tips out there that is new to my proactive self. Most things that have been proposed, I have considered and revisited periodically due to changing circumstances, and done the business case to see if it is worth adopting, buying or doing. I am challenged by the minimal opportunities of what else I can do within my control and rely a lot on, currently, on industries' green innovations in the form of products and services and, importantly, market demands on things to bring them within my affordability. Which brings me to my second condition.

I used to be more able, more willing maybe, to suffer for my passions and ideals when I was younger. I gave up meat for a whole year, 20 years ago, even though I hated vegetables then, and was/am an ardent carnivore. But as I grow older, I am somehow more reluctant to compromise on my quality of life. I am happy to eat less meat but am in no hurry to turn vegetarian or try plant-based meat. I am more inclined, and now more able to, splurge a bit on ethical farming and animal husbandry produce. I am unwilling to give up my travels but will offset them as best I can and "stinge" and work extra hard in other areas to make up for it. My second condition is my own perceived value of my quality of life and that forms the foundation of my business cases in this area. I love avocados but I have given them up and not eaten or bought any for a few years now. I do miss avocados, but apparently not that much, because my business case says "no".

USE YOUR WISDOM – HOME-MADE SOLUTIONS

On the above basis, for the lean green drive in my household, I found the number two of the lean attitude – "Use your wisdom first, not your money" – to be a huge driver and facilitator. This drives my reuse (full or partial) and recycle agenda. Unlike consolidating and multi-uses, this is for things that will otherwise be thrown away.

There are two ways to do this. I find and create ways to use things that I am otherwise going to throw away (or council recycle) or I need something or solutions that I have to buy.

Some examples of homemade solutions using packaging or things to be discarded:

  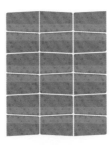  

| Amazon delivery box as a drawer in a cabinet | Soda bottles as tissue dispensers | Wine cork as a heat mat | Vertically hung shoulder strap from a bag with hooks for caps | Soda bottles as herb pots |

Other green home solutions using our wisdom look out for ways to engineer the correct behaviour to non-wastage. For example, I got this idea in a B&B on a Filipino island. They had velcroed the air-conditioning remote to the headboard of the bed, which was accessible at any time for temperature and strength control. The bed was situated just next to the room entrance so you could easily reach out and turn on the air-conditioning as the first thing you did on the way in and turn it off as the last thing you did on the way out. This is the point of use, making it easy and inducing the correct behaviour. You'd be surprised how many people don't turn off the electrics in hotels, wasting a lot of energy and cost. You may think it's not your home and don't pay for it but you do as it gets built-into the asking price.

I have since Velcro-ed everything wherever I find the opportunity, including the unsightly TV/media remotes under the edge of the coffee and side tables, within easy access for everyone. We're all too lazy to switch gadgets off and it is astonishing the amount of energy we waste leaving things on standby. Use standby savers, timers, remotes etc. to engineer the surroundings to make it easier for us to turn things off. What else is wasteful in your own surroundings that you can use your wisdom to combat?

SHOPPING

Prevention is better than cure, i.e., not incurring waste is better than finding ways to reuse and recycle. The less coming in the door, the less clutter and things you have to throw away. Refrain from buying unless you really have to. Avoid bringing absolutely unnecessary things into your space by not accepting stuff just because they are free, e.g. charity branded goods like pens and calendars in exchange for donations, promotional stuff given out at events etc.

I have my own usual suspects of monthly charity contributions, but not wanting to mention any names, two were sending me "stuff" and updates costing more than I gave them. I've repeatedly requested them to take me off the gifts and postal list but to no avail. I have since cancelled their subscription and found two other charities to replace them that have better processes, are less wasteful and more deserving.

With further regard to charities, I speak for myself but believe many are like me. I use my cast-off contributions to justify buying more. I reuse an Amazon delivery box that fits my wardrobe floor as a "charity box" to facilitate my 5S clothes procedure. If I try something on more than 5 times but still never wear it, this goes in the box. That plus the 1-in-1-out protocol. I currently fill that box up about 2-3 times a year. I realise this just makes me feel better because I'm giving to charity but does not solve the root cause of frivolous purchases. I am not there yet but have started by making a small step-change to a smaller box and I allow only a once-a-year fill-up.

I have another People and Planet's pledge which I really like. I have 10 shop links in my charities folder on my browser favourites. They are my first port of call when I need to buy gifts and presents for whatever reason. I am a huge Sea Shepherd fan, among other charitable organisations, and they have clothes, belts, trinkets made from sustainable materials and ethical labour. These make wonderful gifts and the money goes to help causes close to my heart, making it money well spent. They usually come in compostable packaging which I reuse once and then throw in the black-bin guilt-free.

Reuse of good quality zip-lock plastic shower cap packaging instead of clingfilm.

The last bit about shopping I'd like to bring up is packaging. I realise that we the consumers pay for it, whether we want to or not, as it's built into the price. I buy what I buy and do not overtly make my choices based on packaging. To offset this I try my utmost to reuse as best as possible and where it's impossible, recycle. One thing I try very hard to do, which is annoying and time-consuming but very in line with Space Utilisation, is to crush or flatten everything, including plastic soda bottles, beer cans, tetra packs etc., so they don't take up unnecessary space in the recycling bin and, in turn, the recycling truck collecting them, meaning fewer trips and emissions. I find flattening every cardboard box and separating tape from them especially annoying when they are taped up like Fort Knox. This gives better-quality recycled material for higher grade use. According to my value-based business case, this is apparently not a waste and worth doing, so I persevere even though I really don't like doing it.

TRAVEL WISE

A lot of the topics touched upon in this section should be no different from what we normally do when not travelling. I chose to put most of them in this section instead of home, as more consideration may be needed when we're not in our own backyard, where we take some services, choices and freedom for granted. At the same time, if we are doing most of this stuff at home, what excuse do we have not to do them when we are away?

Think global, shop local – Experiencing the local cuisine and trying traditional food is a huge part of the travelling experience. Choose and support local produce over imported food. It makes no sense, for example, to be eating feta couscous salad in China!

Support local businesses – Many travel destinations rely on the injection that tourism gives them, so choose a small, independent hotel, local eatery or bar rather than just heading for familiar chains. Think local AND global. Avoid useless and pointless souvenirs and gifts. Most holiday destinations have an array of tacky trinkets specially targeted at tourists, but most of these gifts are popped in a drawer never to see the light of day again or, at worst, in the bin. You can pick up a fridge magnet from pretty much anywhere, but giving something useful and produced by local artisans, handcrafted and high-quality is a more thoughtful gift that is sure to be treasured. This will give the local economy a much-needed boost.

Consider the transport pyramid – When we travel, we often use a very quick and fast method of transportation. That's lean, but lean sustainability means we need to consider the transport pyramid wherever possible and convenient.

If you can, go for the least detrimental one. For example, if you've travelled to Thailand via plane, get a tuk-tuk to your hotel instead of a taxi and hire a bike to get around the next day instead of taking the bus if the journey isn't too far. Make sure that transport with the greatest emissions is used least frequently at the top of the pyramid and transport with less impact will be your go-tos at the bottom. I almost always walk everywhere once I arrive at my destination. As far as consolidation goes, this double-ups as exercise and earns my holiday eating. I pre-plan and build-in these walks in my one-page travel schedule and pace my days to get quality over quantity.

Avoid Bottled Water – Now this might seem like a complete turnaround from the usual advice to drink bottled water when abroad, but plastic bottles are a plague to the planet we love to travel around. 350 million plastic water bottles are used globally each day! It is said that there will be more plastics in the ocean than fish by 2050! There are usually safe water sources available when you travel, so look for them and pack a re-usable water bottle and do a little research before you head off. A compromise, I usually buy the first bottle and use that for the whole trip and throw it in a recycling bin if there is one at the end of the trip.

Bring Your Own Toiletries – You will find advice to buy toiletries at the destination on most packing blogs, as a way of packing light. This is indeed an option but my stance is to always bring your own wherever possible. With all the packaging and containers we throw away at home, there is no excuse not to consider up-cycling those old containers. If you don't have space even for these most essential things, you are not doing it right. Check out how to squeeze the required amount of toothpaste into an existing toothpaste tube here.

Bring your own shopping bag – Plastic bags cause thousands of tons of landfill waste every year, and some countries do not have the facilities we have at home to recycle them effectively, so you can pretty much guarantee that every plastic bag you use is having a detrimental impact on the environment. Take a reusable tote bag on holiday and you'll always have something handy to help carry those holiday essentials, such as sunscreen, towels or groceries back to your accommodation.

Use Reef-Safe Sunscreen – The UN Ocean Conference 2017 revealed that coral reefs provide close to US $30 billion each year in goods and services. Plus, coral reefs are invaluable to human beings considering the role they play in the subjects of air quality, food web, erosion prevention and medicines. Reef-safe sunscreen is produced without oxybenzone and octinoxate, two chemicals toxic to coral reefs and other marine life. Toxins in oxybenzone are absorbed through the skin every time sunscreen is applied. The Environmental Working Group (EWG) believe that oxybenzone is linked to hormone disruption and tests have shown it acts like oestrogen in the system, altering the sperm counts in many animals and causing endometriosis in women. It has also been found in mothers' breast milk and causes skin allergies. So, corals or not, oxybenzone is bad news. Simple and there's no excuse not to use reef-safe sunscreen, if not for the corals, then for ourselves.

Animal welfare – Sadly, animal cruelty is present in every country in the world. As evolved and humane global citizens with considerations towards animal welfare, it can be an intensely upsetting experience to witness the mistreatment and exploitation of animals while on holiday and it's just as bad to unwittingly contribute to the practice.

As travellers, interaction with local wildlife can be very educational and memorable, but these experiences should always occur in the best interest of the animal. Do your research as it is easy to say we didn't know. For example, not many people know that the bulls in Pamplona are kept in the dark running up to the event, before being forced out into the light with electrical prods to create more frenzied behaviour. Animal tourism is big business, but some less reputable attractions have poor standards of animal care and welfare. Don't get caught out by "ethical animal attractions". If it doesn't look or feel right, just don't get involved.

HEALTH – FOOD AND FITNESS

I believe that improvements start with ourselves and doing what we can within our circumstances and improving those practices continuously throughout our life, in the quest for perfection. On top of that, I am happy to say that my own stance and consistent actions on food and fitness have made a huge difference and directly influenced five other people I can think of in my circle, to be lean in body and mind on this subject. I have written much on this subject in the earlier Food and Fitness chapter but will like to reiterate very quickly, the two key aspects pertaining to sustainability. They are society's wasteful load on the health system due to obesity-related illnesses and food waste.

BEING FIT AND HEALTHY IS OUR DUTY TO SOCIETY

Whether being overweight is due to genetics, learned behaviour, our society, or a mix, we have to accept that morbidity and mortality is dependent on weight at any given time. Obesity and being heavily overweight is associated with causing over 50 different types of illnesses. These common defects that our health system is forced to deal with due to overconsumption and bad choices include high blood pressure, high cholesterol, diabetes, heart/kidney/liver diseases, sleep apnoea, other respiratory conditions and some cancers. Not forgetting the big and complex issue of poor self-esteem with a whole host of direct and indirect societal repercussions.

Poor health due to being overweight is a serious defect especially when it is within our control to do something about it. Time and money are usually cited as the reason for the inability to start or sustain a healthy lifestyle. Dozens of celebrity chefs have shown us through many cooking programmes ways to make cheap, healthy and quick meals.

With regards to time, what more important customers are there in life than oneself? Even in a crashing plane, the advice is to help yourself first, so you can help others. For such an important task, you don't find time but make time. It is our duty to society to stop making excuses and take responsibility for our own bodies and the choices we make. It is our own individual responsibility to understand our customer (our body), what it needs and make sure that we do our best to manage the inputs (quality and quantities) and run it on good processes (lifestyle) and actively get help where required before becoming a liability to ourselves, our family and society.

I truly believe the best start is now and just by beginning to be aware of your food and fitness processes i.e., inputs (man, material, machine, messages), process (how, when, why, what, where), and outputs (quality, cost, delivery) will initiate action in the right direction.

FOOD WASTE

Even with an environmental and waste agement background, it was adopting lean that propelled my improvements and performance in this area. The pull-system advocates the minimisation of all type of waste. By having good processes and Being Lean, the need to be in the know on this subject was minimal. I adopted basic food waste prevention practices that are generally known and recommended. I plan weekly menus and tailor grocery lists to them, which I attribute hugely to my reduction in food waste. For food storage, think meal prepping and go modular (portions). I use freezing a lot and I'm not afraid to buy frozen, things with long durations and ugly foods.

Be aware of throw-away advice, like don't buy in bulk as it causes waste. Whether that is true or not depends on your business case. There needs to be flexibility in solutions as I have stated many times throughout this book. I am a true believer of buying in bulk BUT depending if it is a Runner, maybe a Repeater or occasionally a Stranger. I let the

business cases decide, e.g. bulk buying of Strangers items are OK if they are expensive items with huge discounts and something you will always use but do not have sell-by dates, or very long ones, e.g. honey, hair products, water filters etc.

I push the limits of sell-by dates to find my own level of acceptance on many food products. I am a prolific user of my food sealer and change the original containers to smaller ones to prolong the life of products as I use them.

These simple measures have "automatically" reduced my food (compost). Even with minimal food waste, you can reduce the number of compost bags you use/buy, trips the council waste collector makes and your fuel use by considering lean space utilisation. By giving your food waste a few snips with the scissors in your compost bin, you can half the space it uses.

Bulky food waste, like oranges, bananas and vegetable peel, takes up a lot of space. Crushing your eggshells before they go into the bin helps. This goes without saying for all food packaging, like drink cans, plastic bottles and cartons.

I am persistent in my stance on prevention being better than cure, so not buying more than I need is the underlying guiding principle. But naturally, it is not as simple as that for the layman since there is a web of lean processes behind the scenes to allow "just enough" buying to take place.

I say the same as I did with regards to being fit and healthy – understand your current food-related processes, as the diagnostics will show who contributes, when it occurs, why it occurs, how often and how much food waste you produce, and you can take action from there. Use the lean approach, especially the "how to eat an elephant" (one small chuck at a time) bit to start with, & move forward from there.

CARBON FOOTPRINT

I cannot write about sustainability with regards to food, without mentioning the carbon footprint of food. I am ashamed to say that when I calculated my household carbon footprint by using the various calculators available online, out of the four categories, my Food footprint accounted for 40% of the total. This is not shocking but I did realise how my life revolves around food. This is why data is so important. You know, but you only realise it when you see proof. I did mention previously that I offset my "naughty". My household does very well in the other parts, with a significant conscious effort due to off-setting, and I have a lot to improve on the Food and Travel bit. I urgently need to traipse around the PDCA cycle, re-evaluate my values in those areas and redo some business cases.

WORK – IT'S ALL IN THE BUSINESS CASE

One creative, realised environmental savings idea for an organisation can potentially overshadow and reap the benefits of a lifetime's effort from a family. But let's face it, in my years of business and process improvement with many organisations, the environmental focus comes into play mainly due to legal or customer requirements, "side effects" of cost-reduction efforts or for marketing purposes and to win work. Idealism or sustainable development is seldom the genuine main driver. Organisations need to realise how interwoven People, Planet and Profits are, and stop looking at them as separate entities. Only then can they achieve sustainable development and true market leadership.

From a macro organisational point of view, this is a task of moving mountains. From a micro individual point of view, we can be sustainability advocates who champion the way forward. This is déjà vu as I have known quite a few true lean advocates in my time that do nothing but push rope when convincing their workplace to adopt lean thinking and/or tools for profitability. However, their persistence has paid off as lean is a transferable skill that follows individuals everywhere regardless of the workplace.

Empowered with personal success, these individuals have moved on to better and more influential positions, even branching off to start their own successful businesses. The same goes for sustainability. Taking on lean and sustainability is not necessarily for altruism but topping up on it can only make an individual a more valuable commodity. And if you do take on that mantel, the key is to speak and convince people in the language of business i.e., quantifiable returns in terms of a business case. Whatever it is you are selling; it has got to be good for business.

There are many proposed useful, societal measures but here I want to bring up the earlier mentioned SMART Measures Reloaded. This is especially relevant and apt when it comes to people.

SMART measures -Reloaded!

| **Stretching** - to drive us beyond the comfort zone into real achievement | **Meaningful** - for us, not just for the organisation | **Aspirational** - drive us to deliver and not comply | **Rewarding** - actual reflection of good performance | **Trust** - that processes are being tested first before people |

Very much in line with the lean principle of leveraging human potential (one of the 8 lean waste when unharvested), inclusiveness and empowerment are key.

Very often, people are randomly reprimanded or rewarded for their work based on the System's capabilities. I have encountered many projects doomed from the start due to systemic failure and I see teams working very hard only to be remembered for that last failed job. Then there are other times when hard-nosed incompetent managers get rewarded for successes that had nothing to do with their capabilities. These common work circumstances are huge morale-draining moments that can chip away at people, making them the despondent, jaded workers who make up a huge part of our workforce. There is currently no trust that processes are being tested before people and very little rewards are given in line with actual good performance. Working harder is emphasised instead of leaner and smarter.

Organisations impose training and improvement activities on staff, so for most staff, Doing Lean is something you do on top of your "day job". This is meaningful and benefits the organisation but does nothing for the individuals. Being Lean on the other hand paves the way for staff to adopt the continuous improvement ethos and empowers them through building up the relevant skills and capabilities that enable them to choose and make meaningful improvements and do it willingly in order to drive excellence in delivery and individuals.

Whether it is an organisation creating this or you, yourself proposing a set of fit-for-purpose Reloaded SMART measures that drive the correct behaviour, and whether it is skills or process – e.g. an NRFT-based set of measures – this will certainly lead to the desired economic effect on the organisation and individual.

Relationship of Construction Industry KPI's to Lean Q,C,D,H&S Measures

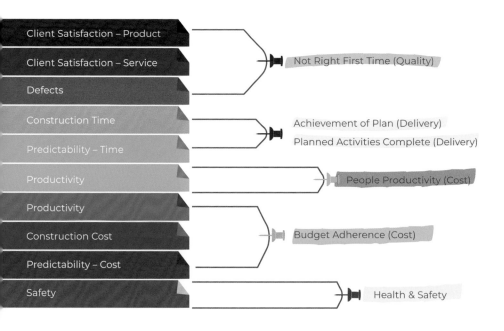

PROFIT – BALANCED LEAN MEASURES

Construction has a set of industry key performance indicators, and in relation to that, lean has come up with custom measures that drive the required behaviour in line with the KPIs.

Organisations will be very good at coming up with ways of measuring outputs. Lean proposes the need for balance from these measures. However, whatever ways or sets of custom measures you create there is a need to measure the quality, cost, delivery across the board. It is important to use more than one measure when assessing the current situation.

You will want to ensure that concentration on one measure will not have a detrimental effect on something else. For example, throwing labour at a job in pursuit of the Achievement of a Plan can affect cost and H&S, or a classic pursuit of Budget Adherence can adversely affect Quality.

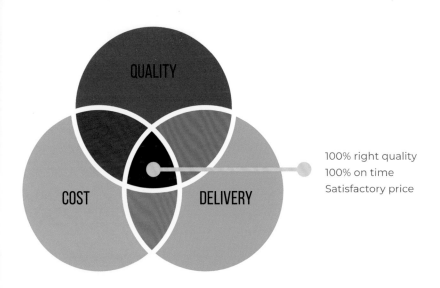

100% right quality
100% on time
Satisfactory price

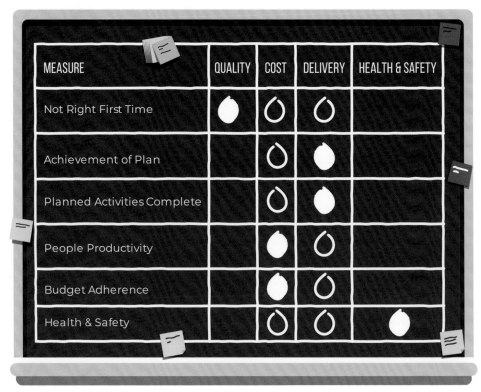

MEASURE	QUALITY	COST	DELIVERY	HEALTH & SAFETY
Not Right First Time	⬤	○	○	
Achievement of Plan		○	⬤	
Planned Activities Complete		○	⬤	
People Productivity	⬤	○		
Budget Adherence	⬤	○		
Health & Safety		○	○	⬤

You will see that NRFT is a processed-based measure that affects measures from across the board. I consider it a classic "super" Reloaded SMART Measure that tests the process first but fairly reveals people's problems, regardless of who they are, when an analysis of NRFT causes is conducted.

Going back to the 5S van examples, you will see that the benefits of conducting 5S on them have resulted in reduced carbon emissions from fewer trips and less fuel usage, not only from the reduced trips but also from less inventory weighing down the truck.

This just goes to show that even when you have no thoughts for the planet, improving processes for profit's sake can benefit the environment. The generic benefits stated in the diagram can all have cost savings attributed to them, making them powerful business cases. If anything, take this element more into consideration and include leveraging it from a marketing perspective and be more competitive.

If you do it often enough, you might actually believe it. This is a great example of evolving from Doing to Being Lean, whether you plan to or not.

ATTRIBUTE SPECIFIC COST SAVINGS TO THESE BENEFITS FOR ORGANISATIONAL BUY-IN.

Less resources (raw material, water, energy) required due to quality processes and outputs

Right first time reduces carbon footprint & emissions

Reduced raw materials required for replacement product/materials

Reduced defective/ruined material requiring disposal

Less energy usage for extra transportation of material

Less energy required for lighting, heating etc.

Longevity of possessions reducing need for new

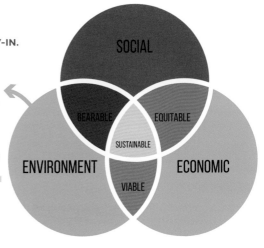

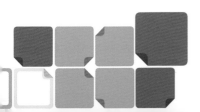

AFTERWORD

Having come to the end of this book, I realise that I may have been writing this book to my younger self of 30 years ago. Looking back, it would have been really helpful for my journey. I would have had a few extra years to spend doing the things I love if I'd known then, what I know now. I've now had the experience and understand the difference Lean living can have on my life and my goal is to ensure that others don't make the same mistakes that I did back then – much like a doting parent nagging about the importance of education. I'm now in a position that I can appreciate how much Being Lean has changed my life for the better and I can only hope that it does the same for you.

Being Lean incorporates every part of my life and has even helped me to structure this book in a coherent and hopefully, easy to follow way. When I finished it, I felt incredibly lucky that I had been doing Lean for such a long time and so consistently that I was able to follow through, fill out the chapters and achieve the flow.

I say lucky, but is it luck really? I dare say that somewhere down the line, I crossed from doing Lean to Being Lean because nothing in my Lean living is random. I followed a structured approach and engineered my way through. It became more automated than I realised. Finishing this book is really a testament to Being Lean, as a methodology in my quest for a good quality of life.

I reiterate my wish made in the beginning of the book; to provide you with lean thinking, tools, techniques, and examples to get you started on your own Lean journey towards self-improvement. My goal is to help you to be YOUR own life coach and do the things that are important to you, without compromise.

Understanding that there are others out there experiencing the same battles you are and wanting to change them is a massive part of your Lean journey, so the tools and support don't stop here. Lean living is collaborative, it's about aiding one another and sharing tips and tricks along the way. It's about acknowledging problems and finding waste removing solutions.

As individuals, we already know some of the biggest things hindering us from living the life we want. But sometimes it's not quite as easy to overcome them as we might think. My website www.beinglean.net was created with this in mind. It's a platform specifically designed for you, providing helpful products, discussion boards and blog content to give you that extra assistance and encouragement when you need it most. You took the time to finish reading this book because much of it resonates with you. Take the time to communicate with other Lean practitioners or Lean novices and share best practice. I sincerely hope that this book has opened your eyes to what's possible and the wonderful things you can achieve by Being Lean.

Index

BEING LEAN
WEBSITE & RESOURCES

Congratulations on taking the first steps on your Lean Journey! I hope this book has helped you recognise some key areas in your life that could be changed for the better.

But Being Lean isn't just about reading a book, it's about putting everything you've learned into practice. It's important to live life to the fullest and making your lifestyle leaner will give you the time and energy to enjoy every single second.

While developing a new Lean lifestyle is a great thing, some habits can be hard to break and we all need a little extra support and confidence boost every now and then. I still often need someone else to point out that one of my processes still includes a lot of waste. So, our Lean journey doesn't end here. The Being Lean website is packed full of Lean content and goodies to help you along the way. You'll find helpful downloadable exercises, LeanPac travel bags, perfect for your next adventure, and our Lean Exchange lets you connect with other Lean lovers to share great tips, knowledge and experiences.

You're not alone in wanting to make a change and together we can take Lean living to the next level.

To get involved visit www.beinglean.net

I'll see you there!

Michelle

Blogs
Knowledge is power, read more, know more & get inspired!

Lean Exchange
Have something to say or share? Join our Lean Forum!

Resources
Downloadables to help your journey to Being Lean!

Lean or Mean?!
Vote on activities, whether they are lean or over-the-top!

Contests & Competitions
Let your lean experience win you something!

Shop
Get the book or other evolving products, visit us & have a look!

Contribute & Collaborate
Whether you want to contribute Lean content or collaborate for cross promotions, product development or training! Call us!

About the Author

Michelle's background in construction resource efficiency and her pioneering research into the root causes of material and environmental waste led her naturally to discover the revolutionary improvement offered by lean construction. Together with colleagues, Michelle introduced lean to the construction industry in a government funded Construction Lean Improvement Programme (CLIP). She was later part of the team that translated and developed the Business Improvement Technique (BIT) NVQ qualification into Construction from the manufacturing industry. Michelle holds the highest level in that qualification and is an accredited assessor. Having been a lean practitioner for almost 20 years, she has facilitated over a hundred organisational changes within the UK & Europe. Michelle's quest for perfection in living life to the fullest makes her staunch advocacy and adoption of lean in everyday life inevitable.

Home - Always challenge status quo! This is a photo I sent in my family group WhatsApp, with a message exclaiming how I cut my vacuuming time by 40%! Who says don't fix what's not broken? I was flabbergasted by the performance of this new vacuum, compared to my decade old one! Never occurred me to question it as long as it was working. All that wasted time! But better late than never!

Fitness - My weight training was stalling, so I engineered my circumstances to push myself to make improvements. I declared my performance on a Facebook post a couple of years ago. I was stalling at 50kg deadlift & I'm currently lifting 55kg. Slowly, but steadily.

Food - LOVING my food, I NEVER leave it to chance hence I have not had a mediocre restaurant experience for the past decade. It started with researching & planning for holiday restaurant visits as I cannot afford a bad experience while on a hard-earned holiday before I realised enjoying meals at home is just as important. I started planning my weekend restaurant visits & that led to me to question why I value my every day, homecooked meals less. Thanks to Lean, now, ALL my meals are "luxurious" & highly enjoyable!

Travel - Like most people, I started out planning only the components of my travel that I felt were important to a good trip. As Being Lean gradually kicked in, more & more components seemed important to achieve flow. In the end, every minute became vital to enabling me & my travel companions to enjoy our holidays to the fullest. All that legwork of researching, thinking & decision-making upfront before holiday starts, contributes to greater quality time, allowing me to do MORE of the things I love.

Sustainability - Applying the modular concept to cooking has allowed me to explore my love for fine dining at home. It has helped me reduce cost for this expensive hobby and definitely minimise otherwise inevitable food waste that comes with it.

Quality of Life - I've been practising Lean for two decades. The first 10 years, due to trial and error and no guidance I was always wishing, aiming & striving. Now, I'm finally reaping the rewards and am doing & living instead of wishing and striving. I've been to more concerts in the past 10 years then I did in the 25 years of adulthood before that!

Business Case
Reality Check
Smart Choices
Resting Heart Rate
Types of Procrastinators
Habits Building

Healthier Lifestyle

Fag Pack Calculations